D0363994

CRICKET WONDERFUL CRICKET

Also by John Duncan

How to Manage your Bank Manager

CRICKET WONDERFUL CRICKET

JOHN DUNCAN

With a foreword by Tony Greig

metro

Published by Metro Publishing
an imprint of John Blake Publishing Ltd
3 Bramber Court, 2 Bramber Road,
London W14 9PB, England

www.johnblakepublishing.co.uk

www.facebook.com/Johnblakepub `facebook`
twitter.com/johnblakepub `twitter`

First published in hardback in 2011

ISBN: 978 1 84358 316 5

British Library Cataloguing-in-Publication Data:

A catalogue record for this book is available from the British Library.

Design by www.envydesign.co.uk

Printed in Great Britain by CPI Mackays, Chatham, ME5 8TD

1 3 5 7 9 10 8 6 4 2

Papers used by John Blake Publishing are natural, recyclable products
made from wood grown in sustainable forests. The manufacturing processes
conform to the environmental regulations of the country of origin.

Every attempt has been made to contact the relevant copyright-holders,
but some were unobtainable. We would be grateful if the appropriate
people could contact us.

For Helen, Alistair and Ged

All author profits from the sale of
Cricket Wonderful Cricket
will be donated to
The Lord's Taverners.

CONTENTS

FOREWORD

BY TONY GREIG

One of the many wonderful things about being a professional cricketer is having the chance to travel the world and meet people that you might otherwise never have known. So, when I started to think about what might be appropriate for this foreword, I was intrigued by the list of people that John has persuaded to talk about the game. I haven't met all of them by any means and, of the few I have, some only in passing.

Nonetheless, I could easily write at length here about Prince Philip, Buckingham Palace and the corgis; Michael Parkinson and World Series Cricket; Tim Rice and his generosity; and many others in the book's 20-strong line-up. But that is all best left for another time and another place. So I'll restrict myself to just the one story, even if it does revolve around someone who is only in the book 'second hand!'

I first met the Rolling Stones, including Bill Wyman, in Trinidad when one of the England team spotted Mick Jagger sitting in the crowd through binoculars. It wasn't difficult because he was wearing pink pyjamas! So we sent the 12th man over to invite him to come into the dressing room at the close of play. To do this, he had to come into the Members' section at the Queen's Park Oval and, not surprisingly, there were one or two complaints about his dress. So, when we invited him to have a drink again the next day, we asked him not to wear his pyjamas, but to dress properly. When he appeared, he was dressed all in pink again, but this time it was a pink satin suit, with pink shoes and a pink stetson. The suit probably cost as much as a motor car. What a performer!

So, what am I doing writing this foreword? You may well ask. As a player, and subsequently as a commentator, I've always felt that there has been something special about the relationship we have with cricket lovers of every kind, including those that you can enjoy reading about in *Cricket Wonderful Cricket*.

I originally arrived in Sussex from South Africa in 1965, but it was probably another four or five years before I became aware of JD, as the Sussex boys soon labelled him, when he started to cover some of our matches for BBC Radio Brighton. Stanley Allen, a Brighton solicitor, was the original and 'senior' commentator, but we gradually began to see more and more of this cricket-mad NatWest banker.

Over the years, JD became almost an honorary member of the Sussex squad; travelling with us to away matches, bowling in the nets, perching in the dressing room and taking his fair share of the sometimes cruel humour on offer. To be quite honest, he talked a far better game than he played. His military medium should have been court-martialled. And he still claims to have taught me all I know about cricket commentary! I don't think so.

It was in the early seventies that he came to do a pre-match interview with me at my flat overlooking the Hove County Ground. After the usual round of cricket questions, he suddenly asked me why I hadn't bought a house! And that kicked off my first venture into the property market. My then wife and I found a place we liked, he organised the finance, and soon we were living in a home of our own.

And, for forty years or thereabouts, during more than thirty of which we have lived at opposite ends of the globe, we have managed to keep in touch. He has stayed in our home in Sydney and we have stayed at his in London. But a lot less often! Much of the contact nowadays is through the magic of Skype, the internet call system. The problem with this is that he usually wants to chat when I have just got out of bed, bright eyed and clear headed, whereas he is about to stumble in the opposite direction, having normally consumed the best part of a bottle of Rioja...

Which is an appropriate note on which to end this foreword. Cricket, communications, a glass of wine and JD are inseparable. His lifetime love of the game has helped him to produce this splendid book. It's very different from the usual run of cricket books and all the better for that. I hope you will enjoy it as much as I did.

Tony Greig,
Sydney, January, 2011.

INTRODUCTION

The anecdotes, the humour, the memories, the heroes and the issues aired here are those of a disparate group of people united by a single thread; a love of cricket. For some, it is a lifetime's passion of an exceptional and ever-lasting intensity. For others, it is a calmer and more passive affection, but one that is an important part of life, even when pads and gloves gather dust in a corner cupboard. It is a love that glues ears to Test Match Special, *eyes to television sets, bums to seats near the boundary and, increasingly, surfers to cricket websites. It is the eccentric and magnetic allure of cricket.*

I sat bolt upright in bed one morning – a major achievement in itself! It was three o'clock and I was suddenly wide awake. The previous evening I had finished reading an absorbing book of interviews by Gyles Brandreth, called *Brief Encounters*. He had talked to royalty, politicians, actors and many more. The result was a book that I had enjoyed enormously.

As well, and as usual, that day I had been watching cricket, reading about cricket and thinking about cricket. The wonderful game has been a part of my life since the day I was born. Our house in Sussex, opposite Henfield cricket ground, was situated at deep midwicket to a right-hander when the bowling was from the village end. It was so close that a six once bounced down the hallway and landed in the dog-bowl, near the kitchen back door!

I played the game moderately well in itinerant fashion for a number of teams who seemed to be moderately happy to have me on board. These included Henfield, of course, Blackstone, Brighton Banks, Shoreham, Hove Aldrington, various Westminster and NatWest Bank XIs, and even Sussex, in occasional benefit or social matches. My medium paced trundlers, even though despatched from a good height, generally caused little alarm or despondency amongst opposition batsmen, although there was one long and weary season when 100 wickets were taken in what seemed like as many matches. I was no all-rounder, failing ever to reach the 50 mark with the bat, albeit on one occasion I had made 42 off 14 deliveries (with the aid of two dropped catches while still on nought!) when my heartless captain decided to declare!

Since the launch, in 1968, of BBC Radio Brighton, where I freelanced for a decade or more, I have from time to time commentated on and written about the game. And, when Sussex at long last became county champions in 2003, I even cried about it.

And so it came to pass that the book, and communications, and cricket came together in the early hours of that particular morning and, three sleepless but thoughtful hours later, I crawled out of bed, fortified myself with a mug of coffee, sat at my pc and started to record my initial thoughts on what has become *Cricket Wonderful Cricket*.

I was already aware of a number of high achievers who were simply cricket mad. Some of them even featured in Brandreth's book. Despite forging very successful careers in their own chosen walks of life they had still had the time and energy for cricket, albeit in varied and individual ways.

I knew that I would need to find the right people to talk to and then persuade each of them to give me an hour of their time. I wanted to 'recruit' a diverse group of people with one common denominator – a love of the game of cricket. But, to ensure total objectivity, my self-imposed rule was to be that they had remained outside the boundary rope. In other words, they must not have played first-class cricket. That said, at least four came very close. David English had been on the ground-staff at Lord's, Michael Parkinson had Yorkshire trials, Ian MacLaurin had opted for a business career rather than a Kent contract and Christopher Martin-Jenkins played for Surrey 2nd XI.

Through various involvements with such distinguished organisations as the BBC, MCC, Sussex County Cricket Club, NatWest, Inchcape and, more recently and very importantly, The Lord's Taverners, I had met an array of candidates who met my criteria. So the initial recruitment exercise was not too challenging. Nevertheless, I was delighted when, in quick succession, John Alderton, Barry Norman, Chris Tarrant, Victor Blank and Richard Stilgoe came on board. They made the next stages far easier than might otherwise have been the case.

Although there were several other prospects with whom I was acquainted, if only fleetingly, it was getting closer to cold call time. It meant approaches to agents and managers, personal assistants and secretaries. Some of these intermediary filters were brilliant, some obstructive, some simply didn't respond. Nevertheless, the internet was 'Googled', letters were dispatched, phone numbers were dialled, and emails 'pinged'. A series of postal strikes was not helpful. Nor was the banking crisis, which cost me one of my prime targets. And there was a grim time when I felt that I had hit a brick wall. I was close to calling a halt to the whole silly enterprise but was persuaded to keep going. Then the tide turned, with the emergence of more candidates bringing a new surge of energy and confidence.

At this point I ought to mention briefly that, about three months before my 3am bedroom 'road to Damascus moment,' I had been diagnosed with Parkinson's Disease. There are, of course, worse things that can happen but it's not a massive amount of fun, particularly on the bad days. But I sometimes surprise myself with what I can still do, aided and abetted by a steady intake of pills and potions. And the occasional glass of red wine! Other sufferers have achieved far more than me but I hope that this book, apart from modestly helping a wonderful charity, will also, at least to some small degree, inspire fellow Parkinsonians to keep on keeping on.

Having said that, this would seem a good stage at which to mention briefly The Lord's Taverners, the official charity for recreational cricket and one that I have been pleased to be quite heavily involved with since the mid-nineties. Its focus is very much on helping disadvantaged and disabled young people, through cricket and a wide range of other sports, including rugby, football, tennis and basketball. For example, the charity manages and supports youth cricket competitions and programmes, donates cricket equipment and puts on the road, at the rate of about one every week, the familiar green, specially-adapted minibuses, which give young people vital transportation and access to sport and recreation. For more information, visit www.lordstaverners.org. It is The Lord's Taverners who will receive every penny of any profits that I make from *Cricket Wonderful Cricket*.

Now, where was I? Oh yes, recruitment! Some of the responses were instant, others took an age. One approach, through an agent, I had virtually written off as it seemed to be going nowhere. Then, one Friday, the target himself emailed me, suggesting that we meet three days later! It was also encouraging that only one person, once committed, had to withdraw, although a few dates changed – and one major difficulty was never satisfactorily resolved.

The interviewing process was, almost without exception, pure unadulterated pleasure. To have the opportunity to relive so many matches, and summers, the triumphs and occasional disasters, to hear amazing anecdotes and share in so much laughter. All of my interviewees, if that is what I should call them, have been more than generous with their time, their memories, their favourites and their opinions. We have talked in palaces and offices, in clubs and homes, in bars and hotels, in cricket grounds and restaurants. I have been given some wonderful contributions by this special group of cricket fans. I cannot thank them enough.

When I set out to write this book, I hoped that those I spoke to would have a tale or two to tell and that they would not all sing the same song, but offer some variety, some different perspectives. At no stage was I disappointed. Surprised? Yes. Disappointed? Never! Indeed, as I have said, the only obvious common denominator has been a deep-seated love of the game. Other than that, what emerged was a patchwork quilt of anecdotes and achievements, favourites and failures.

In more than twenty-four hours of cricketing conversations, I learned how Hitler put an early end to a budding Yorkshire career, met a man who created his own cricket ground, enthralled to hear about a team called Dusty Fleming's International Hair Stylists, shuddered at the thought of watching cricket while sitting next to Robert Mugabe, thrilled at the re-living of both the only televised hat-trick at the Oval, and an innings of 1,792 not out, and much, much more.

Most of the twenty people that I spoke to will not, I am sure, object to being described as "mature", so it is not surprising that they tend to talk about cricketers from a bygone age rather than those currently active in the first-class game. The names of Bradman, Hutton, Compton, Laker and Miller roll off many a tongue, but I hear little of players from today's games, which was something of a surprise. Apart from Ponting, that is. He and another Australian, Warne, have a select group of admirers; as have England's Gower and Botham.

'Too much cricket', both at international and domestic level, is a frequent cry, and it was to be expected that the word 'corruption' would be on a lot of lips following the spot-fixing incidents that surfaced while the book was being compiled. Slow over rates are a major irritant, while the use of technology on umpiring decisions has mixed reviews.

I have decided to include a glossary of nearly 200 players whose names appear in these pages. For serious students of the game this section may well be irrelevant but, for others, a potted guide, particularly to those lesser known cricketers such as Showkat Baksh, or that fine fast bowler Charles Jesse Kortright, may be of some interest. These pen pictures are not meant to be comprehensive, comparable or complete. Merely compact and comprehensible!

But now it is time to say thank you. Along the way, I have been aided, enabled, supported, encouraged, advised and counselled by a wonderful group of people. In particular, Ian MacLaurin, David English, Alan Davies, David Tossell, Rachael Heyhoe Flint and Matthew Patten opened doors to people who might otherwise have been difficult to reach. John Alderton opened the batting for me in more ways than one, so as to make what followed easier than it might otherwise have been.

Tim Dickson, Ian Griffiths and Ged Duncan generously offered their collective publishing, writing, editing and, in the first two instances certainly, drinking skills when they were most needed. Mike Gatting, J K Lever and Clive Radley talked to me freely from 'the other side of the ropes.' Over a splendid lunch at *The Forge* in London's Covent Garden, that talented actor Struan Rodger introduced me to John Blake and, by dessert, I had a publisher. And, had it not been for a very special lady, Paula Goldstein, I would not have read *Brief Encounters* and this book probably would not have happened.

The many wonderful people who have helped me so much in making contact and appointments include Sarah Dalkin, Feona McEwan, Caroline McCrink, Adrian Mundin, Anne Stenson, Eileen Heinink, Marina Purser, Teresa Rudge, Vanessa Burgess, David Lazenby, Samuel Turnbull and Susan Willer.

I thank my publisher, John Blake, for having the faith and wisdom(!) to invest; my editor Joel Simons, for getting me up to speed and staying the course; and Liz Mallett and the rest of the team at Blake Publishing. Emma Lewendon, Shona Langridge and the other special people at The Lord's Taverners, as always, provided the perfect cocktail of energy, enthusiasm, expertise and experience.

Writing a foreword at a distance of more than 10,500 miles in the middle of an Ashes series was never going to be easy. But somehow Tony Greig, as good mates do, sat in Sydney and came up with the goods.

And now a hat-trick of people who deserve a special mention.

Mary MacLennan transcribed impeccably every interview, coping with noises off including an over-enthusiastic pianist, ladies that lunch and chattering children, along the way. She produced from my digital recordings more than 175,000 words and for those many hours of work she resolutely refused to take one penny. Mary, you have always been and always will be, a star.

Before sending each chapter to the publishers I felt that I needed someone to cast an expert professional eye over what I had produced. A former City Editor of *The Times* and a friend for more than thirty years, Mike Tate has given freely of his time, experience and his abundant skills in far more detail than I had ever expected in filling that role. A great man to have on your side.

Some things are best said privately. And have been, I hope. So I will just put it like this. I simply couldn't have produced this book without my wife, Helen. She has kept me going, lifted me up, calmed me down, even sometimes put my socks on and pandered to me every single inch of the way. No Helen, no *Cricket Wonderful Cricket*. It really is as simple as that.

My heartfelt thanks to all of these remarkable people who have supported and helped me in so many different ways. And also to those that I may inadvertently have forgotten to mention.

The later stages of this book were completed against the background of the record breaking Ashes series in Australia. England's triumph, the quality of their cricket, so many outstanding performances and the final outcome were magnificent. And demonstrated emphatically that cricket is undoubtedly a wonderful game.

I hope you will enjoy reading this book as much as I have enjoyed producing it. And that the Lord's Taverners will be able to do just a smidgeon more for those with special needs as a result.

JD
London, January, 2011

JOHN ALDERTON

'...HE TURNED ROUND, THE BALL HIT HIM FULL IN THE MOUTH AND HE WENT DOWN LIKE A SACK OF SPUDS.'

John Alderton was born on 27 November 1940 in Gainsborough, Lincolnshire. He is an actor, best known for his roles in Emergency Ward 10, Upstairs, Downstairs, Thomas and Sarah, My Wife Next Door, Wodehouse Playhouse *and for the lead in the long-running series,* Please Sir! *He has often starred alongside his wife, Pauline Collins, and has made many West End stage appearances, including roles in Alan Ayckbourn's* Confusions *and Harold Pinter's* The Birthday Party. *His film appearances include* Zardoz *and more recently* Calendar Girls, *and he narrated the children's series* Fireman Sam *and* Little Miss.

We meet in the kitchen of John's Hampstead home, the scene of many splendid gatherings after days of golf, cricket and any number of theatrical occasions with Pauline. A number of times, to my certain knowledge, reasonable quantities of fine chilled white wine have been consumed, but on this grey December morning it is to be mugs of hot coffee and warm memories of cricket.

Every Yorkshireman wants to play cricket for Yorkshire and

John was no exception. But to play for the county you have to be born there and that was a big problem for John, a proud man of Hull. 'I wasn't born in Yorkshire. I blame Hitler for that because, in 1940, three weeks before I was born, that despicable man nearly ruined my life. The Luftwaffe used to fly over Hull to Manchester to drop their bombs, but they couldn't always find their targets. They would return down the Humber on their way back to Germany and offload their bombs on Hull. One night the city took an absolute hammering and they hit the local maternity hospital where I was supposed to be born. My mum had to go to Lincolnshire and I was born in Gainsborough – but only because there was no maternity hospital in Hull any more. So it's as simple as that; it was Hitler's fault that I never played for Yorkshire.

'Even so, when I was a kid, that was still the dream – that I was going to play for Yorkshire. I used to go to the county ground in Hull and always took my tennis shoes in case Yorkshire were a man short, always thinking that one day it would happen, that they would ask if there is anyone out there who plays a bit… It was always a dream. They want your autograph, you're going to play for England… And then…

'So it was a case of hero-worshipping Hutton and anybody who was playing for Yorkshire. They were all my heroes, although I never saw Hutton in his pomp. Then there was the excitement of the Australians coming up to Leeds, seeing the great players. And that was the first time I was ever on television – running on to the field at lunchtime, patting these big, brown, sunburnt Australians on the back and beaming into the camera. So, for me, cricket and television came together for the first time in that little moment.'

Once he had come to terms with this earliest and gravest disappointment, John next had to accept that football was not where his sporting potential lay but there was ample compensation in his instant love of cricket. 'At school, I thought I could bowl a ball and keep wicket a bit, and be quite good. I didn't have to do a lot of running, because I never scored many runs, so I didn't have to get too fit! Nobody in the family had played – my dad certainly didn't. But I enjoyed the mechanics and the pace of it all – even though, when I was eight, I got a smack on the nose – broke my nose – because we didn't have helmets or anything and there were one or two who could ping it down. That didn't put me off so I kept going. Basically, I played a little bit of knock-about stuff, and school cricket for the first XI, but it was not really until some time after I came to London that I became a regular and reasonable player.'

My research shows that John, in his prime, was a more than reasonable player. Whether it was a product of modesty or memory, or a mixture of both, is a difficult judgement to make, but he has to be reminded that he once made a ton for the Lord's Taverners against a useful Sussex side at Hove. After the briefest of pauses, he chats on, seemingly unmoved by this achievement! 'Although I didn't play for a long time I eventually started to get involved in charity cricket and the Taverners, although there were other sides, like The Stage and the Cricket Society. To play with these heroes was a great thrill and, of course, what was so good about it was that you were in awe of these people. You'd see them – Denis Compton, Bill Edrich, Johnny Wardle, Eric Hollies and all these people – but they were also fans of what *you* did. There's always been that wonderful, wonderful mutual respect, even going back to the 1870s and 1880s, when there were charity benefit games. Half were show business and variety people and half were from international cricket. It's always gone on and the great players have always liked to be a part of that.

'You know that they all give their wickets away once they've scored a few runs – although Boycott never did, until he did to

Cloughie [Brian Clough].' This prompts us to start shuffling through the papers that litter the kitchen table – the combined results of our pre-interview research – until one of us comes up with a scorecard. It is for a match played on 18 August 1975, at Lord's, between the President's XI of MCC and the Lord's Taverners. And there it is – *Boycott caught and bowled Clough 68*. John is suitably pleased. 'Yes, that was it. It was, I think, the Taverners' Silver Jubilee match on the main ground. We used to get big crowds because in those days there wasn't any other cricket, or any other sport, played on a Sunday.'

John played in the Taverners' match against *Tiswas* that Chris Tarrant describes elsewhere in this book, a match he remembers for his part in a very painful accident right at the start of his innings. Fred Rumsey was captain of the *Tiswas* team and he told me how he had been having problems with Chris, who had been nattering to a broadcasting colleague from ATV, Peter Tomlinson. Fred had to swap fielding positions with him and was still making his way to backward square leg when Josh Gifford bowled the first ball of the innings. John takes up the story.

'Josh bowled a long hop down the leg-side and I hit the ball out of the meat of the bat as hard as I could. It was going at a rate of knots towards the back of Fred's head as he was walking away, which would have been all right, because he's got a thick conk. Chris shouted, "Fred!" and when he turned round, the ball hit him full in the mouth and he went down like a sack of spuds. Absolutely spark out. We all ran over to him – there's blood everywhere – and when he came round, Fred said, "I've lost all me teeth." I said, "No you haven't, Fred – I've got some of them here!" He went to hospital, where he had 12 stitches and found he'd lost four teeth. He came back from the hospital and said to Ed Stewart and me, "That's great. There you are, having a party and chatting up the wife while I'm away." I

4

bought him a bottle of nice red wine for each of the stitches: 12 bottles of red wine and four bottles of beautiful white wine for each of the 'pearlies' he had lost. But, from that day, he had to grow a moustache to cover the scar underneath, and that's the only injury Fred ever got in cricket.'

It may or may not have been poetic justice, but John himself was destined to sustain injury, when playing for Surrey in a benefit game at Beare Green, a small village near Dorking. Arnold Long, the regular wicketkeeper, didn't want to go behind the stumps but John readily agreed to do so. 'So, Robin Jackman is bowling and it is on a lively green wicket. Pat 'Percy' Pocock, fielding at slip, says, "John, wind him up. Go and stand up to the stumps and when he turns round, tell him he's not as quick as he used to be." So I go up to the stumps, Jackman turns round and I say, "Percy says you are not as quick as you were." He says, "Get back, get back." So I go backing off, the gag's over, but I don't back off quickly enough because the first ball broke my finger. I don't know this at the time but I know it hurts and it is swelling up. All the professionals are hurling the ball in like Exocets from the boundary, as they do. When we throw a ball in, it goes up in the air and comes down again, but when the pros throw, it seems to come in hard and flat. So it is hitting me, and banging me, and at the end of the day I can't get the glove off. Jackman asks, "What can I do for you? I'm terribly sorry." I told him not to worry and mentioned that I was due to play against him at the Oval. I said, "I've always wanted to hook a ball at the Oval. If I'm in and you're bowling, drop me one short, second ball of the over, and I'll be able to…"

'So when this game does take place at Surrey's ground, he comes in and I know this ball is going to be the one. He digs it in so short, down by his own toes, that by the time the bouncer gets to me, it's coming down again! I'd gone through with the shot, made no contact, the bails are off and Pocock laughed 'til he wet himself. The umpire wasn't quick enough to call no ball, so off I walked, the only guy ever to be bowled at the Oval by a bouncer!

'In a match for Denis Amiss's benefit, I played against Warwickshire for Vic Lewis's XI. A young Bob Willis was bowling for them but he didn't quite know what charity cricket was all about. Michael Parkinson opens the batting and Willis comes haring in, big mop of hair all over the place, and fires one in at 150 miles an hour. Parky doesn't even see it, let alone play it. He's castled, stumps are all over the place and the umpire again doesn't shout no ball. I'm first wicket down and go out to bat and Parky, as he is passing me says, "Just wait! Just wait 'til it's Willis's benefit!" He was livid. So I'm thinking that by now somebody must have told Willis to slow down, but he comes tearing in, second ball of the match, and I don't see it as it brushes my eyebrows! And they all went up to him and said, "This is an actor, Bob. He doesn't bat – he's an actor, not a batter!" It hadn't entered his mind. So first they slowed him up, and then they took him off and sent him off to field on the boundary.

'I know I've mentioned it before but to be out there with these guys is just wonderful. Going back 40 years, for example, to a game for the Taverners against Old England, with such a rich mix of Test players and celebrities on both sides. Reg Simpson, Jack Ikin, Bill Edrich, Ken Barrington, Godfrey Evans, Johnny Wardle and Doug Wright were all in the England side. We had Don Kenyon, Peter Richardson, Jack Robertson, Doug Insole, David Frost, Brian Rix, Harry Secombe, Don Brennan. And I was in the midst of this array of stars, coming in at number four on the bill! It was simply a knockout to play with these guys. It was like meeting Hollywood stars when Pauline was nominated for an Oscar – and finding Gregory Peck sitting next to you!

'Talking of Godfrey Evans, he once took me to an event which was a part of Percy Pocock's benefit. Godfrey, after we'd done the speeches, suggested that we go to the Sportsman Club near Marble Arch. This is Godfrey all over: he always liked to gamble. I am not a gambler but we go, and there is nobody there. Tables are up and running and we go on to the roulette. We had 200 quid chips, only had three or four bets and in four minutes we had won £800 each. He said, "That's it, come on, let's go and have dinner and just enjoy ourselves."'

John's close relationship with Yorkshire cricket resulted in him being invited into the dressing room at Lord's by Brian Close. 'I think it was an MCC game against the Australians and it was Graham Gooch's first England trial. He got a big 70 or a little 80. Len Hutton was chairman of selectors at that time and young Gooch was 21 years old. He's sitting with just a towel wrapped around his waist and Hutton says he wants to talk to him. I'm also sitting there on the bench, with Goochie between me and Hutton, and I can hear it all as Hutton asks him who he plays for, where he fields, can he catch, and so on. This is the chairman of selectors – he should know all these things! Nevertheless, the England team is announced at 12 o'clock on the Sunday and Gooch is in against the Australians.

'That day, I'm playing in Essex somewhere, in a Lord's Taverners game. I'd played with most of my fellow team members before but not with Bill Edrich, who looks at me – and thinks I'm Graham Gooch! For some reason, he's got it into his head that I'm Graham Gooch, because I look a bit like him. So I go into the dressing room and he says "Congratulations – nice batting." And I'm thinking, I got 50 last week for the Taverners; maybe someone has told him. Then we chat about the Australians until we go out to field, where the ball is chasing me a bit, and he's looking at me, thinking, "He's not a natural athlete, throwing the ball in with a polythene arm." He's watching this and looking at me a bit quizzically, but he still thinks I'm Graham Gooch. We go out to bat together and he's going to have a look at the new England opener from the other end. It's a pudding of a pitch and I'm hitting it too early, and missing it and nicking it, and he's gone white, because he just can't believe what he's seeing. The following Thursday, Graham makes his England debut at Edgbaston. On the second day, he goes out to bat with England three down. Three balls later, he's back in the pavilion, having been caught behind for a duck. In the second innings he manages to last seven deliveries before Jeff Thomson removes him – again without a run to his name. Edrich is not surprised; he is absolutely not surprised. But it's not until months later that somebody tells him that it wasn't Graham Gooch that he had played with in Essex!'

John then moves swiftly from one case of mistaken identity to his suspicion that he might have been involved in another, of an altogether different kind. 'One day I get a call from someone who says he is the Queen's Equerry and that Her Majesty would like me to come to lunch. I immediately think that this is a mate winding me up and said, "Yeah, who is this? Who's calling?"

"No, this *is* the Queen's Equerry."

So I said, "Who else is coming?"

"I'm not allowed to say."

"Is the wife?"

"No, not invited."

"What dress?" I asked.

He said, "Buckingham Palace."

"No, no, I know where she lives – what do we wear?"

"Oh," he said, "just a lounge suit."

'On the day of the lunch, I suddenly see Colin Cowdrey's Jaguar, with its MCC number plate, parked near the Palace and I thought, "Right, I know you're going to lunch, otherwise you wouldn't be here." So I jump out of my taxi and say, "I know you're going, so give us a lift." Colin drives up to the gates, winds down his window, and the copper leans past him and says, "Good afternoon, Mr Alderton. I hope you have a very pleasant lunch." Colin is sitting there, staring forward, wanting to know where to park. "Well, mate," explains the copper, "what you do is you go through there, turn right and you'll get a sandwich and a cup of tea with the other drivers." Colin never batted an eyelid and when we told the Queen, she absolutely loved the story. She thought it was the funniest thing that one of her coppers should think Colin Cowdrey was my chauffeur. And that is why he always addressed me as "Dear Boss".'

Then a sudden change of direction from John, and an unexpected view on the physical dimensions of the game as he ponders the length of the cricket pitch. 'It was an arbitrary length, to do with the measurement of a chain, which was 22 yards. It was easy to measure because every ground apparently had a chain. Whether or not it was right for underarm bowling or any other type of bowling in 1780, I don't know, but that's what it was. It's remained 22 yards – but these guys are now bowling at 150kph! So it's not 22 yards any more, really – it's 20 yards, because the bowlers' front foot is on the popping crease and the batter is on the other popping crease. That's 10 per cent less, facing 100 per cent faster. So I think maybe somebody has to take a fresh look at the actual dimensions of the bat, the ball and the wicket. Should there be changes to get the balance right? It has still got magic, all the history, and if you change it, of course, the record books will need to be rewritten. In the old days, the wicket was two stumps with one bail and if the ball went between them, it was not out. And there wasn't a popping crease – there was a hole. The way you stumped people, or ran them out, was not to take the bails off but to get the ball in the hole before the batsman put his bat there. So wicketkeepers had their fingers ground to pulp by the ends of bats. Going back a long way, there was no such thing as a cylinder mower at Lord's. All you had was shears – or sheep! Whenever they had a match – Gentlemen v Players, or whoever against somebody else – it was all timed according to when the sheep came through St John's Wood. They put them in the ground overnight to take the grass off. But there was no way of getting it really short. The pitch was marked up anywhere the opposition's bowler wanted, and his choice would be where, just on a length, there was a load of crappy grass or a sod of earth, or something equally bad. If anyone made 10 runs, that was terrific!

'But looking at the future of the game, I think it's old-fashioned now, because it's the longest game played. Once, when I was in New York, I tried to explain Test cricket to somebody. He looked a bit confused when I told him that it went on for five days and was usually a draw. We've now gone crackers with Twenty20, and people do like it, but it will be too much of a feast, I think. Although a lot of the traditional skills are shown in Twenty20, it is basically "crash bash, thank you ma'am". There's nothing wrong with that, but I do believe that five-day matches are largely dead. Unless it's a Test match involving Australia, England or South Africa, only eight people want to see it. And nobody wants to see County Championship matches – unless you're winning.

'But I must say that, for me, cricket is the subtlest, cleverest, most demanding game where, however much you have watched, however many games you have seen, however many twists and turns, you can never be sure of the final outcome. We've all seen situations when you think, "You can't get out of this" or "You can't lose this one" or "You can't win this one." But it's not true – it's simply not true. That is the joy of not knowing the script. As an actor, I know the script, I know how the third act finishes – I'm used to that and I love it. But with cricket, where it could go and wherever I think it might go, it doesn't. It never does.'

Quite suddenly, John feels it is time to stop. 'That's it. That's me done.' It is typical of the man that he knows when he has had enough, when he has said what he wants to say, when he wants to lower the curtain. I quite like that!

SIR VICTOR BLANK

'CLIVE FLUNG HIMSELF TO HIS RIGHT, HIS HAND MOVED OUT IN THAT CONCERTINA WAY AND HE TOOK WHAT WAS THE MOST EXTRAORDINARY CATCH.'

Sir Victor Blank was born in Stockport, Lancashire on 9 November 1942. He is a businessman, who became the youngest partner in the law firm Clifford-Turner before joining the merchant bank Charterhouse, where he later became chairman and chief executive. He has been chairman of three major companies – Trinity Mirror, GUS and Lloyds TSB – and a director of the Royal Bank of Scotland. He is now a senior adviser to the US private equity group TPG Capital and was knighted in 1999 for services to the financial industry. Among a number of charitable involvements, he is chairman of Wellbeing of Women.

I am sitting in Victor's office, which is situated little more than a cover drive from Claridge's Hotel, in the heart of London's Mayfair. Beside his desk is a small table bearing an array of cricketing and celebrity photos and caricatures; among them I spot David Frost and John Major. Victor is a man who loves cricket so much that he has his own cricket pitch in the grounds of his Oxfordshire home at Chippinghurst.

'More than 20 years ago I looked at this wonderful river meadow that I owned. It was flat and looked as though it could be made into be a cricket pitch,' he recalls. 'I went into Oxford where I saw the Christ Church College groundsman, Morris Honey, and asked him if he would come out and have a look at this field. So he came and saw that the grass was eight feet high. I asked him, "Can I turn that into a cricket pitch?" and Morris said that I could. "To start with, you need to chop it down, then cut it and roll it and eventually you will have a decent grass field. After that we can do some work on the strip itself."

'We started with a local farmer's threshing machine that chopped the tall stalks down and then kept cutting and rolling the whole field. Then Morris came in with some loam and topsoil, and dressed it and did all kinds of clever stuff. But, for about five or six years it was a very flat, but very dead, wicket. And then Morris sadly passed away. He was succeeded by a groundsman called Dick Sula, who looks after the pitches at the Parks used by the University in Oxford. We decided to do some real work to improve the wicket. Dick took about nine inches out of the strip, put in a proper foundation, then loam and then topsoil, and according to the guys who play on it now, it's as good as most first-class wickets.

'But because the ground is really part of the back garden, it is not suitable to open it for public events. So my games are all private cricket matches. But the ground has a nice ambience and it seems to work. We always try to make our events a family day because we always hated going out to a corporate event at the weekend without the children. There are lots of facilities, so you see loads of kids with their faces painted, queuing up for ice creams, and on the bouncy castles and that sort of thing.

'We put on both charity and benefit matches every season for the Lord's Taverners and Wellbeing, and for professional cricketers. I have held benefit matches for Mike Atherton and for John Emburey, and some of the other Lancashire and Middlesex players over the years. I thought the idea of doing a Taverners cricket match would work. I was, at that time, chairman of a merchant bank in the City, and I believed that it would be quite easy to get a six-a-side competition running. If the charity brought along some celebrities and also some great cricketers, and if the banks brought their team and put something into the pot, and if I threw in the pitch, the marquee and the lunch, then we would raise some decent money. It's a formula that has worked. One of the nice things about the City is that I only have to make five phone calls every year and I've got the five teams – the sixth being mine. People just like doing it. They can contribute to the Taverners and have a nice day out in the country at the same time.'

From the charity's point of view, Victor's event is a successful and enjoyable occasion. But it's a modest affair compared to the match played as a substantial fund-raiser for the charity Wellbeing of Women [WOW]. It is a misconception that Victor became involved with WOW because of his own mother's death. His commitment to the charity, of which he is now the chairman, began rather differently.

'It is a very happy coincidence, because she died of ovarian cancer when I was 12, and Wellbeing has done a lot of research into the disease and its causes. My becoming involved, though, was wholly down to David Frost. There was a big fund-raising Lunch for Life being held at the Savoy that Princess Diana was attending. Off the back of that lunch, the charity wanted to raise a lot of money and David went to see a number of people, including me. I remember getting the call late one rainy, November afternoon. David was just round the corner, and asked to come and see me. He arrived in a very benign mood, complete with large cigar, to explain that he was raising money and could we at Charterhouse help? He was looking for quite chunky sums – more than we gave to charity – but I told him I could lend him a cricket pitch. David is an old friend who, interestingly, had looked at Chippinghurst before we bought it.

He had thought of buying it and so he knew the house. I explained to him that I had this cricket pitch and why didn't we raise money for Wellbeing by having a pro-am cricket match? He could get some great players and I would go around the City and get some money out of my chums to play with the greats. So he said, "That's a wonderful idea. How much do you think you'd raise?" And I said, "I have no idea, but let's assume it will be £25,000." So off he went.

'Three months later, I called David and reminded him of our conversation. The following week he rang to say, "Right, Victor, I've got Imran Khan, Dennis Lillee, Clive Lloyd, John Edrich and Mike Denness – will that do for starters?" So I then had to go out and raise the money! Which we did, and in that first game in 1989 we raised £125,000. We've gone on every year since, and have raised about £4.5 million over the 22 years, just on this one game a year. It's the same formula: a private event at which we have a lot of City firms and business and industry friends, who come for the day to watch and to support us so well, alongside the charitable trusts and our other friends. But the pros come willingly, usually having been asked by David, and have supported us massively and enthusiastically. We do really manage to attract some of the top players from all over the world. You name 'em – we've had 'em!

'The first time Warney [Shane Warne] came to play, on his first tour of England in 1993, he had just bowled Mike Gatting with that extraordinary leg break. And everyone – Brian Close, Mike Denness and Mike Brearley – all wanted to watch him. So they insisted we play an extra five overs, just so they could watch Warne bowl a few more deliveries. But I think highly of the man for a number of reasons. First of all, I think that he is the greatest bowler, certainly spin bowler, I have ever seen. But more particularly because, on one of the occasions on which he had agreed to play, he had to withdraw because he had been banned by the Australian Cricket Board from playing for a year. Although David Frost and I appealed to them, they said he couldn't play, not even in a private game in England. So we called him and said, "Come anyway, it would be a privilege to have you here. Come and spend a nice day with us." So he came along and when he arrived immediately said, "Look, I can't play but I can bowl in the nets, so why don't we auction half a dozen overs and I'll bowl to some of your punters." So he put on his kit and his war paint, and he went down to the nets and bowled half a dozen overs to people who had paid £200–£300 an over to have Shane Warne bowling to them. And then, without me or anybody else asking him, he just stayed in the nets with about two dozen kids, from 15 down to six years old, and he taught them how to bowl 'leggies'. There were plenty of people he could have spent time with, there was plenty of good wine in the marquee, but Warney decided that was what he wanted to do. I thought it was a spectacular piece of generosity and I will never forget it. And those two dozen kids will never forget it either.

'Then there is Clive Lloyd, who I am privileged to have as a friend now. He is somebody in cricket I always admired for the ease and grace with which he batted and extraordinary athleticism with which he fielded. The last time he played down at Chippinghurst – he still comes but doesn't play now – he was fielding in the covers when Sunil Gavaskar stroked, as he does with great elegance, a cover drive. Clive lumbered a couple of paces to the right, stooped half-heartedly, but the ball went beyond him and I thought, "Oh dear." Everybody groaned, and Clive just smiled and went back to his position. The very next ball Sunil hit harder into the covers. It was six inches off the ground and Clive moved with the speed that took you back to his heyday. He flung himself to his right, his hand moved out as it used to in that concertina way, and took what was the most extraordinary catch. Afterwards somebody said to him, "Clive, how come you looked as if you were half asleep one minute and the next you took one of the most brilliant catches ever?" Clive said, "Ah! In Kingston, Jamaica, in 1974, I dropped Sunil in the covers and I resolved then I would never ever do it again." It took him the best part of 30 years to fulfil that resolution!

'On one occasion, Mushie [Mushtaq Ahmed] bowled an over to Mike Procter, getting him out with the last ball. Mike came off the field and said that, in the whole of his career, he had never faced a better over.

'Also, at another match, there was a marvellous example of how enjoyable it is for the amateurs as well. Company director Nigel Wray, who is a terrific supporter of the Taverners, and of Wellbeing, was batting. Normally you try to ensure that people who have paid to play actually get a decent innings. Wasim Akram was bowling to Nigel and the last ball of the first over was one of those dipping, late inswingers – one of those yorkers that doesn't get played by anyone! The umpire said, "Oh, we'd better call that a no ball," and Nigel said, "No, it's a privilege to be out to a delivery like that!"'

I know Chippinghurst well from the Taverners' Sixes but in 2010 my wife Helen and I went to the Wellbeing match for the first time, as Victor's guests. As we walked past the giant marquee to stroll around the boundary, we were aware of the plethora of very smart cars and an amazing and impressive collection of cricketers on and off the field. As we ambled, I tried to list them: Jeff Thomson, Mike Gatting, Mushtaq Ahmed, Adam Gilchrist, Gordon Greenidge. Then, a little later, Mike Atherton, Mark Nicholas, Brian Lara and many more. No wonder that the day is so successful, and no wonder that Victor is so pleased with how productive his converted river meadow has become. 'The first match we had, I remember standing by the fence at the edge of the ground watching Dennis Lillee bowl to Clive Lloyd.

I am watching two of my heroes and just thinking that this is heaven. These guys are playing on my pitch and we are raising all this money for the charity.'

Chippinghurst is clearly at the very heart of Victor's love of all things cricket but I wonder whether Victor, as a chairman of large public companies, found it difficult to watch cricket as much as he might have wanted. 'Ideally I would have seen more matches, preferably at Lord's, but I have had a business life that has been very full and that has enabled me to do all kinds of things, including my involvement with cricket. I probably wouldn't have had a chance to do that in other circumstances, so there are pluses and minuses to the hectic round of business.

'When I do watch, I am primarily a Test match man. I also used to love the John Player League, the 40-over games on Sunday afternoons, but Twenty20 I don't enjoy as much. However, the number of people it attracts, the amount of money it brings to the game, means that it is here to stay. How can you turn down a formula that has that kind of attraction? The big question must be whether longer forms of the game will survive. But grounds here still get filled for Test cricket, and I think they will continue to do so.

'There is a social element to watching cricket, as well as a purely sporting one. People go for the pies and the beers, and into boxes, and make an occasion of it. We will always have the national pride to want to have international teams continuing to play each other in Test matches. The problem is between Twenty20 at one end, which brings the money in, and the Test matches, which I believe people want to watch. But what do you put in between to make sure you have got the skills to play the five-day game, bearing in mind the county game attracts very few spectators?

'I also think we probably have got too much cricket and we should either amalgamate the counties or reduce the number of games they play, something the county chairmen would almost certainly resist. But if you take a stratospheric view and look at the number of counties, and you take self-interest out of it, then you have to say something needs to give. Self-interest leads to bankruptcy. We haven't had enough reforms in the county game. Ian MacLaurin did a great job as chairman of the ECB [England & Wales Cricket Board] but he was never really allowed to finish the job because his proposed changes to the game didn't suit a lot of people. I don't know how you make the change, because the vested interests of the counties really dominate the ECB and make it very difficult to push significant change through. We have made a lot of progress, though. We've got the central contracts, and money does get down to the counties. But to improve things further, I hope cricket can attract to its hierarchy and administration more of the talented individuals who love and know the game.'

As a boy, Victor lived in Stockport, just outside Manchester, with a father who enjoyed cricket. They would play in the back yard, which was in effect no more than a long piece of concrete. 'My father tried to persuade me to become a left-arm spin bowler, because he thought that was actually much better than being a right-handed bowler. But I never managed to do it. There are those who'd say I never really improved after the age of eight, which is probably closer to the truth! But I always enjoyed it. I played at school, and a little bit at university – not particularly well – and I've played it socially ever since. I've never been a great cricketer, although I would like to have been – but the skill just wasn't there!

'Though you should know, John, that I was once 12th man for Lancashire, in a sort of honorary way. It was something given to me after doing so many Wellbeing games, as a thank you. I had to turn up at Lord's at noon with my kit, for a one-day Sunday league game against Middlesex. So I go and have lunch with the team, get changed with the team, have nets with the team, spend the afternoon in the dressing room with the team, take out the drinks and the kit – the only thing I couldn't do was actually play! But that was fun, and Lancashire won, but no thanks to me!

'The most memorable time for me at a Taverners game was when Rory Bremner was fielding and went off at some point, took the microphone and started doing impressions of everyone who was on the field. It was just hysterical. You couldn't play serious cricket while it was all going on! He would announce that Nelson Mandela had turned up to watch the match and imitate his voice – and then it would be John Major, and then a stream of others. Quite remarkable!'

Victor began watching cricket when he was taken by his father to one of the most famous of Test match grounds, Old Trafford, as a seven or eight-year-old schoolboy. 'I still have this image of Brian Statham opening the bowling for Lancashire with everyone except two players standing behind the bat. He had four slips, two gullies, a point, a leg slip, wicketkeeper and a mid-on and a mid-off. My father explained to me how this worked – how a fast bowler aimed to get the ball to move one way or another so that it would hit the edge of the bat and fly into the slips and so on. So that was my introduction to first-class cricket and from then on I used to go to Old Trafford in my summer holidays. I'd get the train to Piccadilly station, buy a box of sandwiches and a glass of orange juice when I was there, and then just sit and watch. My most memorable time at Old Trafford was watching Jim Laker get his 19 wickets against Australia in 1956. I saw him get 17 of them and after that, how can you not love the game, be excited by it and become a cricket fan?'

Victor has put so much into cricket in all sorts of different ways and particularly in the charitable sense, but is there is anything he has taken from the game that has been significant in his life? 'Well, first of all I have had immense pleasure out of it because I have met people I would never otherwise have met – people who are prominent in the game that I love, people who I admire. As I said before, heroes have come and played on my own cricket pitch, which is a great thrill.

'What I have also taken from it is the immense decency the game has engendered in virtually all the people who have played, in contrast with other sports. While money may be a factor in football, for example, you rarely find it so in the cricketing fraternity. Those who get to the top of the game in international cricket probably get fairly decent rewards, but those who are just quality county players are still quite modestly rewarded, and it is difficult for them to get jobs when they finish playing. I have tried to help a number of people over the years and just feel sad that it has to be that way.

'If you go back 30 or 40 years, local shopkeepers or manufacturers supported the cricketers who came out of county cricket, with the job of salesman or marketing director or whatever. That worked well, but it's more difficult now in a world that is changing. We were talking about Mike Atherton before. Mike did brilliantly: he was at the top of his profession and has managed subsequently to do very well in the media. Not many people can do that. Some do, but most can't, because they haven't got the skills and don't get the opportunity, and there are far too many who are left struggling. Fortunately, the Professional Cricketers Association [PCA] and ECB give advice and guidance on the educational and career options open to players, particularly once they have finished their playing careers. I do sincerely hope that this is solving the problem.'

As I leave Victor's office, he asks whether David Frost will feature in this book. When I tell him that I haven't been able to make contact, he immediately offers to do so on my behalf.

SIR VICTOR BLANK

Despite some of the tough challenges that Victor has had to face in his long business career, this typically helpful gesture again demonstrates his caring and friendly nature, whether it be to retiring cricketers or humble writers!

RORY BREMNER

'BILL TIDY WAS ON THE BOUNDARY AND COULD SEE
THAT I WAS A BIT NERVOUS. I WON'T EASILY FORGET
HIS WONDERFULLY ENCOURAGING WORDS. "DON'T
WORRY, RORY – THE WORST THING THAT CAN HAPPEN
IS THAT YOU WILL BE TOTALLY HUMILIATED!"'

*Rory Bremner was born in Edinburgh on 6 April 1961. He is
an impressionist, comedian and political satirist. His first television
series* Now – Something Else *on BBC2 was followed by a
move to Channel 4 for* Rory Bremner, Who Else? *and*
Bremner, Bird and Fortune, *both of which have won numerous
awards. He has made many other appearances on radio and
television in programmes such as* Parkinson, Breakfast with
Frost, Mock the Week *and* Sunday AM, *and presented a
BBC Four documentary,* Rory Bremner and the Fighting
Scots. *He has also translated two operas and a play from French
and German into English.*

Peter Jones, a department store in Sloane Square on the
corner of Chelsea's King's Road, is where ladies who lunch,
lunch. It is also where, in the Top Floor restaurant, Rory
Bremner joins me at noon for a light snack and a remarkable
hour of cricket. He sits across the table from me with his
notebook open in front of him, so he can work through a list of
topics he has prepared for our meeting. For most of our time

together, I am a one-man audience for a performance by the country's top impressionist. Rory is quickly into his stride, describing his introduction to the Lord's Taverners.

'I had done my first television show at the end of 1984 and was getting reasonably well known on the cricket benefit and charity circuit in the following year. It was then that I met Brian Johnston, who said, "Bremmers, we must get you into the Taverners." So he got me to join and, as a kind of thank you, he invited me to do "View from the Boundary" on *Test Match Special* at Edgbaston. England were beating Australia by an innings when, in the BBC box, Johnners said, "Can you do an impression of Richie Benaud?" As I started with "Good morning, everyone, and it's a lovely day here at Edgbaston," I noticed everyone in the box falling about laughing. I suddenly realised that there was somebody behind me and, of course, it was Richie himself! Johnners had done one of his classic set up things. So there was Richie, who said, "Very funny, very good, but what about the royalties? That's what I want to know!"'

'That was my second encounter with Johnners. Another was in a tent, at an Eve of Test Match Dinner before England played the West Indies who, in those days, were beating everybody. Johnners was on his feet, talking away, when the rain started to pound on the roof of the tent. Johnners just looked up and said, "Is that rain, or are the West Indies pissing on us already?"'

When Rory was on *Desert Island Discs* he chose *Test Match Special*'s "He just didn't quite get his leg over" commentary from 1991, when Ian Botham was out hit wicket. It is abundantly clear that Johnners's humour and sense of fun had a particular appeal. 'Absolutely! I think the reason I chose that was because it was just sheer joy. I felt that if I were to be on a desert island, I would like some of the humanity, the warmth of a human just reduced to helplessness by laughter. And that obviously was it. "Oooh, oh stop it, Aggers!" and then in came the new batsman, "Syd" Lawrence, amid more roars of laughter. "Aargh, oooh, Aggers, stop it!" I think you had to hear the original, but Aggers tried to commentate and he couldn't do it. It is just timeless. It is just a joyous thing. There are stories of people pulling over to the hard shoulder of the motorway that day because they were crying with laughter. I think it is still impossible to listen to without bursting out laughing yourself or without feeling that wonderful joy just spread over you. Because here was somebody completely helpless. Most of us have been in that situation where you get the giggles and you are trying to control it. It is a completely unwinnable battle.

'Thinking back, the mid-1980s were what you would call the Gower/Lamb/Botham era – the three musketeers. There was a lot of fun to be had and while I wasn't quite in the front line of all that, they all became friends of mine over the years. Whenever I was in Hampshire, I spent a lot of time going to see Mark Nicholas and David Gower playing down there. On one occasion we took Ian Botham and Gower out to dinner. We mis-ordered and, at the end of the meal, they said, "We're sorry, we have one bottle of wine too many for you." We were just about to send it back when Botham just puts his hand out and says, "No, it's OK, I'll have that," and he went back to his room, finished off the last bottle of red on his own, and came out to bat again the next morning!'

Rory then moves from Botham to Boycott and a One Day International in the Caribbean in the late 1980s. 'The Yorkshireman was going round in the morning telling everyone, "I'd have a bat, I'd definitely bat, I'd bat." So England batted – and got absolutely trounced!

'Another Boycott interlude was in Pakistan, when I went to see some friends in the commentary box and he said, "What are you eating? Don't eat the local muck – here, 'ave some of my food." And he shared an apple with me, saying "It's OK, we'll see you right. Don't you worry." On meeting my wife in Cape Town in 2010, he said, "Now then, he's made enough out of me, so I hope he gives you some of the money."' Several years ago, when Boycott was having a little bit of local difficulty with his girlfriend, Rory wondered why would any woman go to bed with him. 'He'd be at you all night. "No, no – bad technique is that. You've got your legs in the wrong place…" Fortunately, I think you do have licence as a professional comedian, and people you impersonate usually realise that if they get too stroppy about it, they are going to make themselves look stupid. It is rather like the Royal Family, who you always assume have to have a sense of humour.

'Allan Lamb, for example, is just a great character and to this day we always have enormous fun. He gets himself into all sorts of scrapes and I still love his use of English, because he's the kind of person who will say, "I'll tell you about this bloke, but you'd better be careful because he doesn't take any pensioners!" Lamby's greatest moment was with Ian Botham in the Imran Khan libel trial in 1996. The story goes that the prosecutor said, "Now, Mr Lamb, do you condone cheating?" and Lamby replied, "Absolutely. I completely and utterly condone any form of cheating!" His lawyer had to stand up and say, "Your honour, I think Mr Lamb means 'condemn'."

'I always tease him about John McCarthy, who I played a couple of charity games with in the early 1990s. One day I told Lamby that I was trying to get hold of John McCarthy. And his response? "Is that the bloke that was held hostage in Debenhams?" I was out in Cape Town in 1995/96, doing a show for Allan Lamb's testimonial, and it was the first time I had done an impersonation of Nelson Mandela. So we made up this thing about Mandela being asked to do Robin Smith's benefit and saying, "Why are we going to do Robin's benefit? I spent nearly 30 years on Robben's bloody island!"'

It was at Clifton Hall School, near Edinburgh, that Rory first played any organised cricket. 'That was where I learned to bowl leg breaks and came to love the game. I can remember being very excited with my first Wisden cricket bat – that had to be oiled in those days – and how I practically went to bed with it. As a teenager, at Wellington College in Berkshire, I developed as a player, although the competition for a place in the first XI was usually pretty strong. I was never good enough, to be honest, so I was either in the second or third XI, where I just bowled my leg breaks. I was always more a bowler than a batsman, although now I love batting. After Wellington the cricket lapsed, before I got a chance to play in charity games with the Taverners and others.'

In 1993, at Wormsley, an Old England team beat an Old Australia side by 20 runs and for some reason Rory was the only non-professional player. Batting at number four, he made a useful 23 and added 68 for the fourth wicket with Clive Radley. 'I remember going out to bat when Mike Denness was out. Bill Tidy, lovely Bill Tidy, was on the boundary and could see that I was a bit nervous. I won't easily forget his wonderfully encouraging words. "Don't worry, Rory – the worst thing that can happen is that you will be totally humiliated!" The great thing about that day was facing Dennis Lillee. That was wonderful. The ball was bending like a banana, even though he wasn't bowling anything like his normal speed – he was barely medium-paced. He dropped one short and I thought I would hook it, played the shot and looked up to see the umpire signalling four. I looked down to fine leg, then to square leg, to see where the ball had gone and Lillee said, "Other way, mate!" It had come off an edge and gone down to third man, a total fluke!

'One painful memory was when I broke my hand in a charity six-a-side game at Althorp, near Northampton. As I went out to bat, Charles Spencer, who was playing on his own home ground, had apparently suggested to Chris Cairns, the New Zealand all-rounder, that he might "ginger it up a bit." The first ball came through very quickly and the next thing I knew was that it was whizzing past my head. It was a bouncer, but not close enough to do any damage; it was certainly the quickest ball I had ever faced. The next one was quite quick and as I prodded a forward defensive, it hit the back of my hand and broke my knuckle. So I went off and had it checked out at hospital and sure enough, there was a fracture there. I had to give a speech in the evening and was full of wine and painkillers, so I can't remember what I said, but it apparently went OK! And that was my one cricket scar.'

In July 2000 there was a memorial game for Malcolm Marshall at the HAC ground in London, in which some of the truly great names from international cricket took the field. They included Gordon Greenidge, Desmond Haynes, Viv Richards, Joel Garner, Michael Holding, Courtney Walsh, Shane Warne, Mike Gatting, Graham Thorpe and Alec Stewart. Again, Rory was the sole non-pro cricketer and he nearly spoiled the party. 'I bowled Brian Lara. I think he was trying to hit me into the sea from the City of London and it was just one of those flukey sort of leg breaks that, to the great left-hander, pitched on middle and off, turned and hit middle and leg. He'd only got 10. I wish I hadn't done it, because it must have massively disappointed the crowd. They didn't come to watch me bowl, but they certainly came to watch Lara bat. So in retrospect it was the most stupid thing I could have done. But then it wasn't exactly my fault.'

Over the years, Rory spent a lot of time with Colin Cowdrey, occasions that he enjoyed enormously, not least for the lovely man's fund of wonderful stories. 'Evidently somebody once turned up for a shooting weekend in a brand new suit.

Colin just walked up, felt the material and, along with his typical colloquial mannerisms, said, "Urgh, urgh. Well, why pay more?" I was down at Angmering, where he lived, on the day in 1997 that it was announced he had become a lord. There was nobody else there and his wife, Lady Herries, was away for the night at a race meeting somewhere, so it was just he and I sitting at opposite ends of the table. The phone kept ringing – people congratulating him – and Colin was so modest and so self-effacing. He would just keep saying, "Urgh, urgh, I am so sorry, another piss-taker, another piss-taker!" Then he would get up to take another call and I could hear him say, "Hello, hello, that's very kind. Isn't it lovely about Peter O'Sullevan?" So he straight away moved the conversation away from himself and on to Peter O'Sullevan, who had been knighted in the same honours list.

'Lovely man, Colin Cowdrey – just so kind and generous, and the Cowdrey stories are legend. He was facing Thomson and Lillee for the first time and at the drinks break he took his glove off, went up to Jeff Thomson, and said, "Urgh, I'm not sure, urgh, I don't think we have ever met. My name is Colin Cowdrey. How are you?" Colin hated sledging and, if somebody was really sledging very hard and getting very worked up, he would go and see them after the close of play. Then he would say, "Urm, you seemed very bothered about something out there. Is there anything I can do? You seem very upset."

'Colin loved his Don Bradman stories. He saw Bradman, I think when he went out for the Melbourne Cup, and they were able to spend some time together. He particularly liked the story of Bradman at Lord's. "It was the first time King George ever took a wicket! Australia were doing quite well – and then King George arrived. He met the teams and on resumption Australia immediately lost a wicket. Out came Bradman, who scored a not-out 100 and whatever it was, between tea and the close of play. As the Don walked off at the end of the day, the steward opened the gate at the bottom of the pavilion steps and said, "Well done, sir. Well done, Mr Bradman." The Don turned to him and said…' At which stage Rory stops, smiles and says to me, 'Sorry, John, I don't know why I am doing this as Brian Johnston – it's Colin Cowdrey talking!' After our laughter has subsided, Rory resumes the tale. '"And the Don said, 'Yep, nice bit of practice for tomorrow.'"'

Looking to move on to the subject of his recording of 'N-N-Nineteen Not Out', I embark on what might be the worst link of all time. I tell Rory that I came here from Islington on a bus and inevitably it was a number 19. 'Oh, very good, John, very good. Yes, "Nineteen Not Out" was a bit of a boost because at the beginning of the summer in 1985 it went to number 13 in the singles charts and I found myself on *Top of the Pops*. I was obsessed with cricket and cricket commentators and stuff like that, and I used to do some voices for Andrew Sachs' son, John, who was on Capital Radio. I was messing around doing these things when Paul Hardcastle's number one hit "19" came out, and it just popped into my head. I can't remember exactly how the idea came around, but it was one of those great things that happen sometimes. I think I suggested it to people I worked with and, out of nowhere, the next thing I knew, Kim Fuller, the comedy writer and director, became interested. Kim is the brother of Simon Fuller, a massive agent, artist manager and producer, and the man who discovered and managed Paul Hardcastle. Because they were brothers it was much easier to get the permissions to do a parody of the original "19." So we did it, and into it went the John Arlott "It's a long, slow, lazy delivery, but it's the best I can do" and Brian Johnston, Richie Benaud and so on.'

The enormous range of impersonations that Rory has accomplished, of both players and commentators in cricket, is impressive to say the very least. But I wonder whether there have been any that have been too bland, or too tricky, to master? 'To be quite honest, if they were too difficult I just wouldn't do them. One that I am quite pleased with is David Gower. I think it is fair to say that his is not exactly an obvious voice, but he's got that slight laugh, and the self-deprecation. Also, he speaks very obliquely. He doesn't say, "That was plumb lbw," he will say, "I think it is fair to say that was not un-adjacent." Or he won't say, "Went out last night and got pissed" – he'll say, "I think it is true to say a fairly good time was had by all, a certain amount of alcohol was consumed and we went home tired but happy." Or, if he hits a six, a huge six, he will say, "It's always fairly nice to get some form of contact and, obviously, if the ball disappears over the ropes, then so much the better." So there is a wonderful way about him and it is one I'm pleased about.

'But they are all great characters. David Lloyd – good old Bumble. "Eh, look at that, eh." The value he gets out of names like Shane Warne and Ashley Giles, and that wonderful Accrington accent. His brilliant story about having his box turned inside out by a delivery from Jeff Thomson – he contrasts it with Andrew Flintoff being hit in the box by Cardigan Connor. Lloyd came up to Flintoff and said, "Cardigan Connor? You can consider it an honour to be hit by Cardigan. Do you remember Jeff Thomson? I was hit amidships by him, and it was not a glancing blow. I was wearing one of those old boxes – you know, the pink ones, like a soap dish. It ended up that everything that was supposed to be inside the box had come outside the box – through the air holes!"

'And Bumble tells of batting with Colin Cowdrey on the 74/75 Ashes tour and thinking that Cowdrey, by then in his early forties, might like a bit of protection early on. So he thought, "I'll protect him, take a bit of the shine off the new ball. I'll take a bit of heat out of it." So he hogged the strike for a bit, just to blunt the edge and give Cowdrey more of a chance.

After a few overs, Cowdrey strolls down and they do that thing where they prod the pitch and do a bit of gardening, and Cowdrey says, "I say, this is rather fun, isn't it?" Bumble says, "Fun? Fun? I don't know what you call fun. Call this fun?"'

The stories continue to roll off Rory's tongue as the time for him to leave approaches, and he manages one more before he goes. 'The South African born pair, Allan Lamb and Robin Smith, are batting together for England against the West Indies. The umpires were the Jamaican, Steve Bucknor, and David Constant. Lamb supposedly went up to Constant and said, "Here David, I've just realised – you are the only English f****r out here!"'

How do you follow that? Perhaps by looking for his personal take on the wonderful game. 'Well, I suppose you would say it is the sunshine game. I just associate it with summer days, with great times, whether it be in Cape Town or Antigua, or Lord's or the Oval, or any ground. Summer afternoons, and that smell and the sound. And the friends that I have met through the game have been some of my best acquaintances. Even to this day, and it is probably a weakness on my part, I can't fully understand or warm totally to anybody who doesn't enjoy sport, particularly cricket. The personalities, the characters, the contests are everything, and when you throw in the sunshine and the locations it is just the best.'

The hour has flown by and I have a recording that would make a thoroughly entertaining CD or radio show. Rory often seems more comfortable when he is the voice of someone else and as a result, not only do I have a collection of cricket anecdotes but I've also had the best seat in the house and been right royally entertained. It is no wonder that I am still chuckling as I set off to seek another number 19 bus.

LORRAINE CHASE

'I REMEMBER WHEN I WAS IN EMMERDALE THAT I USED TO HAVE THESE WONDERFUL FALSE NAILS, AND IF THE BALL WAS COMING HARD TOWARDS ME, I HAD TO DECIDE WHETHER I SHOULD WORRY ABOUT MY NAILS OR ABOUT STOPPING IT!'

Lorraine Chase was born in Deptford, south London, on 16 July 1951 and is an actress and model. She made her name in a Campari TV commercial in the 1970s, with the catchphrase 'Nah, Luton Airport'. She has appeared on television in the BBC quiz show Blankety Blank, *the children's programme* Worzel Gummidge, *the sitcoms* The Other 'Arf *and* Lame Ducks, *and in the long-running soap* Emmerdale. *She has made frequent appearances on stage, at home and abroad, in plays such as* Shirley Valentine *and* Dead Guilty, *at the Edinburgh Festival and in films such as* Love and Bullets.

I arrive at the bar at the Ritz Hotel in London's Piccadilly in good time, jacketed but tie-less. I had forgotten – no tie, no entry. The bar staff are not new to this situation and produce a box containing a selection of ties that may have been smart, perhaps even fashionable, once upon a time. I select one at random and once it is approximately in place, I am permitted to pass through the golden gates to await Lorraine's arrival. When she appears, dressed in a black leather coat and tastefully

35

'blinged', she is as eye-catching and poised as ever, and a pleasure to be with.

Her love of cricket is very different from that of the other people I speak to while putting *Cricket Wonderful Cricket* together. She does not claim an in-depth knowledge of the game, nor does she pretend for one moment to be a keen supporter or spectator. But in her own way she is as involved as she can be and has been prepared to learn from the time she first began to play. 'I had some coaching at Lord's about 12 years ago from a lovely man whose name I simply can't remember, but I do know that he was very nice to me and very patient. It was just before my first trip to Guernsey with the Taverners and we were going to play a match in Sark. I decided that I wanted to do it properly and not let the side or the charity down when I went out on the field. So before we flew out, I had a couple of lessons in the nets in the indoor school and I felt a lot more confident and ready to give it a go.'

Clive Radley, a different lovely man, was MCC head coach at the time. He remembers Lorraine coming for coaching and tells me, 'It was most unusual for someone who knows that they will probably only bowl a couple of overs and maybe face a few deliveries in a game to make that sort of commitment. She could have just shown up at a match and signed a few autographs but that's not her style. Instead, she took it very seriously and made sure that she could bowl a decent ball and play straight, which is a lot more than I could say of one or two others I know!'

When Lorraine got to Sark, she had more lessons from one of the Taverners people in nets at the Governor's House, and she obviously appreciates the help she was given. 'I suppose having lessons at Lord's, and then in the Governor's House, wasn't the worst preparation that anyone has ever had for their first game of cricket!

'In fact, I think it was their first match in Sark and Guernsey, so I was the first celebrity ever to go with them. And, from there on I've tried to play whenever I've been asked to, and have done so every season since that first trip. Every so often people say to me, "Oh, what are you doing this weekend?" and I tell them that I am going to play cricket. I have been going over to Guernsey ever since the matches started 12 or 13 years ago, but they still say, "What do you mean? You really play? Is that why you go over there?" And I have to explain to them that I like to play, to take part, to be one of the team – if not one of the boys! I have a bat, try to stay in for a while, maybe make a run or two. When we field, I am not the fastest bowler in the world – I certainly won't be a killer bowler – but I can bowl over-arm and get it straight to the batsman well enough. I don't pretend to understand the game in great detail but I like it, I like playing and I enjoy the great camaraderie. But I feel that to put my name to cricket without making a real effort would be almost insulting. As a result, Mike Gatting and John Snow, and a lot of other lovely cricketers, are very sweet and very good to me, and actually don't mind if I'm in their team.'

One of those lovely cricketers was the charismatic Graham Roope, who died suddenly in Grenada in 2006. 'I loved Roopy. He was a very kind man, generous with his time and with his knowledge. He was always trying to teach me to bowl that bit better and talked about anything that might help me to enjoy and understand more about the game. It made me want to try even harder when I was out on the pitch. I can remember once doing something very stupid when I was fielding, although now I look back I am so glad I did it, even though I was in a lot of pain as a result.

'It was not long before Roopy died, and we were playing for the Lord's Taverners at Headingley in Leeds. We were supposed to be playing outside but it rained, so we decided that rather than not play at all, we would use the indoor cricket school.

While we were fielding, I missed a ball that I really should have stopped. I shouldn't have allowed it to hit the back wall because when you are playing inside, that counts as something like four or six runs. I saw that Roopy, who was captain, was looking a little aggravated. The next time the ball came in my direction, it was like the one that I'd missed, although it was travelling quite a bit faster. I stuck my foot out to stop it, it hit my instep and I swear to God that [Lorraine now demonstrates a seemingly impossible series of contortions] my toes stayed there, the heel stayed there, but the whole foot went like that and then came back again. And everyone on the pitch, everyone, went deathly quiet, until I squeaked, "I'm alright, I'm alright." Roopy was more concerned than anyone, and afterwards he said, "Thanks for stopping that one – the runs you saved would have lost us the match." I told him that I was all right, but it did hurt my foot and was a very stupid thing to do. But that man, I didn't want to let him down.'

A couple of years after Graham died, a memorial match was played by the Taverners at Woodhouse Grove School in Yorkshire, where he had been the cricket coach for many years following his retirement from the first-class game. Organised by the school, the match supported not only the Taverners but also a new Memorial Fund that was to be established in Graham's name to assist in the development of cricket in schools within the Leeds and Bradford area. Lorraine was in the team that narrowly won the contest. 'It was a long way from my home to the school but it was worth every mile of the journey – I just wouldn't have missed it for anything. I bowled a couple of overs, signed some autographs and we won by three wickets – I think it was off the last ball of the match. But in the end, it was all about Roopy.'

In 2009, Lorraine was on parade for a game in Lincolnshire between a Taverners team led by Chris Tarrant and Bourne

Cricket Club. 'I batted with Chris for a little while and scored two runs, before the wicketkeeper stumped me. I always think of Chris as the geezer who does *Millionaire*. He just takes the mickey out of me mercilessly, but I've often been on his team, and he's another one I love very much. I realise I'm usually put in as the joker because, as you know, I am not terribly good, but I can bowl and not only that, I've opened the batting at Lord's and in Sark, so I must be doing something right! From the time I first started to play I decided that if I was going to do it, I didn't want to just be the token. My dream is to hit a six. Oh, to hear that noise and to see it go for miles! To hit it out of the blooming ground, instead of getting caught… I see the lads playing so well and whacking it time after time – that's my dream, that's what I want to be able to do.

'Someone who is always very kind to me is Mike Gatting. I often borrow his pads and gloves, and I've got a red cap he gave me, which I always wear when I'm playing. Because if you've got all your gear, then you look the part. I am very proud of my whites, for instance. Very proud. I hate it when they play in different colours. I think it's horrid. The same as I hate people playing tennis in colours. I love all that white. I love all the tradition and the styles. And I have to say, when I'm playing in a match and I can turn up in my whites, I am all lovely and comfortable! And I've got my plimsolls, my lovely flat shoes. And I don't have to put on too much make-up; it would look pretty ridiculous if I was overly made up. So that is quite nice, because you're kind of one of the boys.

'I have to find a toilet to change in, because there aren't too many ladies' dressing rooms available! But I often have to go gingerly to where the men are changing to ask to borrow pads or helmets and things. I love all that, maybe because it's a bit like dressing up to go on stage, to perform. It could be the acting thing, that the cricket ground we play on is the stage. Maybe that's it.

'They look after you when you're out on the pitch and teach you how to field properly. Now I know to be more careful with my foot, and also the way to kneel down, so you stop it with the side of your leg rather than doing daft things. I remember when I was in *Emmerdale* that I used to have these wonderful false nails and if the ball was coming hard towards me, I had to decide whether I should worry about my nails or about stopping it! Then you have to remember that you're there for the charity and for the entertainment, because if it all gets too serious, then it spoils it – as well as your nails! So they always used to look after me, guide me and protect me. Mike Gatting would say, "Lorraine, come here – come and stand just over there," making sure it was somewhere that I could be fielding safely and that I never got into an area where the ball would be whacked and hurt me. He would work out each batsman to decide where to put me for safety. It's a lovely feeling, being looked after like that.'

Mike Gatting and Lorraine Chase turn out to be something of a mutual admiration society, as the former Ashes-winning captain is happy to confirm. 'She is a really bubbly lady and she throws heart and soul into it. We get on very well. She just loves being around, enjoys the Taverners and she always turns up when she says she will. She has put in a lot of effort to make sure that she is able to bowl properly. And that's all credit to her, because she knows what she is doing and can actually do it. It's always great when she's at a match, because you know that she will sign autographs 'til her arm falls off and will talk to everybody. And, of course, she always wears the red cap!'

At this stage in the evening, our quiet conversation is being almost drowned out by the incessant braying of a suited individual on his mobile phone. 'He's very loud, isn't he?' is Lorraine's understated comment. My gripe in response is that I hate mobile phones at the best of times. These people never seem to me to need a phone because they can be heard anyway about a mile away. Later that evening I wonder why an establishment that demands a tie condones this noise pollution. But time to move on!

When Lorraine was in *Emmerdale*, she played the part of Stephanie Stokes, a nasty individual, and that made things interesting for her on and off the field. 'It was very difficult because before that, everyone knew me as the nutty person I am – and hopefully as a nice person. As far as acting was concerned, I used to get offered the lovely fairy and that sort of thing, but since *Emmerdale*, because I played this woman, I now get all the wickeds – Wicked Queen, Wicked Fairy and so on. Fortunately, the *Emmerdale* cricket team recognised the true me and we had a great time when we played. Roopy was an outsider who was very much involved in the side with actor Chris Chittell and the others who played, like Patrick Mower. The *Emmerdale* team played quite regularly every season. We had a lot of fun and raised a lot of money for charity.'

Lorraine's place in the world of cricket and her achievements, from a standing start, in making the very best that she can of her involvement, are now well established. But she has a tale that she is obviously dying to tell because of its importance to her. 'When I took on the role of *Shirley Valentine*, I was going through a pretty hard time in lots of ways. I was touring Hong Kong, Bangkok and Singapore, and it was quite lonely because unlike the film, you are the only actor in the original stage play. You didn't have the company of other actors – there were only a couple of fellows who were on the technical side of it. Anyway, when I was in Singapore, I went to the theatre early to see what the set-up was, because the play took place after dinner. And I heard this voice I recognised. I followed it and it came from the bar – and who is sitting there but Ian Botham and Allan Lamb. They were out there with a tour or something and up to no good, I suspect. But I have never, ever been so glad to see two old mates. I went up behind them and said, "How are you, alright?" and Botham turned round and said, "Crikey! What the hell are you doing here?" I said, "I'm doing a play – don't you look at the posters?" So I will always remember that moment. Someone to talk to, to laugh with. Friendship, familiar faces – when I needed them most. And all because of cricket.'

Lorraine then took me back to when she became a member of the Lady Taverners, having met Jean Ratcliff, a past chairman, at a function at The Dorchester. 'There aren't enough words to say how wonderful Jeannie is, what she has achieved, how brave she has been. She introduced me to the charity and I became an honorary Lady Taverner. From then on, I always used to go with her to places where it was hard to get people to go. It's quite easy to get people to come to things in the West End, but a challenge when it was to go out in the regions. So we would go to Wales, or up north, and that really got me involved in the Lady Taverners and before long I was asked to take part in the cricket. As I've said, Jeannie is a wonderful woman and throughout the charity as a whole, there are some lovely people. It's a great charity and long may it be so, because it isn't political: it isn't people playing at a charity. We do enjoy ourselves, we do have a good time, but we raise money while we are doing it. We don't go, "Oh this is very difficult, this is very painful." We just get on and do it, and I like that. I like that honesty and I like that fun.'

But it is cricket that we have met to discuss and it is cricket that Lorraine wants to get to understand even better than she does already. 'The Tavs' captains nearly always seem to be able to ensure that matches would have a very close finish, even if it is the Taverners who win. There are tactics that they can use, such as where to place the field, to get the result they want. I know there are tactics involved in the game, and I have often thought there is more to this than meets the eye!

'So I love it. I like being part of a team and I don't mind going round with a blanket for everyone to throw the money in and chatting to people. As I say, you are part of the team, and that's off the field as well as on. It's going out there and mucking about and teasing, but also talking to people. That's what you're there for. You're not there just to enjoy yourself and you're not there to have a miserable time, but you are there to work. And I enjoy doing it. I'm particularly thrilled when the Lord's Taverners ask me to play cricket because – and this is going to sound strange in a way – it's nice to be one of the boys. It's not that I'm an unmarried woman and I'm in amongst men – but I like to be not just a woman, but one of the team. And it is a nice feeling, too, that I can also spend time with all the wives that are there, people like Jenny Snow, and they all love you and look after you. Yes, cricket, I love it.'

This has been a very special and enjoyable conversation because this lovely lady, cockney and proud of it, has provided me with a completely new and refreshing perspective on the wonderful game. She simply bubbles over with energy, enthusiasm and laughter in a way that is totally infectious. Towards the end of our chat, we are joined by Lorraine's friend Brian who runs Tramp, the club in nearby Jermyn Street, and has just returned from America. After a suitably warm embrace, I take my leave of them, rid myself of the dreaded tie and stumble off into the Piccadilly night, simply feeling good.

ALAN
DAVIES

'I PLAYED WITH ARTHUR SMITH, A COMEDIAN FRIEND OF MINE, WHO HAD A TEAM CALLED DUSTY FLEMING'S INTERNATIONAL HAIR STYLISTS.'

Alan Davies was born in Loughton, Essex, on 6 March 1966. He is an actor, comedian and writer, who starred in the BBC mystery series Jonathan Creek *and is a permanent panellist on* QI, *the BBC comedy quiz programme. He also has the leading role as a celebrity chef in* Whites, *which started its BBC run in September 2010, and has made numerous appearances on other radio and television programmes, including* A Many Splintered Thing. *He is an award-winning stand-up comedian and his autobiographical book,* My Favourite People and Me, *was published in 2009.*

Alan Davies and I are both Islington residents and we meet in Trevi, a restaurant just off Highbury Corner. It is well regarded, modest, family-orientated and Italian, and busy even on a hot weekday afternoon. Alan arrives at three on the dot and orders linguini fruta de mare while I nurse a coffee. He is a pescatarian and tells me that this dish will be 'a bowl of pasta with bits of squid sticking out of it'! It's an encouragingly relaxed start to a chat with a man I have not met before and who, as well as being an Arsenal supporter, has been watching cricket since he was a schoolboy.

'My brother and I were taken to Lord's in the mid-1970s to see England play against Pakistan. Then there was England against the West Indies at the Oval in 1976, when Michael Holding was bowling, and he would walk out nearly to the boundary and then turn round and run in. He was fantastic and took loads of wickets – and the whole field was brown because of the hot weather. When I was 10 or 11, I was also taken to see Essex. They never seemed to have done anything at all until 1979, when they won the Championship for the very first time, led by Keith Fletcher. I can still remember their names: Pont and East, Acfield and Graham Gooch, as well as Lever. Whenever I look at Essex in the newspaper I somehow still think it is going to say Acfield, East, Pont…

'I was taught how to score by my dad, so I bought little score books and went over to Woodford Wells Cricket Club, which is near where I grew up and not far from here. Most of the time we didn't know the names of the players – we didn't even know who the other team was! – so we would make up names. We would find some characteristic in the player, so if he had a short-sleeved jumper or bald head or dark hair or flat cap, then that would help us find a name. 'Wrongfoot' was my favourite, because my dad was very hot on any bowler who bowled off the wrong foot. I remember Mike Procter used to bowl like that and whenever he was on television, every time he bowled my dad would ask why he had bowled off the wrong foot. So I might write in my scorebook: *Baldy, caught Black Cap, bowled Wrongfoot, 14.*

'We also had a game that we used to play which my granddad, I think, maybe invented, called Dob Cricket. You stuck a pin in the obituary notice of the newspaper and each letter of the alphabet or number represented something that happened in the game of cricket. I can't remember many of them now, except that "M" was three runs. Every time you stuck the pin in was a delivery and if you didn't get a letter then it was a dot ball. It was quite a good representation of a game of cricket: you didn't get silly scores so no one ever made 280 not out.'

But apart from scoring and Dobbing, there were times when Alan actually played the game, initially in the garden with his older brother. 'We had one pair of batting gloves and they were getting a bit dirty so he said I couldn't wear them. Then I got my thumb trapped between the ball and the bat handle, giving me a blood blister that looked like a black 10p piece. I was screaming! I'll never forget the pain. Dad came out and asked me why I wasn't wearing the batting gloves. I wailed, "He wouldn't let me wear them." But that apart, when I was batting, I just wanted to slog it. I had no patience with building an innings or playing myself in, or any of the things I was taught by my dad. So no forward defensive shots or keeping my elbow up – I just wanted to slog it!

'I played very little cricket at school and it wasn't until later on, when I was in my twenties, that I played with Arthur Smith, the comedian and a good friend of mine, who had a team called Dusty Fleming's International Hair Stylists. Dusty Fleming was a hairdresser who had a series of commercials on television, in which someone would be desperately in need of a hair-do on a film set or whatever, and Fleming would suddenly run across and say, "Dusty Fleming, international hair stylist" and would fix their hair. Arthur thought this was so funny, which is why he named his team as he did. We played four or five times each summer, usually against his friend Chris England's team, which he called "An England XI".

'All kinds of people would play in those games, some quite well-known comedians or actors. I remember Hugh Grant, who was at university with one of the other guys, playing one game. Arthur would always have a dinner and dance at the end of the season, which was over a pub in Wandsworth. He would make his own awards and my favourite was always "Best Catch Taken Whilst Smoking". I was playing every summer, but then Arthur got really ill and as a consequence he had to stop drinking completely – and that really was the whole point of the cricket. It really was. It started in the pub and finished in the pub. But it's died out now – plus Chris England used to take it very seriously and Arthur thought that was really boring. Arthur wanted to play 20 overs a side and back to the pub. Chris England would always want to get in and bat and play for as long as daylight lasted.'

In the course of our conversation, Alan reveals an intriguing and diverse group of cricketing heroes, but one in particular stands out as almost a god. 'Botham can't put a foot wrong for me. I just think he's fantastic, and the way he played cricket – I've never seen anything like it, before or since. Sometimes you watch someone play and you think it's just luck, but as a teenage boy, watching him in 1981, it was amazing. He doesn't even look like he's got his eyes open half the time, yet he's swinging that bat like a great bit of oak that he's pulled off a tree. He doesn't even take any notice of the delivery. If he wants to go down and hit it, he'll go down and hit it. And if they bounce him, he is quick enough, despite his size, to react and swat it. Pure instinct. Just talent, incredible reactions and hand-eye coordination. And you'd think, "Well, that's a one-off." But the fact is, he would go out and smash 50s and 80s all the time. Just like that day at Headingley against the Aussies when he hit 149.

'It's also really extraordinary that he's done something like 12 charity walks, covering around 20 miles a day, day after day, and has raised £10 or £12 million or something. It is unthinkable. My mum died of leukaemia, so the Leukaemia Research charity is important to me, and I think what he has done is extraordinary. He received a well-deserved knighthood.

I thought it was wrong to dish out MBEs when England won the Ashes – you shouldn't get an MBE for winning; you should get it for contributions over a long time. But honours like Botham's knighthood are well and truly deserved. Astonishing bloke. Sometimes he got into trouble and got such a bad press. In fact, the worse the press he got, the more I liked him! Just leave him alone. He is what he is. I felt sorry for his wife sometimes but yes, amazing. One of the greatest English cricketers – perhaps of the century.'

Next it's a long haul, to India in 2009, for two players who made a very big impression on Alan. 'I was lucky. I was in Chennai for the wedding of my wife's friend when, because of the terrorist attack, they moved the Mumbai Test match there. So I got to go to the Test with Danny Morrison, the New Zealand pace bowler, who is not only good fun but also got tickets for me. England batted laboriously but built a good lead, setting India about 380 to win when they declared towards the end of the fourth day. They thought they could get the openers out before the close, but Sehwag came in and hit 80-odd in about 10 overs. It was really exhilarating: the crowd were electrified, and I've never seen hitting like it. If you said to me, "Sehwag is playing at Highbury Fields," I would run round there right now! I mean, there are not many people I could say that about!

'Tendulkar went on the following day to make a hundred, and to watch him is amazing. He can play any game you like. He can drop anchor for three days or he can score 200 in an hour. He can do anything he wants. I watched him in the field on the third and fourth day. The fielders walk in as the bowler is running up, and everyone watches. After the delivery, when Tendulkar turns round to walk back out again, all the crowd cheer and wave until he turns again, and then they stop. So I imagine that when he goes around the world, or goes around

India, people just wave and cheer. That's what they do every time they see him – he is an absolute deity.'

After Botham, Sehwag and Tendulkar, Alan Knott of Kent is someone he rated highly. 'Alan Knott was my childhood hero, partly because he has the same name as me! He was always in the England team; he won 95 caps and played for England for about 15 years, virtually unbroken. I used to follow Kent, even though we lived in Essex, because I had a thing about Knott. He was always in the picture, doing exercises, and he caught the eye. I always liked the slightly odd, eccentric players, like Derek Randall. I was always a sucker for a brilliant cover fielder, and I liked that he couldn't stand still. Randall was outstanding, and David Gower was as well. Gower was like lightning in the covers, even though he wandered about with his hands in his pockets most of the time. He could pick the ball up and get it in better than anyone.'

For his home county, John 'JK' Lever, a fine left-arm bowler, was always one of Alan's favourites. JK now coaches at Alan's old school, Bancroft's, but Alan mischievously claims, 'He is actually the creator of *Harry Potter* under the nom de plume Rowling! I am pretty sure about this. After all, have you ever seen Lever and Rowling in the same room?' When, a few days later, I tell JK about Alan's claim, he replies, 'I have to say he obviously hasn't tried to read my autobiography!'

Alan then tells me about the best match he has ever seen. I have to confess that I had never heard of Bermuda's Cup Match, even though it has been played every year since 1901. 'This is worth going to if you are a real cricket fan. Somerset and St George's, teams from either end of the lovely island, play over two days in a game simply called Cup Match. I went to watch the first day, at this ramshackle ground in the middle of Bermuda, with this really nice, brightly coloured pavilion and corrugated iron sheds all around the boundary. The thing I remember most about it is that as one of the batsmen was approaching 50, some guys came out and walked around the boundary with a hat, making a collection for him. People were throwing in coins, all sorts of money – and a few empty beer cans! When he got his 50, they ran on the field and presented him with the hatful of money. There was music playing, there were barbecues going on – it was packed out. It was on the radio: the concierge at the hotel had a transistor radio on the desk listening. It's a huge event, and well worth a visit.'

Alan was in Australia during the World Cup in 1992, staying in Adelaide with his aunt and uncle, and he went to see Australia play Sri Lanka. 'The visitors, who at the time were a bit hopeless, posted less than 200 in their 50 overs. In reply, Moody and Marsh put on a hundred plus for the first wicket, but got them very slowly. Whatever you say about Twenty20, it's better than the 50-over game, it really is. Eventually Dean Jones came in – the Jones Boy as they call him – and he blocked a couple and scored one or two and then suddenly hit a straight six over the bowler's head right up on to the bank. It got the whole place on its feet. It was an immaculate straight six, but by that time they only needed about 12 to win. I wanted Sri Lanka to keep bowling another five or six overs, just so I could see a bit more of Jones.'

I had been to Lord's the evening before this chat for a Twenty20 floodlit match that had pulled in a crowd of 17,000, and Alan had visited the Chelmsford ground the previous summer when it was absolutely packed. 'It's never usually that crowded. The cricket is quite well supported by the Essex public and it is a good, well-run club, but this is unheard of. The bars are packed, the merchandise is flying out the tent and they just want it every day of the week. The odd thing is that nobody really cares about the cricket, because it's just a silly slog, I think. Maybe if the game is played more it will settle down, and players are going to take it more seriously if there is more money in it. I think when it started they just put on their pyjamas, the music was playing, and they just went out and had a whack. They didn't care.

'But it is changing the way the game is played. The reverse sweep was something that was absolutely frowned upon when I was a boy. No one would even try it, because if you got out to it you were crucified. Now it is a "legit" shot – Eoin Morgan does it all the time. There are a couple of Indian guys, who run a shop at the end of my road, cricket fanatics. They love Twenty20, even though I tell them that it's not cricket – it's silly, it's obscene. It's like Arsenal playing Chelsea at five-a-side. It doesn't matter. And they always argue that it does matter, because England has won the World Cup, and I thought, "Well, apart from the fact that South Africans and an Irishman won it for them!" I can't really get interested, but OK, maybe I will get into it in the long run. We won't be talking about Twenty20 for years to come in the way you do about Test match cricket. But I think kids will grow up and learn about the game, and get enthusiasm for it, through Twenty20.

'I must say that I don't see the point of the long One Day International series that they play, quite often after the Test matches. I just get tired of it and would rather have seven Tests than that. I don't understand the one-day game any more. I don't know what a "power play" is and I can't follow the fielding regulations. Like rugby union, which I played at school, I don't understand the rules any more. If they have to keep changing the rules, there's something wrong with the game.'

Not having taken to Twenty20 and tired of too many one-day matches, there is no doubt that Test match cricket reigns supreme for Alan. 'That's what matters. That is all that matters. What is your Test average? That will tell you at the end whether you are a good player or not. I love Test cricket. It is the best. It is perfect. You can be gripped by every session, no matter what. And it doesn't get any better than it did in 2005 and those amazing games against Australia. Every session was on a knife-edge. Every wicket counted. I mean, still to this day Glenn McGrath treading on the cricket ball was the best thing. It was the most significant incident in the whole series. What was he doing playing touch rugby?'

The last traces of linguini disappear from Alan's plate and he declines the offer of dessert and coffee. Having completed the task of sorting out the inner man, he moves on to talk about the coverage of cricket on TV. Alan is most in tune with the commentators who don't take themselves or the game too seriously. 'Well, David "Bumble" Lloyd always tries to make sure that there is never a dull moment – never a dull remark. Very astute, very knowledgeable. Never says anything you think, "Nah, that's not right." Michael Holding has got such a wonderful voice and is just a joy to listen to. And he smiles and says the right thing. You just want a little bit of insight into what it feels like to be there, what's going through their minds. That's what they can offer. But I don't really like the way that if you are an ex-England captain, you get to go straight on the box. I just feel they line up the ex-England captains and in they go.

'And I don't really like Atherton's writing. I think it's extremely negative and critical and humourless. I don't know why he's so hard on people. I'm baffled by it. He won an award for his writing but seems to hate everybody who plays. Although he's not too bad on Sky Sports. To be honest, I think all the cricket writers are really hard on the players, really hard. I feel as though, with each delivery in a game, you can look at what the bowler did, or what the batsman or the fielders did, and either they did it well or badly. If you're a batsman in a Test series, your head's on the block every ball. You might make an error. You might hold your bat too far out or flash at something, be deceived and you're out. But a lot of the journalists just have a go at them.

'I've been in that press box at Lord's, that sort of sealed room they built at the end of the ground. Not only can you not hear what is going on outside, you can't even hear the ball hit the bat, never mind the crowd cheering. But no one speaks in there. It's like being in a library. It's no wonder that you end up writing a lot of angry stuff! You want to say to them, "Lighten up! It's only a game of cricket." It's one of the things you come to for fun.

'Brian Johnston was, I think, the greatest radio broadcaster there has ever been. It was the humour as much as anything. You can't sit there with a stony face and take cricket super-seriously for six hours a day, for five days of a Test match. I mean it is inhuman. So I really liked Johnners. When I was growing up there was also John Arlott, Jim Laker, Peter West and Tony Lewis. There was a slightly different atmosphere about it with all of them. And Arlott had such a wonderful voice.

'The only sad thing about cricket for me is that everyone doesn't love it. With football you can go anywhere in the world and it is so popular, but with cricket you have to punch away because I think you have to have been immersed in it as a boy. I was drawn completely into it by my granddad and my dad. My older brother loves cricket; he's played club cricket all his life. And so whenever I hear the commentary on the radio, it still takes me back to being in the back of the car in the 1970s and hearing that the Australians had six slips and two gullies. Terrifying! My dad used to complain about the way they appealed, because they did it so ferociously that he thought the umpire was just going to give it out anyway. He might have had a point. But it does stir up that nostalgia in you from your childhood. Cricket is hard to get into unless you have been led by the hand. It's complicated and difficult to understand, a wonderful game, and there is something beautifully addictive about it – there really is.'

As we prepare to go our separate ways, I feel as though I have been chatting to a mate I have known for years. But it is not the last time that I will see Alan that day. A few weeks earlier, when we were fixing up this meeting, he had invited my wife, Helen, and me to a recording of the comedy quiz programme *QI* on the South Bank. Presided over as usual by Stephen Fry, this particular edition turned out to be the Christmas show – ironically recorded on one of the hottest days of the year! Being brilliantly entertained by a panel that also included Lee Mack, Graham Norton and Daniel Radcliffe was the perfect way to end a day that was, at the very least, 'quite interesting'.

H R.H. THE DUKE OF EDINBURGH KG, KT

'I THOUGHT I WOULD TRY A GOOGLY. I LET THE
BALL GO... I HAD NO CONTROL OVER THE BLOODY
THING OF COURSE, AND IT SAILED WAY UP INTO
THE AIR, HE DUCKED, AND IT HIT HIS WICKET!'

*Prince Philip, Duke of Edinburgh, was born on the Greek island
of Corfu on 10 June 1921. After leaving Gordonstoun School,
where he became Head of the School and Captain of Hockey
and Cricket, he joined the Royal Navy as a cadet in 1939. He
gained a series of promotions during and after the Second World
War, rising to Commander by the time he left in 1952, on the
death of the late King George VI. He is also patron of some 800
organisations and has a keen interest in the natural environment
and science and technology.*

An introduction to the Duke's Equerry had left the door
ajar for me to present my credentials, a brief outline of
the book and a list of questions I would like to ask if given the
opportunity. The response to my approach was impressively fast
and pleasingly positive, with a firm date and time for my
audience with Prince Philip at Buckingham Palace soon
confirmed. My chauffeur, Helen, more often seen in her role as

my wife, drives us up to the North Gates of the Palace, where I wave to the gawping crowds – as one does. There is a careful check before we move forward, park and enter through the Privy Purse Door. The Duke's Equerry meets me and takes me up the broad staircase and into the library where, after being introduced, I take my seat on a firm, business-like settee, surrounded by shelves of books towering up to the ceiling.

Once we have checked sound levels on my recorder, I ask the Duke about the cricket that he first played at Cheam School in 1929. 'I don't believe I had a great deal of natural ability, although I made the second XI, but then I left a year early, so nothing very special. I then went to school in Germany for a year where we didn't play cricket at all. So it wasn't until I went to Gordonstoun that I had the chance to play again. There were only 20 of us in the school when I first joined, so everybody had to play everything all the time. We only had a couple of masters who could play cricket and we didn't have any playing fields, so we had to go to the public park in Elgin and play there.

'The one thing you are coached at school is batting, but I really decided that I would also learn to bowl, because at least then I would have something to do when we were in the field. If I could do some bowling I would not have to stand endlessly down at third man. I tried – as everybody does, I think to bowl fast and straight, rigidly, before coming to the conclusion that it was much too energetic. So then I thought I would see if I could bowl off breaks, which sometimes worked and sometimes didn't!

'After I left school I went on playing, but then the war came and I went into the Navy. So there wasn't very much cricket – we never really stopped anywhere! Once every six months or so we managed to get a game, but it wasn't very serious. After the war I played a bit at Windsor, where there were two clubs. I played a couple of times. I was also persuaded to play in some charity matches; I think probably the earliest charity cricket matches. I believe the first was against Hampshire at Bournemouth. Then I played at Arundel, Badminton and at Highclere, I think once a year, in these sorts of matches.

'I remember a cartoonist called Jackie Broome, a retired Royal Navy captain, who signed his cartoons simply with a drawing of a broom. I was playing cricket against him at Windsor and although I usually bowled off breaks, occasionally I could bowl a leg break, and I thought I would try a googly. I found that by doing something like this [he demonstrates the delivery] it did actually still become an off break having come the long way round! Anyway, I let the ball go. I had no control over the bloody thing, of course, and it sailed way up into the air, he ducked, and it hit his wicket! Broome produced a cartoon of this event, which I have hanging in the loo at Sandringham.

'In what must have been the early 1960s, I was playing in one of these charity matches at Arundel, and I was bowling to Tom Graveney. I don't know what he did, but I had a fine leg and he was caught there. Sheer fluke, I think. Every time I saw Tom afterwards, he always said, "I'm your rabbit" or something like that. I remember that one, funnily enough, because he kept reminding me of it! And his son's going round saying it now!

'When I played, it was mostly with first-class cricketers. One of them was John Reid, who was captain of the New Zealand side. He was quite a small chap, I think, but had forearms the size of my leg. He was colossal and he belted the thing around – scored, I believe, the fastest 50 ever. [According to Ted Dexter, who was Reid's opposite number in the 1962-63 series, Reid hit the ball as consistently powerfully as anyone he had ever seen.] So I did see some quite remarkable performances. There is a certain enjoyment in playing these games with professional cricketers. They are brilliant at fixing a game for charity purposes and they really can get the whole thing to finish in the last over. They knew how to bowl to you, let you have 15 or 20 runs, and then it gets serious! I once played in a village cricket match – in fact, it's the only one I did – and I was given out first ball – lbw. The fielding team were absolutely stunned. Lovely!

'Of course, the great thing about those matches was that they were played on very good pitches, and that was new to me because, in Scotland, we played on land that had recently been grazed by sheep or something. Most of the games I played in – well, apart from when I was at Cheam, where they had a very good ground – most of the grounds were not brilliant and then suddenly to play on a county ground, which is like a billiard table, was absolutely spectacular. I probably got less turn with my off breaks but on the other hand it was easier to bat, because you had a certain amount of confidence about what was going to happen.'

How strange it must have been for the Duke, given his rather special status in life, to play in these matches. How was he treated in changing rooms – notorious for being places of great joshing, bad language and jockstraps? 'Oh yes, and that is exactly what they remained. I think, like all these things, if you get involved you become one of the participants. Exceptional circumstances don't come into it and that applies to all the organisations and sports that I got involved in. I didn't get special treatment in yachting, or in polo, in carriage driving or anything. In fact, when I was carriage driving, I was also president of the International Federation but I still had to perform in front of the chairman of the Driving Committee, who was a judge on these occasions, just as part of the competition, which was odd sometimes.'

One slightly tongue-in-cheek thought on his active cricketing days: had he ever set up a cricket net here at the Palace and sneaked down the backstairs to practise from time to time? 'Not here, no! The trouble is, this is the office – people don't very often play cricket in office hours. So no, it didn't happen here.'

The Duke was still only in his twenties when he effectively gave up cricket and started to play polo. It's abundantly clear that he had enjoyed cricket and I wondered whether he had simply been attracted by the idea of playing polo or had made the change for some other reason. 'In 1949 I went out to the Mediterranean as second in command of a destroyer and my uncle, Lord Mountbatten, was commanding the First Cruiser Squadron. He was a polo fanatic and he literally said, "My boy, you are going to play polo." He provided some ponies for me and from that start I went on to play polo for 20 years. I suppose I did play some cricket in Malta – I think I might well have done – but Malta wasn't a great place for cricket really. Even so, if I hadn't been encouraged into polo, I probably would have gone on with cricket, I suppose. It was great fun, but I found I couldn't really play both games, so I rather drifted out of cricket.'

Despite this, he became involved with the Lord's Taverners almost as soon as the charity was founded in 1950. 'They asked me whether I would be Patron and I told them that I thought it was awfully pompous and silly for an organisation like the Taverners and wouldn't it be better if I was 12th man. It wasn't a question of not liking it – it just seemed to me that if it is a sort of boozing cricketers' thing, then Patron seems rather out of context. I also thought it would get me out of having to play! So I am described as "Patron and 12th man".

'When they started, they said they wanted to raise money for cricket and I asked them if they had any idea what that entailed. I explained that they would have to get people to apply for grants, to go through the applications, go and check on what they want and so on. It's a complicated business, making grants, and I said that until they really got going, why didn't they give any money they raised, and wanted to go into cricket, to the National Playing Fields Association? I suggested that they tell the NPFA what they wanted done with the money, get them to organise it and if it was to go to cricket, find appropriate people to receive it. "Once you're big enough and have enough people, you can organise it yourselves," I said, "but it would be the easiest way to get started." That's what they did and they still today make an annual donation to the NPFA, although I don't know whether they limit it to cricket or not.'

Since those earliest involvements with the charity, have there been other practical ways in which he had tried to help the Taverners – other than simply lending his name, that is? 'No, I have never got very closely involved. As President of the Royal Yachting Association, I got much more closely involved and when I was President of the International Equestrian Federation, I chaired all their executive meetings, and that was hands on. But with the Taverners, I am perfectly happy to be a figurehead. What tends to happen is that I am a figurehead when the thing is working well and then if it goes wrong, they come along and say, "Can you help?" and then I can try and do something about it. But I don't want to tell them what to do.

'But yes, there was one instance when they asked if I would go to a charity ball. I said, "Come off it!" Charity balls! I don't know if they happen so much now but they did in the 1950s and 1960s, and they were a great way of raising money. However, I asked, "Why don't you do something original? Have a cricket match in the ballroom." So they had one ball that had a cricket match, which was quite funny, and they had a rowing match in another, and then I can't remember whether they played football or something like that. Then I think it became too much trouble to organise, so they dropped it.

'A classic case, in which I did get seriously involved, was Outward Bound, which had effectively gone bankrupt for various reasons, which I had seen coming. I was chairman of the trustees of the [Duke of Edinburgh's] Award Scheme and we happened to be quite flush at the time, so I suggested we take it over. We put it under the trustees of the Award Scheme and then built it up, changed its constitution, got some new trustees and hived it off again. So that was quite an interesting exercise. There had been times before when Outward Bound had run out of money, and one of the principal causes when these things happen are personalities. When you get a personality clash, the whole thing falls to bits. Management would be dead easy but for people!'

Turning to MCC, I reminded the Duke that he became president for the first time in 1949, when he was 28. 'Yes, I suppose I was twenty-something or other, and with all these very distinguished characters in the game, I wasn't going to tell them how to run cricket. It would have been ridiculous. They were all very enthusiastic cricketers and they couldn't have been nicer. I have to admit that I did say to them that I would try to do what I could but that it might not be much because, in those days, I was hideously busy doing all sorts of other things. I mean, I was perfectly happy to do things when asked. I attended a couple of AGMs. One of them was quite interesting, because it was when honorary membership of MCC was given to 26 leading English professionals. This was the first recognition of the professional cricketer by the club and, I suppose, the beginning of the eventual "professionalisation" of cricket. I didn't really know an awful lot about it but it seemed to me that, if they wanted to do it, then that was that. It did occur to me that it was going to change the face of cricket, because the professionals were going to need more cricket to make professional life possible. I did suggest that one way of doing it was to have the County Championship at weekends, over three days, and that the professionals should join together and make up teams, not necessarily county teams, and play mid-week but in a different league. I think the saddest thing about professional cricket is that it has completely cut off the progression from club cricket to county cricket. Amateurs play for their club and that's it, and the whole of county cricket, and international cricket, is now professional. Which I think is a pity.

'Later on, I became President of the International Equestrian Federation and it was just at the time when showjumping went professional. Professionals do have their interests and they do have their influence, but they very often look on the sport from their own point of view – for which I don't blame them at all. It is slightly different if it is your way of earning a living.'

When the Duke returned as MCC President 25 years later in 1974, had his approach to the role been different from his first term? 'No, no, I don't think so. It was great fun and I got to know quite a lot of the people. You know what it's like if you sit around with people who know about cricket discussing the game. There's much more to talk about in cricket than in practically any other game, because there is this curious combination of individual and team exercise, which is unusual. It is unique.' I suggest that the game also calls for a mixture of brawn and brains while wrestling, for example, is very much brawn. 'Yes, I suppose so. But if you're going to be good at any sport you need a modicum of brain, I think. At least, if you don't, you very soon see the result!'

I wonder whether, particularly as a schoolboy, he had cricketing heroes or players that might have been role models, just as cricket lovers from other walks of life do. 'As a boy following cricket, you couldn't help but notice Hutton, and watching the films of the Ashes series in Australia, and matches like that, seeing the bodyline bowling, being aware of Larwood and Bradman. They were remarkable players, as was Sutcliffe. Compton and Edrich were really outstanding. Compton I got to know quite well, because he took an interest in various things that I was interested in. He was a great chap, I thought – he was so casual.'

H R. H. THE DUKE OF EDINBURGH KG, KT

Despite his involvement in cricket and many other sporting pastimes, the Duke is not a great spectator or television watcher. 'This really is so. I go and watch it occasionally, but I would rather be doing something than watching it, frankly. After all, nowadays you are just watching people earning a living! I am not a fanatic. I quite enjoy watching other things too, although as you say I am not a great spectator. I follow the Test matches and very often turn on the sports channel if there is a series going on somewhere, just to see who's playing, what's changing, what's going on. I go to these Taverners' charity matches we have at Windsor every year and recently somebody came up to me and said, "The President of the Afghanistan Cricket Association is here – can I introduce him?" Of course I agreed, because I was absolutely fascinated. If you remember, in the last World Twenty20 Tournament, there was an Afghanistan team playing. I think they were probably refugees in Pakistan during the Taliban period, who went home again and kept on playing cricket.

'I've made a lot of very good friends and met a lot of very entertaining people in cricket. It is very curious, the cricket community, quite different from any other. I think, on the whole, they have a better sense of humour than most. I think that if you figure the Lord's Taverners as a sort of archetype, the idea of combining cricket with enjoying yourselves seems to me something that works rather well. I mean, most cricket teams are based on the pub anyway!'

This splendid thought leaves me with just enough time to ask whether he might have learned anything from cricket? 'Well, I suppose I must have done when I was at school, although I don't think I have learned much from it since then. I certainly learned from all team games, not just cricket, that they are very much a social classroom. I think they teach people who take part an awful lot. For instance, they teach you respect for the law, because in games you have to abide by the rules.

65

There are an awful lot of people who, when they go out on the town, don't feel there are any rules. If they have had experience of team games, I think they are more likely to abide by social rules. But I think also the great thing about team games is that you have to sublimate – you may be bloody good but you have to play with 10 other people, and so you have to learn to cooperate. That's also a very important social lesson, because people have to cooperate in communities. So I think there are various and very valuable experiences for young people to take from the team game.'

I say that we have probably covered the ground and thank the Duke for agreeing to see me. He smiles. 'Well, you've now got to try and write something!' There is a garden party at the Palace that afternoon, all part of a busy day for someone who celebrated his 89th birthday only a few days before. I remind him that he also has a St James's Palace dinner tonight for the Lord's Taverners. He clearly does not find this at all onerous. 'Oh well, you've got to have dinner somewhere!'

When I try to get to my feet, I fail miserably. Parkinson's has kicked in and I am dangerously close to tipping over the settee. The Duke immediately offers to give me a hand before planting a knee on the seat and a hand on the arm of the settee to steady it, enabling me laboriously to lever myself upright. I am slightly embarrassed by the episode and can only stammer, 'Thank you very much. I am sorry about that.' The Duke smiles and says, 'That's all right,' before we shake hands and he leaves the library.

As I emerge into brilliant sunshine to join Helen, the Changing of the Guard is reaching its conclusion only a few yards away. We are then politely requested to delay our departure until Prince Edward has arrived and while we wait in the car, Helen is desperate to know how it all went. 'I think it was OK, apart from a shaky finish! But my overriding impression? What a thoroughly nice man.'

DAVID ENGLISH
MBE, CBE

'I SAID WE WOULD GET ALL THE BOYS – PHIL COLLINS, BILL WYMAN, RINGO STARR AND ALL THAT LOT – TO TURN UP, BUT ERIC CLAPTON SAID, "THEY DON'T KNOW HOW TO PLAY." I SAID, "IT DOESN'T MATTER. WE'LL JUST GIVE THEM THE WHITES AND THEY CAN GO OUT THERE, AND THE CROWD WILL BE HAPPY!"'

David English was born on 4 March 1946, in Isleworth, west London. He is a record producer, author, actor and charity fundraiser. After seven years with Associated Newspapers he joined Decca Records in 1971 for two years, before becoming president of RSO Records, where he worked with Eric Clapton, the Bee Gees and many more. He has appeared in films and on TV and written 17 books. Since the mid-1980s, his Bunburys cricket team has raised substantial funds for charity and to support the English Schools Cricket Association. He was awarded a CBE in 2010 for services to charity and cricket, having previously received an MBE in 2004.

I have never met anyone quite like David English. He is charismatic, eccentric, entertaining, hyperactive, witty, charming, charitable and a raconteur, who is variously and affectionately known as The Loon, Dr Dave and Arthur (after Arthur English, the old actor and comedian). He lives in a north London country cottage, swimming in what he describes as his paraphernalia. Two large glass cabinets are crammed into the hallway, each stuffed with cricketing memorabilia, including several trophies and caps donated by Geoffrey Boycott, Rod Marsh and Viv Richards among others.

The desk in his office is reached along a narrow walkway, hemmed in on either side by letters, brochures and piles of other papers of every description, together with more caps and sweaters and a prized birthday present from Ian Botham: his 1986/87 Ashes-winning blazer. The walls in every room are covered with cricket photographs, posters, cartoons, scorecards and caricatures, alongside gold and platinum discs from the chart-topping days with Eric Clapton and the Bee Gees. Amidst this chaos, and without a computer, typewriter or secretary, David has handwritten thousands of letters and raised millions of pounds for charities.

Once he has cleared just enough space on the settee for the pair of us, we sit down to talk. I cannot help but notice one item of a non-cricketing nature: a 6ft high, fibreglass blonde model in a very skimpy outfit. 'Barry Gibb and I were walking down the road in Miami and this beauty was in an antique shop,' David explains. 'He said, "Dave, that's your type isn't it – blonde and big boobs?" I just said, "Yeah," and didn't think any more about it. I got back here and a week later the Post Office rang and said, "Mr English? I've got something for you from Mr Gibb in Miami, Florida, with his best compliments." And Barry had sent it to me. There was a note with it: "Lots of love, Baz." And there she stands, blonde and curvaceous, like my ex-wife! But everything else you see is to do with cricket. They all tell a story and I remember everything vividly. The reason I've got all these pictures and things up is that they remind me what happened and when. So I'm surrounded by my memories and when I go, maybe they could make this into a little museum or something similar.'

Putting those memories to one side, we move on to talk about his earliest taste of cricket, which turns out to have been at an unbelievably early age! 'I remember my mother, who used to wear a belted camel coat and looked like Lauren Bacall, the American actress, pushing my pram through Hendon Park to the Burroughs district of Hendon, where we used to get powdered milk, cod liver oil and orange juice. On the way home I remember seeing a game of cricket in the park. I would have only been about six months old but this is the truth. She used to push me through the park every day and I remember the activity, and seeing the cricket, at a very young age. My father didn't play but when I was four or five, I used to go to Hendon Park and try and coerce anybody I could to come and play cricket with me. Up against a tree, or wherever there was space to do so. I just used to love playing and when the holidays started I used to go and play every day in Hendon Park. It is just something I love doing. I can't think of anything more pleasurable than whacking a ball around, or hurling a ball about, and just bowling whenever I had the chance to do so.

'At primary school, which was quite a rough place, we just played in the playground where we had three stumps chalked on the wall. There wasn't anybody who coached cricket there but when I went to a prep school, there was a guy who told us how to hold the bat and so on, which was a start! Then, when I was 12 or 13, we used to go to the Middlesex Indoor Cricket School at Finchley once a week, which was a great learning experience. I was so much in awe of the coach, Jack Robertson, who would always be wearing his Middlesex sweater with the three seaxes badge. He had a bat that had been sawn in half and we used to have to hold it in one hand, with the other hand behind our back, and hit the ball cleanly.

'In 1963 I joined the ground staff at Lord's. Len Muncer was MCC head coach and we used to flog score cards and bowl to the members and do whatever else we were told to do, and for me it was just exhilarating. Don Bennett picked me for the Middlesex second team quite a few times, and I played for MCC and scored a hundred at Lord's for the Cross Arrows. I was on 99 and a bloke called George Hepworth, a Yorkshire lad, hit me on the pads. I was plumb lbw and a Lord's hundred was slipping away from me, even if it was on the nursery ground, so I ran down to the other end to the umpire who was about to give me out. I said, "No, no, please!" He put his dreaded finger down and I was able to make 100 not out. Hepworth swore at me, "F★★★★★g 'ell, you bastard!" Soon after, I asked Don Bennett, "Look, do you think I am good enough to play professionally?" and he said, "I don't think you've got the attention span. You love the game, but would you be willing to get to the ground at 9 o'clock, nets at 9.30, cricket from 11 until six, every day of your life? I think you would be better off doing what you are probably best at, which is all sorts of different things." I think I probably could have played first-class cricket to a certain level but I would never have been Gower or Botham, so I went off and worked for the newspapers instead.'

Having taken Don Bennett's advice, David moved into a whole array of different activities before cricket beckoned once more. But it beckoned in a very different way and resulted in the creation of his own cricket team, known (in due course) as the Bunburys. 'It all started in Eric Clapton's garden, where I first suggested to him that we start a cricket side and call it Eric Clapton's XI. I said we would get all the boys – Phil Collins, Bill Wyman, Ringo Starr and all that lot – to turn up, but Eric said, "They don't know how to play." I said, "It doesn't matter. We'll just give them the whites and they can go out there, and the crowd will be happy!" So he told me that if I could get it all together, then he would turn up.'

Their first game was at Ripley in Surrey and despite the non-stop pouring rain, it attracted a crowd of 5,000 or more. David remembers it all too well. 'I promise you, John, it was absolutely peeing down but I had been in touch with all my musical contacts and despite the weather they all turned up to play. Most of them didn't have a clue. Eric was looking the wrong way, drinking red wine, and somebody else had a cigar on – it might have been Gary Mason. But I do know that 26 grand went to the Royal Marsden Hospital as a result. We used to play every Sunday after that and, because of Eric obviously, we used to get very big crowds.

'I always used to try and keep him out of harm's way so we could protect his fingers. One day we were playing at Penn Street in Buckinghamshire and although I didn't want him to, he was fielding in the gully, probably so he could chat to the boys. The bloke who was batting whacked it and the ball broke Eric's finger! So I've now got visions of lawyers and litigation and all sorts of problems because Eric is about to go on a tour to Japan. But that wasn't the end of the affair. As he walked off, a bumblebee stung him on the other hand, so he soon had both hands in buckets of water. He just sat there looking at me and said, "Right, Arthur, that's it. I'm retiring." As a result, the name of the team had to be changed, although as it turned out Eric was able to do the tour!'

The team was rechristened the Bunburys, with a little rabbit as the club's logo. The name is based on another of David's 'different things'. 'I wrote 14 children's books, called *Bunbury Tails*, all about little rabbits who play cricket. There was the BBC, the Bunbury Broadcasting Corporation, with Bunny Johnston and Richie Bunnow as commentators, and the Bunburys had Ian Buntham, Rodney Munch and Dennis Lettuce playing against the cats from Whisker Town, managed by Chairman Miaow, with Mike Catting and Imran Kitten in their team.

'Some of the things that have gone on in Bunbury matches have been crazy. I often saw drinks and fags on the field. Bill Wyman used to smoke, even when he was bowling his leg breaks. He's not a bad bowler, although most bowlers use sawdust when it's wet, not fag ash! I wouldn't have to ask him to bowl – he would come up and say he wanted to bowl there and then, more often than not right in the middle of an over. He took the only televised hat-trick ever at the Oval. [Bill tells the tale elsewhere in this book.] The game was to mark the 50th anniversary of VE day and I had Keith Miller and Denis Compton there, and Sam Fox bowling with Devon Malcolm – it was all very surreal. Everyone was wired up for sound for the live coverage on Sky, but the language was unbearable and at one stage Foxy [Graeme] Fowler shouted a four-letter word at Syd Lawrence. The producer went absolutely mad because viewers were phoning Sky to complain. He screamed into my earpiece, saying that I had to get them to stop swearing and to stop discussing "who had or had not had their end away in the last week"! It just went on and on, and I couldn't control them. At one stage there were five blokes chatting away in the slips and at the end of the over they wouldn't move, so we then had five mid-ons! I tell you, John, it is all so much fun!'

That had been evident when I saw David in action at one of the Bunbury matches, an annual fund-raising fixture against Norma Major's XI at Alconbury in Cambridgeshire. He seemed to be permanently surrounded by players, sponsors, guests and friends, and introduced many of the latter as a son or a daughter when very often they obviously were not! At lunch, he played the part of the stand-up comedian like a seasoned pro, entertaining his captive audience with a string of gags that nearly brought the marquee down. When the cricket eventually got under way, Test players Robert Key and Charlotte Edwards were in the Bunbury side, alongside an array of footballers and personalities who gave a sizeable crowd autographs and entertainment as a part of the afternoon.

When I asked Bill Wyman about David as a cricketer, he told me, 'Blimey! He bowls fast, or at least he used to before his knees went. Or was it his hips? He bowls fast, and he's a bloody good batsman, oh yeah. He always got 30, 40, 50. Really quick as well. He's a bit of a slogger. Good eye. Often dropped catches, though, in the field.' Rory Bremner is also a great fan. 'He is a great character and has done very well in terms of getting a lot of very good players. These matches are one of the big reasons why I enjoy playing the game. Having said that, I stopped playing for a while because it became a bit like a circus! You would turn up and there would be 18 playing for the Bunburys. I used to enjoy fielding in the covers but I would find there were already four fielders there, which tended to make it a bit congested!'

For 25 years David has succeeded in getting many famous people to play cricket for the Bunburys. They come back week after week and play for nothing. David believes the reasons are quite obvious. 'They have a good day out, the public loves to watch them, and it gives them a nice feeling to know that they are helping so many charities. Over the years we have been able to help worthy causes such as Cancer Research, Age Concern, ChildLine, the NSPCC, Addenbrooke's Hospital and very many more. I get all these letters from charities and I decide which ones I am going to support. I particularly like the children's charities and the ones that help old folks.

'I like to go and see the children – not just send the cheque but to actually see where the money is going and how it might help. I'm a patron of When You Wish Upon A Star [the charity dedicated to dream making for sick children]. Each year they charter planes to take youngsters who are very poorly to Lapland to meet Father Christmas, and this is something we did. Just to see these children – many of them terminally ill – to see the wonder in their eyes and the glow on their cheeks is very moving. I said to one little chap, "Do you like football? Do you like David Beckham?" And this little voice said, "You think I'm a boy, don't you? I'm not – I'm a girl!" and she burst out laughing. She had leukaemia – no hair. And was still laughing. I could easily have cried.'

To support the charities, David needs annual sponsorship of the Bunburys to supplement what is raised by the clubs hosting the matches. He rejects the notion of writing letters in the hope of getting positive responses. 'Forget it, John, it doesn't work at all. I get sponsors by making lots and lots of friends in the highest places I possibly can. You've got to meet people. Once they have agreed to be sponsors they come in for a season. They get their logos on the shirts and sweaters, advertising and editorial in the brochure, a table at every game and they bring their clients along. So we get wonderful support from Shredded Wheat, CostCutter, Bentley and people like that. The club we are playing normally gets sponsorship as well as raising funds in other ways. We played at Lord's in 2010 and, largely through the auction, raised an all-time Bunburys match record of £178,000 for the Myeloma cancer charity. In our quarter of a century, we have raised more than £14 million in total.'

In 1986 David was approached by Ben Brocklehurst, the former Somerset player and publisher of *The Cricketer* magazine, who introduced him to Cyril Cooper, the general secretary of the English Schools Cricket Association, which plays a crucial role in the development of schoolboy cricket. ESCA's annual Under 15 Cricket Festival was in trouble through lack of funding. 'Cyril told me they hadn't got a sponsor and asked me if I could help. I told him straight away that nothing would make me more proud and I've been involved in what is now known as the Bunbury ESCA Under 15 Cricket Festival ever since, during which time 52 boys who have played in the Festival have gone on to play for England, including Michael Vaughan, Paul Collingwood, Graeme Swann and Andrew Flintoff. And there are 193 guys who have gone on to play county cricket. In the pre-Bunbury years, Mike Atherton, David Gower, Ian Botham, Mike Gatting and Nasser Hussain all came to be noticed during the Festival.'

The year 2008 was particularly memorable for the ESCA, with a game on the main square at Lord's. 'Keith Bradshaw plays for us regularly each season and is a brilliant bloke,' David explains. 'As you know, he is chief executive of MCC and he's the man who made the first ever match between the England Under 15s and Under 16s possible. It was terrific: the match was tied and that day, 10 September, was designated National Bunbury ESCA Day. And that evening we had a wonderful dinner to celebrate the 60 years that the ESCA had existed.'

David has effectively dedicated most of the past 25 years to the Bunburys and all that this entails. But what does he get out of it? 'The most pleasure for me as a Bunbury is watching the boys play in the Festival – seeing them arrive, lining up in their blazers and being presented with their regional caps. I love to see them play, dealing with a combination of adrenaline and nerves; they are so talented. And that's the start of a lifelong friendship. They go on into first-class cricket but they all come back to play in my celebrity team. Ronnie Irani, Ian Bell, Freddie Flintoff – they will all turn out whenever they can.

'The second thing that I enjoy when I captain the Bunbury side is the banter, because it's priceless. The things that get said by players from all different parts of the world! They may be cricketers, actors, musicians, footballers, it doesn't matter – it's amazing. They all get on so well. The banter that goes on in the dressing room is quite extraordinary – it's worth recording! Jeff Thomson and Ian Wright together have to be heard to be believed, and I like being the catalyst. I remember years ago, probably late 1970s, when Robert Powell played Jesus Christ in the TV series *Jesus of Nazareth*. Brilliant he was, too, but the lads used to upset him by phoning for Judas Iscariot! And Robert used to say, "No, Jesus Christ, f★★k you!" Actually, whenever all this was going on he would get quite chirpy – he could be quite full of himself!

'The only thing I would add to all my cricket chat – my anecdotes and my memories – is this. Like you, I love the game. And I just want to help as many people as I can and have a good day out.'

My time spent with David has never been less than interesting. Seeing him in his two-tone blue-and-white shoes, blue cords and cricket shirt, surrounded by his chaotic cricket memorabilia and closely watched by his pair of 19-year-old ginger cats, it is easy to understand why Mike Atherton wrote of him in *The Times*, "He teeters just on the right side of that fine line between eccentricity and madness." In fact, his remarkable achievements in the world of music, for the ESCA and for charity, all clearly demonstrate that he teeters very strongly in the right direction.

AINSLEY HARRIOTT

'I SAID, "CAN I CALL YOU BLOWERS?" AND HE SAID, "ABSOLUTELY, AS LONG AS I CAN CALL YOU AINERS!"'

Ainsley Harriott was born in Paddington, London, on 28 February 1957, and is a celebrity chef and television presenter. He has worked at a wide range of restaurants in London, including Verrey's, The Strand Palace, The Dorchester, Brown's, The Hilton, The Westbury and Quaglino's, and was head chef of the Long Room at Lord's. On television, he was resident chef on Good Morning with Anne and Nick *and subsequently the main presenter of* Can't Cook, Won't Cook *and later* Ready, Steady, Cook. *He has published a series of cookery books that have achieved worldwide sales of more than two million.*

As we drove from Buckingham Palace and my audience with the Duke of Edinburgh to Wandsworth and a warm welcome from Ainsley and his wife Clare, one thought was uppermost in my mind. 'This is what *Cricket Wonderful Cricket* is all about. A rich mix of people, all happy to talk about the game from their own unique perspective.' Soon after our arrival Helen, my wife and chauffeur, and I are sitting in the garden under a blazing sun, enjoying cooling fruit drinks from a giant glass jug and a lively stream of cricket chat from Ainsley.

Although he is probably best known for his frequent television appearances, this is the man who once made beef baps for England! His catering career had started as an apprentice at Verrey's restaurant in London's Regent Street. 'I remember an Irish chef there saying to me, "Do you want to earn yourself some more money?" And I did, because it was such bad pay then. I was on £12 a week, which was just no money at all, although you know that's how it is when you first start out in catering. The chef said that now the cricket season was on, if I went to Lord's on my day off I could get some part-time work and be paid something like £3.25 an hour. How could I resist? So that's what I started to do, although you were only ever at Lord's for about three weeks of the year. You probably had two five-day Test matches, the NatWest Final and not much more. If Middlesex were playing particularly well, or they played Surrey, or if there was a one-dayer on a Sunday, it might get busy, but otherwise it just wasn't very hectic at all.

'But I had never made so many bloody sandwiches in my life! You walked in there, and you made five or six hundred rounds of sandwiches every day. Ham, lettuce, tomato – right, that lot's out of the way. Seal them up, put them away. A few of the guys working there got bored with that, so one sarnie got half a pound of ham and the next one got a little slither! But I always tried to maintain standards. And then I got promoted and went to work in the kitchen. There I got to know the chef quite well and he would call me when the big games were coming up and there was plenty to do. God, I loved it! I was put in charge of the Warner Stand, where the members and their guests sit, and they sang my praises because I really looked after all the punters up there. It was very busy at lunchtime but I just organised everything and still had chance to watch the cricket. It was a fantastic viewpoint and I could see all my heroes.'

Ainsley was promoted again after the executive chef told him that they were having problems with the Long Room restaurant in the members' pavilion, and that they wanted him to take over. 'By the time I got there, the Long Room beef bap had already become a tradition. Although the players would have lunch laid on and would have had their early morning nibbles, a lot of them used to send down, because they just wanted a real, proper beef bap. Graham Gooch loved them with a bit of extra horseradish, and Mike Gatting did as well. They said he had two jacket potatoes with everything! Apart from the players' requests, the members would queue up for ages, so I used to entertain them by writing poetry and putting it on the Long Room counter. It was crap, basically, but every day, depending on who we were playing, and the plight of the team and stuff like that, I would change my little bit of handwritten poetry and people would tip me according to how good or bad it was. We had such a laugh. I could never be quiet. I used to entertain them, because we were at the back of the Long Room, where you can't see the f★★★★★g pitch! So I had to amuse them myself. I was head chef there for years and until recently I was still getting Christmas cards from the old Long Room faithful. Sadly a lot of them have passed away now. In the winter, Clare and I used to be invited to have lunch with them, at Rules or one of their clubs. It was great to just meet up with those members and talk cricket.'

Ainsley was influenced heavily by his mother, who was an enormous cricket fan, and every time the West Indies came to England on tour, everything stopped. 'We watched all the Test matches on television, and saw every ball bowled. We saw some of the great players who came to play here. When I was at school, quite a few of them arrived on the county scene. I remember Garfield Sobers playing at Notts. Lance Gibbs came over for a while, as did Rohan Kanhai. We all thought we were Garfield Sobers, so you put your collar up when you went to play, and when you bowled you charged in because you were either Charlie Griffith or Wesley Hall. And, dare I say, you also batted like a West Indian, so everything had to be dispatched to the boundary as quickly as possible – it didn't matter whether you lost your wicket or not.

'So this was the start of what, I think, was my greatest achievement in life: to have a love of the game. That's why I would always get excited when I met my heroes and was able to talk to them about their greatest games or their greatest innings. As I said, my mother was a great lover of cricket, while my dad [Chester Harriott, the pianist and entertainer] was in show business. We had quite a nice home and players would come and visit. And they were guaranteed a nice meal – [Ainsley takes on a rich West Indian accent] "some yam and peppy food". I remember when I was a young child in my back garden, people like Lance Gibbs and Clive Lloyd coming to my house, and Jeffrey Dujon, who is a cousin of mine. So when you have that kind of connection, where everybody loves cricket, and you meet some of your cricketing heroes at a young age, you just can't believe how lucky you are. If you have one of these famous guys tossing a ball at you in front of your apple tree in your back garden, you think, "Wow, they've got time to spend with me."'

Given his childhood experiences, I expected that Ainsley's list of favourite players would be made up entirely of West Indians, but this turned out not to be the case. He went for a distinctly international line-up, opening with a South African. 'Funnily enough, Barry Richards is one of the greatest batsmen I have ever seen. Absolutely beautiful. I remember my mum taking us to a Surrey game and watching him make, I think, 80 something for Hampshire. South Africa weren't allowed to play

Test matches from 1970, so he only played four games, against Australia, in which he averaged over 70. Just imagine what it would have been like if he had been part of the Test scene until he retired in the early 1980s.

'As you begin to appreciate cricket even more, you also become aware of the individual brilliance of Allan Border. He went in as captain when Australia were rubbish and he galvanised them; he completely turned them around. He made Australian cricket great again and they just started firing on all cylinders, and he never let them down with the blade. I kind of like that in a captain. I must also mention that I liked the Chappell brothers, Greg and Ian. But, moving on from the Aussies to England, I remember Colin Cowdrey very clearly indeed as one of the truly great batsmen. I loved Atherton, too, and I've always loved Gower. They always said that Gower was a black man, didn't they, because of the way he used to hit that ball. He always got out like a black man, cutting it and caught off the edge every time! I used to love watching Derek Randall and his brilliant fielding; nothing could get past him. He reminds me of a guy called Brendan Nash playing for the West Indies; he's like a little terrier, diving this way and that – it's just fantastic. Then you have the superb New Zealand fast bowler, Richard Hadlee, who also played over here for Notts, and took more than 400 Test wickets.'

At this point, Ainsley leaps to his feet and disappears indoors, returning with what he describes as one of his favourite old cricket books, as a source of additional information. It is no great surprise to find that it is *Beyond a Boundary* by the Trinidadian intellectual CLR James, which is widely regarded as perhaps the greatest sports book ever written. He places it reverently on the table in front of him, where it remains untouched for the rest of our time together – because it is time for the West Indies.

'Without doubt we were all able to walk very tall when the

Windies, who we supported for years and years, had that great team in the 1980s and 1990s. I think I am right in saying that Viv Richards is the only Test captain of the West Indies never to lose a series. Unbelievable, when you think of all the places that he went to play – certainly going down to Australia. One of the greatest things I ever saw was Viv scoring the fastest Test century, off 56 balls. It was against England in Antigua, in 1986. My mother used to sit on the end of my bed and tell me about the three Ws – Walcott, Weekes and Worrell – and all the stories were just fantastic. And having someone like Garfield Sobers come along was just remarkable, because he was something else. It wasn't just because they were black that I supported them, although you definitely go through that as a young kid – you want to have your own identity, you want to support something you really feel proud of. Like my son, who's a mixed race boy: he loved Tiger Woods, which is exactly the same thing – he wants someone who he can identify with.

'But I am very sad about the way the Windies' fortunes have declined now. They just don't seem to be able to do it any more. They are playing like a bunch of individuals at times and I find that very frustrating. It is beginning to change a little bit now, because I think they are realising that something has to be done.'

From the great players to the great, and not so great, writers and broadcasters is an easy step and Ainsley has a splendid anecdote to start the ball rolling. 'I must tell you about "Blowers"' [Henry Blofeld] when he came on *Ready, Steady, Cook*. I've had quite a few of them, like Jonathan Agnew, on the programme and they in turn often interview me on *Test Match Special*, when I end up chatting to them for ages about all sorts of nonsense. But at the start of this particular programme, when Henry was on, I said, "Can I call you Blowers?" and he said, "Absolutely, as long as I can call you Ainers!" Of course, everyone was in stitches and when the programme had almost ground to a chaotic halt, I heard my producer say, "That's enough of that now, Ainers." And that was what I was called for the rest of that series.

'But on a more serious note, I do like Mike Atherton's writing in *The Times* since he took over from Christopher Martin-Jenkins. Besides being a bright boy, he also knows how to get the message across. He doesn't use a long, convoluted word for the sake of it, like some of them do. Then, on Sky, every time Michael Holding says, "one buys two", it's true – there is always another little wicket coming, isn't there? I like his voice, his knowledge and where he's coming from. And I like the little sort of banter with the Lancastrian, "Bumble" [David Lloyd]. He really adds a bit of fun to it, because it can all be a little bit serious, and I like the little cut-away shots that they have of them, chatting away there, especially when they start giggling and stuff like that. You can tell something is going on, and often Botham is involved.

'But although I realise that they are doing a job and that they like to fire off their opinions and comments, I get a little peed off with Nasser Hussain, because he seems to want to hog the limelight a lot of the time. And I do get the odd days when I get put off by Bob Willis, because he was one who was not good enough. He's got that kind of voice, and I just used to think, "Who are you to say that?" He was a good bowler but he was never that great and if it wasn't for Botham, he wouldn't have been in the position to take all those wickets! So some of them do kind of wind me up.'

As a schoolboy, Ainsley thoroughly enjoyed playing cricket, particularly at Wandsworth Boys School, where they had a system for awarding cricket caps that was completely new to me. 'Every time you took three wickets or scored I think it was 50 runs, you were called up in assembly and awarded a cap. I managed to collect a few but apart from that, cricket at school for me was a great experience and I have some wonderful memories as a result. But unfortunately after I left it was very difficult to find time to play, because I decided to take up catering and that doesn't give you much free time, particularly in your early days as an apprentice.

'As I became more established and better known, I started to play again and over the years, I've played in charity matches. Apart from the Lord's Taverners, I just get calls from people and get invited to lovely little cricket grounds, or lovely villages, and I just turn up and play. I played for Sheen Park Cricket Club, near Richmond Park, because an old school friend of mine played for them and every time they were a bit short, he would phone me up. But I wasn't one of their main guys, unfortunately, because as anybody who plays cricket knows, unless you get into the nets soon after Christmas and start to get your fitness back and practise, it's a struggle. You have to have the time, the motivation and the discipline, and I was usually short on one or two of those! Even so, I still play in charity matches and if unfortunately I can't make it, I like to send them one of my juicers and a book that they can give away as a prize. When I have played, I have taken a few wickets, including, I think, those of Graham Gooch, Alan Knott and John Emburey. I've gone for loads of runs but I have had my moments, if not my great achievements!'

As a spectator rather than a player, the most fantastic match in Ainsley's memory was the second Test match in the 2005 Ashes series, at Edgbaston. 'I wasn't there, but I was glued in front of my television, loving every moment, and thinking, "What are you doing? What is going to happen next?" It was so tense. Clare came in and said, "What are you doing screaming and shouting? It's not a game of football." When Shane Warne was ninth out, the Aussies still needed about 60 to win and it looked to be all over. But Brett Lee was incredible. I thought he played with such confidence. I really thought they had had it. Just two runs in it in the end – how close can you get?

'It's those sorts of matches that make me so keen on the five-day game. I like Twenty20, but I am a Test match man. I think it demands special skills. I know there is a lot of feeling in the game that Twenty20 is destroying cricket. It's bringing kids into the game that probably never would have played, because the game just went on too long, but people go to a Test match for a day and they don't care what happens; they don't care about the result. They have been to see their heroes and that's what really matters to them. Twenty20 does definitely offer something different, so sometimes I wonder if the 50-over game will disappear.

Ainsley's love of cricket is as strong as it has ever been, in part because of the high standards of behaviour that the game demands. 'The discipline of the sport is very important – dare I say, a little bit like golf. There are certain laws or rules that should be observed and, in most cases, are. Then, once you are out there on the field, it is gladiatorial: a battle between the batsman and the bowler. I think it is important as well that the character of the team comes out; that you get a group of players that play as a team and don't play, as we have seen so often over the years, as an uncoordinated bunch of players. It's essential to have moments of individual brilliance, with the bat or the ball, but still to know it is about the team working together and everyone pulling in the same direction. When that starts to happen you can sense it. You get this really great feeling that everybody is there, that everybody is working for one another, that everyone is moving together. It can be small things, like at the end of an over when they change ends, everyone is running around and there is a real urgency about it. When you get that in Test match cricket, as it seems to be with England but less so with the Windies, it is a fantastic thing.

'What else do I love about the sport? I suppose it is the history, the tradition that is an important part of it all. You either love it or you don't. I know people that come to cricket but can't stand it – it's like people that talk about golf and say it ruins a walk. It's only when you actually play that you understand the laws of the game. People who don't know or think about cricket can find it almost bewildering, because it is quite complex. Unless you have learned it at school, it is quite difficult to explain to someone. Apart from the laws, the terms can also be a complete mystery. What is lbw, running between the wickets, a maiden over, a no ball, cover point and all the other bits and pieces that go with it? People don't know what they mean.

'But for me, most importantly of all, it is a game that should be protected at all costs. Because it hasn't been around for hundreds of years for no reason at all. It is a great game and you see the way that it continues to develop, for example, with the speed of the game and the fitness of the players. What is going to come now? What's next? I don't know. I just know that I love it, love it, love it.'

Ainsley's expressions of passion for the game are ringing in my ears as I reach the end of the day's absorbing, contrasting and fascinating cricket conversations. Before we leave, he searches his filing cabinet for a picture of himself in cricket gear that I need. He fails in his mission, perhaps because the drawer that seems to be intended for his sports files appears to contain an almost unhealthy amount of Arsenal memorabilia!

LORD MACLAURIN OF KNEBWORTH

"MACLAURIN, THIS IS A CRICKET CLUB, NOT A CHAIN OF BLOODY SHOPS!"

Ian MacLaurin was born in Blackheath, Kent, on 30 March 1937. He joined Tesco in 1959 and rose through the company, ultimately becoming chairman in 1985. By the time he retired, in 1997, Tesco had become the UK's largest retailer. He became chairman of Vodafone in 1998, was the first chairman of the England and Wales Cricket Board (ECB) and is currently chairman of the Sports Honours Committee. He was knighted in 1989 and created a life peer in 1996.

We sit in Ian MacLaurin's stylishly comfortable London home, with *Barclays World of Cricket* – the A to Z of the game – dominating the coffee table. Our focus, though, is not on cricket's ABC but its ECB, an organisation Ian claims to have become chairman of by default.

'Around the time I was leaving Tesco I had several phone calls, including one from dear Brian Downing, the past president of Surrey. He said, "Ian, we are putting the first-class game and recreational game together, as you know, and we are looking for a chairman of the new governing body, the England and Wales

Cricket Board. Will you consider standing?" I said, "Well, if you want to put my name on the list, stick my name on it and see what, if anything, happens." About six or eight weeks later, I had another call from him, and he said, "Congratulations! You are the new chairman of the ECB – well, actually the first chairman of the ECB!" And I asked him, "How many other names were on the paper for the job?" "None," he said.'

Rather less amusing was what happened when, shortly after Ian's appointment in 1997, he went to Harare for the New Year Test match. About half an hour before lunch on the Sunday, Ian was told that Robert Mugabe, President of Zimbabwe, was coming to watch the game. There was a guard of honour as Mugabe came in, accompanied by his Sports Minister, and by Peter Chindoka, the boss of Zimbabwe cricket. 'He sat in the front of the Presidential box and Chindoka said to me, "Go and sit next to the President," adding, "but I have to tell you that we have been warned of a possible assassination attempt on Mugabe's life today." So I went, gingerly, and sat next to Mugabe. There were two television sets up in the box where Bob Willis was commentating and the camera zoomed in on the presidential box and he said, in his very droll way, "President Mugabe is here, the Sports Minister is here, and you can just see the top of the head of the new chairman of the ECB." So there I was, just sitting there thinking, any minute now there's going to be a rifle cracking off.'

When the visit to Zimbabwe was being arranged, Ian was asked by the administrators at Lord's where he would like to stay. 'I thought, "Well, that's rather strange," but said, "I would like to stay with the team, please" – because at that stage I didn't know them personally at all. There was a pregnant pause before they told me that the executives usually stayed in a rather better hotel than the players. I insisted, "No, I want to stay with the players." So I finish up, with my wife, at the Holiday Inn in the middle of Harare. They said, "We've got a suite for you." I said, "Thank you very much indeed," and we go up to the suite, which is actually pretty small and you couldn't open the windows and you couldn't leave the incredibly noisy air conditioning on. It was just appalling.

'The next day I went round the players' rooms with the manager. I went into the first room, then the second and third room, and they were all sharing in these rabbit hutches with single beds. You know what cricketers are like, with jockstraps and all that stuff – it was awful. The only two people that had single rooms were the captain, Michael Atherton, and John Barclay, who was the manager. Meanwhile, Tim Lamb, the ECB chief executive was staying nearby in a very nice hotel, much to my wife's disgust. I said to Tim, "Why are the players all together?" "Oh, tradition," he told me. I said, "Well, Tim, from now on, this tradition stops. They have single rooms and if they want to share, they apply to share, and we will look after them sensibly and well. They are international cricketers." The team went on from Zimbabwe to New Zealand, where all our arrangements were changed so that they all had single rooms.'

The visit to Zimbabwe gave Ian his first close-up of the need for massive changes. But he realised pretty quickly that there were those who were, at best, averse to change. Anything dramatic that he might plan, such as creating two divisions in the County Championship, was bound to be met with tough opposition. 'Well, you have to fight those battles, whether it's in business or cricket. Cricket was difficult. It was absolutely in the dark ages. If you look back, in 1996 we were one of the worst sides in the world. I think only Zimbabwe was behind us. There was very little direction and there was no money in the game. So, one of the first things I did with Tim Lamb, who was a very capable chief executive, was to prepare and publish a tome called *Raising the Standard*. This set out where we wanted to be. It was quite clear to me, with all my retail experience, that we had to brand the England side and that the England side had to be absolutely top in our thinking. But we didn't have any money. When the ECB was formed we had about £30 million to run the whole of cricket in this country, which was absolutely ridiculous!

'I spent a lot of time with Terry Blake, our sponsorship and marketing director, talking to Chris Smith, the then Sports Minister. Eventually we persuaded him to move Test cricket from the A list to the B list, which meant we could negotiate our wares with satellite and terrestrial television. We did this on the clear understanding from Chris that before we announced anything, he had to know about it and pass it. So we did this deal with Channel 4 and Sky, went to Chris, and said, "This is what we want to do. All the limited-over matches on Sky with one Test match, and all the other Test matches on Channel 4." And he said that was fine.'

But the debate rumbles on and there has been a lot of criticism over the non-terrestrial aspect. 'I do not believe that it would now make sense to change it and this daft idea about the Ashes being exclusive to terrestrial television would be very damaging. Cricket has turned full circle. We've got more people playing cricket, we've got money going into grass roots cricket, we've got money going into disabled cricket, we've got money going into blind cricket. The counties, by and large, are pretty well thought of at the moment. They are getting some pretty big grants from the ECB. Now, if you're going to cut that off in any way, you have to be very careful. When we first went to Sky, I was quite vocal, because I had a very clear understanding with Chris Smith that a certain amount of cricket had to be on terrestrial television. But that was kicked into touch, although I still have documents quite clearly stating that it should be on terrestrial television and Sky. But that deal's gone now. Whether it will ever come back I don't know.

'However, as a result of the deal with Sky and Channel 4, our income went up from around £30 million to £90 million. So we could then start to help the counties more. I think about 15 of the 18 first-class counties had basically been on the breadline. They had no money. People weren't going to watch. The whole thing was a bit of a shambles at that time, to be quite honest with you. And the England side itself was made up of a desperate bunch of people. The players were wearing white helmets and pink helmets and green helmets – I mean, the whole thing was a shambles. So we set about putting a bit of discipline into it all.'

A significant part of the extra money went to the National Academy of Cricket at Loughborough, to contracted players, and to hiring Duncan Fletcher after the '99 World Cup. 'This was a very good and important move for us and Duncan did a great job.'

One of the ECB's ambitions was to establish both the England men's and women's sides as number one in the world by the beginning of the 21st century. That has been comfortably achieved by the women but not quite by the men. 'We got very close, didn't we, in 2005 when we beat the Australians? I think we were second in the world. We are probably about third or fourth in the world now. But we are a good side now and you can see the young cricketers coming through. We also have pretty good management – Andy Flower is doing a very good job. I think we went seriously wrong when Michael Vaughan stepped down and they appointed Andrew Flintoff captain for Australia in 2006. To my mind that was crazy. It certainly wouldn't have happened had I still been chairman of the ECB. And again, I think the captaincy going to Kevin Pietersen after that was crass.'

There were, of course, many other big issues that Ian had to address, not least betting and match fixing. 'This became a major concern right throughout my time. I remember bringing everybody to Lord's and getting them to sign declarations. Even then, two nations would not sign. Lord Condon, the former Commissioner of the Metropolitan Police, became head of the International Cricket Council's anti-corruption unit, investigating the game's betting problems. He did a very good job, although it was quite unpleasant and quite difficult. But I think we managed it reasonably well.'

Then there was the issue with the Pakistanis over Alec Stewart, the England wicketkeeper, who was alleged to have been paid £5,000 for information. 'The press loved all that. The Pakistanis felt that he should have been suspended, but Alec had explained the position to us quite clearly. I would always support Alec. I have a huge amount of time for him. He is a wonderful cricketer and he is not, in my book, someone who is going to get involved in sharp practice.'

But sadly the betting problem, coupled with spot fixing relating to individual actions in a match, surfaced again in 2010. Ian's reaction to this is crystal clear. 'Any international cricketer found guilty of match fixing or betting should be banned for life. This is the only way you will stamp out this wrongdoing.'

One major innovation during Ian's time at the ECB was the introduction of Twenty20, which has since had an enormous impact throughout the world. 'It only just got through the counties by one or two votes because they thought we were trivialising the game and that it was wrong. Yet we had actually spent £250,000 on a marketing survey to ascertain what people would go and watch. And Twenty20 was right at the top of the list. So we went to the counties and said we want to launch this, but they were totally against it. I remember the chairman of Durham, Bill Midgley, was adamantly against it. I phoned him up and said, "Bill, I really want your vote tomorrow because we have to give this a try for three years, and if it doesn't work then we'll change it." And he said, "Well, we'll see what happens tomorrow." Next day, at Lord's, we sat the counties in alphabetical order, starting with Derbyshire, then Durham, going all the way round to end with Yorkshire. So we start with Derbyshire: he was for it – so that was OK. Then it was Bill Midgley's turn and I said, "Now Bill, what do you think?" He got up and said, "I think this is dreadful. I think it is burlesquing cricket. I think it is probably the worst thing we have ever had to talk about here – but the chairman has given me such a hard time that I am going to vote for it."

'So I enjoyed the ECB but I have one regret, to be quite honest with you. After six years, it was clear to me that we had to get the management and the directorship of the ECB changed. What was required was a mix of county chairmen and non-executive directors from outside, with a bit of experience in business and raising money and all that sort of thing. I had lunch or dinner with every one of the county chairmen and then I wrote to them and said, "This will be my plan if you want me to stay as chairman for another two years." What upset me, really, was that I only got two letters of reply – having worked bloody hard for six years!'

Even though he was so annoyed that there were only two replies, Ian was not prepared to reveal which chairmen they came from. 'I just thought, "If that's the way they are thinking about it, then I am not going to stand. And I didn't! Nevertheless, I am just very pleased to see the efforts of the ECB and where they are placing their funds – that a lot of money is going not only to the England side, but to counties and also to grass roots cricket. I think that is very healthy and that we are probably in as good a state as we have been in my lifetime. You know, it is so nice to see a game that you have been totally devoted to going the right way, very much the right way.'

In fact, if he was still running the ECB or in a position of authority within the game, there was nothing that Ian would desperately like to see changed or that hasn't been achieved. 'But I do think that, in time, somebody has to grasp the nettle and ask, "Are we playing too much cricket, both domestic and international? And do we actually need to have 18 first-class counties to produce our best cricketers?" A very difficult question to answer, but I think I would prefer to have 12 or 14 first-class counties rather than 18. I would rather the money go into those 12 or 14, so there will be more time for coaching and training and doing all those sort of things.' But Ian agrees that he would have to get over the significant hurdle of saying to four or six counties, sorry, you are not a first-class county any longer. 'Well, it is very difficult, but if you were starting the first-class game now, you wouldn't have 18 first-class counties.'

But away from the ECB there are happy memories of people that he has met through cricket over the years. 'Colin Cowdrey was my cricketing hero, because we were about the same vintage and we played cricket together. He once stood up at a Lord's Taverners' lunch and said, "Among us today is Ian MacLaurin," adding, "I really can't understand why he didn't join Kent as a professional, or even as an amateur, but he went on to become quite a successful grocer." And it was lovely in the House of Lords, when we sat there together on the back benches. I was then chairman of the ECB and he used to send me little notes. "Ian, why don't you do this?" and "Ian, why don't you do the other?" And I would scribble back, "I can't actually do that, Colin." So I had a great association with a wonderful, wonderful man.

'Also, in a very different context, I was young when I went on the MCC Committee for the first time, sitting there in front of all the great and the good. I was really trying to get in and say something which I thought might be halfway sensible. Eventually, I caught the president's eye and I said whatever I said. As I finished, a voice from the other end of the Committee

Room at Lord's, said, "MacLaurin, this is a cricket club, not a chain of bloody shops!" It was Field Marshal Lord Bramall, a fantastic man – someone I got to know well over the years. So cricket is full of super people.'

And of memorable matches. 'Never to be forgotten, without question, was when we won the Ashes in 2005, when Warney [Shane Warne] dropped Pietersen. If he had caught that, what would have happened? I was in the dressing room with the boys afterwards. I mean, that was just wonderful. That was one, and I suppose the other one, which doesn't come high in the history of cricket, was in 2001, when we beat Sri Lanka in Colombo. Graham Thorpe made an undefeated 100 in the first innings and carried his bat again the second innings, when we only needed 70 odd to win. The heat there was intense and I think he lost almost a stone in weight in two days. I mean, that was amazing technique and guts and determination. That was terrific.'

Looking back to when he was a little boy, he recalls that his dad was a cricket nut and that probably one of the first toys he had was a cricket bat. 'So cricket is very much in my blood. I played for my prep school, and then went on to Malvern College in Worcester. I got in the First XI in my first year there and captained the side for two years. I played a little bit for Hertfordshire, not much because I had to work then, but I played for the Royal Air Force during my National Service. I enjoyed Kent 2nd XI enormously, particularly when Peter Richardson came down from Worcestershire, and we were wonderfully captained by Derek Ufton. I was offered professional terms by Leslie Ames, who was then secretary, which I turned down basically because I had to earn more money. I was going out with my wife-to-be at the time and the money in those days for a professional cricketer was pretty small, and I just felt that I would rather play cricket as an amateur than turn pro. So I played for the Band of Brothers, a wandering Kent side, for MCC and a lot for Wimbledon.'

As a player, spectator and from his time with the ECB and MCC, Ian has developed an enormous affection for Lord's. 'The first time I played there, there must have been at least five people in the ground! MCC were playing the USA. They used to have an old boy who opened the gate for you as you went into bat and I remember, as I walked down the steps, he opened the gate and said, "Good luck, sir. Remember all the famous people who have been here before you." And you think, "Wow."

'It has been a huge privilege to be a part of this wonderful game and to meet the people that have been involved. In some small way as a player, as an administrator, with MCC, with the ECB − if you have been able to put something back into the game in a positive way then I think it is a huge privilege to be able to have done that. Not too many people have had the opportunity that I have had to give back to something that I really loved.

'I could go on talking to you about cricket all day. All else apart, it has taught me leadership qualities, it taught me how to get the best out of people, in running Tesco particularly, and Vodafone, and the other businesses I have been involved with. It has taught me the huge importance of teamwork in everything that you do.

'You know,' he concludes, 'it is a very humbling game, so you certainly don't want to get too cocky about anything, because as soon as you get too ambitious or a bit over-the-top, then you are knocked down very quickly.'

As I leave, I thank him for his time, for the cricket chat and, perhaps too profusely, for the coffee: far better than any on offer on the high street and the first brewed exclusively for me by a member of the House of Lords.

THE RT HON SIR JOHN MAJOR KG, CH

'I CAN'T IMAGINE A TIME IN WHICH I WOULDN'T FIND MY HEART LIFTING A LITTLE WHEN I WALK ONTO A CRICKET GROUND AND SEE THE GREEN TURF AND THE STUMPS IN PLACE, READY FOR THE START OF PLAY.'

Sir John Major was born on 29 March 1943, in Carshalton, Surrey, and is the former Prime Minister and Leader of the Conservative Party. He was elected MP for Huntingdon in 1979 and entered the Cabinet in 1987 as Chief Secretary to the Treasury, subsequently serving as Secretary of State for Foreign and Commonwealth Affairs and Chancellor of the Exchequer. In 1999 he was made a Companion of Honour for initiating the Northern Ireland peace process, and was appointed a Knight Companion of the Most Noble Order of the Garter by HM The Queen on St George's Day 2005. Since leaving Parliament in 2001 Sir John has been actively involved in business and charity work.

I sink into the soft cushions of a large, brightly coloured settee, from where I look out through a wide expanse of windows on what must be one of the best panoramic views of the Thames in London. The Houses of Parliament and the London Eye are clearly visible on this crisp September morning. To my right, rows of books on the far wall are dominated by the bright yellow jackets of an impressive collection of *Wisdens*. To my left sits a man totally fascinated by cricket. It is time to talk about the wonderful game with Sir John Major.

It is difficult to imagine how it is possible to get so much enjoyment from cricket when, for most of your adult life, you have been unable to play it. At the age of 22, when he was working for Standard Chartered Bank in Nigeria, Sir John had a very bad car accident which ended all chance of him being able to take the field again. 'People have occasionally seen me waving a bat around since the accident, but not seriously. I haven't been able to play a full match because I broke my left leg in an extravagant number of places and completely smashed the kneecap. I was bedridden for nearly a year, with the constant fear of losing my leg. The fact that I didn't is no small miracle, even though the damage inflicted meant no more cricket. But it did release me to become a spectator, which I have always enjoyed. The amount of cricket that I have played since school was therefore actually quite limited. Would I have loved to have played more? Of course I would. Do I wish I could still play, if only in village games? Of course I do. There is something very exciting about holding a new cricket ball in your hand, or a bat – it is a physical thing. So I miss it terribly, and always have, but I'm philosophical about it because I could be missing one leg. That does put things in perspective.'

Many years later, as Prime Minister during the Commonwealth Conference in Harare in 1992, Sir John did manage to play, opening the batting with Australian's then Prime Minister, Bob Hawke. 'Thousands of people were there, which was hugely flattering to us – except I think they had come to see Graham Hick, who was batting at number three! Bob Hawke and I went out to bat, but he kept stealing the bowling. Then after about half an hour the umpire said, "Right, off you go – time for the real cricketers." As we walked off, I asked Bob, "Did you know we only had 10 or 12 overs?" and he said, "Oh yes – didn't I tell you?" That was the last time I put on pads and held a bat – and the first time I had done so for many years.'

Sir John remembers playing cricket from a very early age when, as a two or three-year-old, his main inspiration was his sister, who taught him how to play cricket in the garden. 'We lived in Worcester Park and on Saturdays and Sundays she used to take me to watch the local cricket club, which is where she may have learned about the game. My sister was in her late teens and the cricket team was full of young men, which might have had something to do with it! But to be fair to my sister, she was a great fan of the Bedser twins and had always followed their careers closely. Although she didn't play much sport, I think she was always interested in cricket – an interest she still retains.'

When Sir John went to Cheam Common Primary School, he played cricket and football. Later, at Rutlish Grammar School in Wimbledon, it was cricket and rugby, and athletics, too. 'I played a lot of cricket at school and Rutlish was very keen on sport. I did very little academic studies at Rutlish, and therefore had a lot to catch up on when I left school. I also needed to pass a banking degree, so I used to get up very early – before five in the morning – including weekends. In the evenings, I was playing politics. So all of that got in the way of cricket, but I played for scratch teams of one sort or another when I was in my late teens.'

As a nine-year-old, Sir John lived in Brixton, just half an hour's walk from The Oval, where he used to spend almost every spare minute. 'I would take sandwiches and a bottle of Tizer and watch the great Surrey team of the 1950s. I think the first game I ever saw was Surrey against Sussex, in 1952. From 1952 to 1957 – those marvellous years when Surrey won the championship every year – I spent the whole of my summer holidays at the Oval.

'I've never been far away from it since, including when I was in politics. The Surrey Committee knew of my affection for the county and were always wonderfully generous hosts. In due course, I was invited to become vice president, which was a great honour. I then became the president in 2000, normally a position held for one year, but one which I held for two.'

This was the period when the new Oval was being planned and Sir John is clearly thrilled to have been so heavily involved with the great OCS stand. 'I think it's the best in world cricket. I spent a lot of time, with others, raising money for that stand and am so pleased we did it, because I think it's renovated The Oval. It made the ground smaller, because we came in 20 yards, but we have increased ground capacity and provided wonderful facilities. It also gave Surrey an opportunity to make money from what is built into that stand, such as conference, seminar and entertainment suites, which produce an income during the winter. So that was my principal involvement as president.'

I suggest that it must have been quite a challenge when he was involved full time in politics, not only to go and watch as often as he wanted but simply to follow the scores. 'All the Test grounds were very generous. They knew of my love of cricket and – given the vagaries of my diary – were always amazingly accommodating, not just towards me but to my protection team too. If I could possibly go for one day of each Test match, then I considered myself very lucky. But it wasn't always possible. As for getting the scores, that was always easy. When I first went to the Treasury as Chief Secretary, my Private Secretary was a Surrey member and as mad on cricket as I was. Nigel Lawson, the then Chancellor, was a cricket lover from Leicestershire, and Peter Brooke, another Treasury minister, knows as much about cricket as anyone I've ever met. My Private Secretary arranged for a television to be permanently tuned in to the cricket during the public expenditure round, and from time to time we'd break off and watch a shot or two. So there was never any problem at the Treasury!

'When I got to Number 10, the Cabinet Secretary was Robin Butler – a very fine cricketer whose grandfather was the great Victorian batsman, Richard Daft. Quite a few Cabinet ministers were also cricket mad, not least Ken Clarke (then Chancellor of the Exchequer), who later became President of Nottinghamshire County Cricket Club. So cricket scores were brought into Cabinet meetings on a regular basis. Initially, Michael Heseltine, who sat beside me, was rather intrigued by this routine. An expressionless Duty Clerk would enter the Cabinet Room and hand me a note. After reading it, I would show it to the Cabinet Secretary, seated on my right. I'd then throw the note across the table to the Chancellor of the Exchequer, who sat opposite me. Ken would read it, pull a face, throw it back to me and I'd tuck it into my blotting pad. Quite naturally, having seen notes pass between the Prime Minister, Cabinet Secretary and the Chancellor of the Exchequer, Michael Heseltine assumed something was happening on the markets. Eventually he was overcome by curiosity and stole a peek, only to find it said "England 52 for 1" or something like that. So cricket, for me, was always subliminal. Subordinate to politics, of course, but in politics – as in any working life – it's vital to have other interests and even in the darkest moments, cricket – for me and for others – lifted the lid on the pressure cooker.

'Of course, the Commonwealth leaders provided additional light relief during our meetings. When an Australian, New Zealand or Caribbean Prime Minister came to London, even if I wasn't inclined to talk about cricket, they were. Michael Manley, the Jamaican Prime Minister, wrote a rather distinguished book on the history of West Indies cricket. The Australians, Bob Hawke and John Howard, loved the game, as did successive New Zealand Prime Ministers. So it was easy to forge close bonds, which is one of the great joys of cricket.

'Cricket is an important part of West Indies life and tradition, so it is rather sad that it's fading because of the American influence and the increasing attraction of basketball. It would be a great bonus to have a West Indian cricket team that was as good as the one they had a couple of decades ago – and I do hope they find their way back. There's a natural talent in the way they play cricket, and you see that difference in the way they bat and the way they bowl. Individual nations play cricket differently, partly because of conditions, as well as physical flexibility and attitudes. If you came from Mars and saw an Englishman playing cricket, you could still tell that he plays it differently in style from a West Indian or an Indian.'

It's hardly surprising that the five-day game is Sir John's favourite form of cricket – a comfortable distance clear of the rest of the field. 'For me, the Test match dwarfs everything else. I like county cricket, and the shortest form of the game, Twenty20, I watch and enjoy but I'm not avid about it. A Twenty20 game doesn't linger in the memory. I can remember things in Test matches that I saw 50 years ago. I don't remember what I have seen in a Twenty20 game, and that is the difference. The 50-over game is more attractive, because you can see more strategy in it. Seeing great batsmen just trying to hit everything in Twenty20 is like watching Red Rum pull a milk cart!

'This is why it's so important that we help cricket to endure and don't kill it with too much of the short form of the game. It raises the money in the short term but the jewel in the crown is Test match cricket, and that should be protected at all costs. My worry is the sheer pressure for the short game that comes out of the Indian subcontinent, where so much of cricket's money is these days. We need to be extremely careful that we don't overcook the goose and damage Test match cricket.'

Since Sir John believes it is important to get the right decision whenever possible, he is in favour of using more technology to help umpires to do their job. 'So often technology shows us that, however good umpires were in the past, they didn't always make the right decision. Legend says Frank Chester was never wrong – well, legend is wrong. Sometimes technology shows things that are almost invisible to the human eye. So, if you want the right decisions, I'm in favour of technology. I think it's going pretty well, although I think there is still a real problem with catches. I think the technology sometimes lies. When you get a catch that just hits the ground and then the hand, I think technology can mislead. But overall, I am pretty much in favour of it.'

We then turn to the worrying and recurring topics of betting, spot and match fixing, and standards in the game generally. 'Well, there is an Anti-Corruption Unit now and I think it has to be very severe on people who taint the game. Cricket has a special social content, more perhaps than any other game, and I think when people are undermining the game in this fashion, you have to stamp it out. It looks as though the recent betting [the 2010 England v Pakistan series] was simply on two or three no balls. You may say it isn't going to affect the game, but it taints it beyond repair. I think it is a minority of people who are doing it – how many I don't know – but once it has been exposed, it needs dealing with pretty firmly by the authorities.

'After all, cricket is by far the most dominant sport in India and Pakistan, and if you go to the Indian subcontinent their love of the game is self-evident. You find kids playing in the street in bare feet and everywhere there's a bit of spare ground, you will find someone with a bat and ball. All the adulation that youngsters have for role models tends to be focused on cricketers, and to find some of them have feet of clay must be pretty devastating. That is why you must deal with the problem firmly.

'It is obviously a key issue, but there are several other things that I don't like. For example, I think Test match crowds are short-changed with only 88 or 90 overs a day. The over rates are often very slow, even when a spin bowler is operating, or medium-pacers without a long run-up. It is not just the fielding team; it is often the batting side as well. You often see the bowler ready to deliver the ball, but the batsmen are having a chat in the middle of the wicket. That is unfair on spectators who, by and large, pay quite a lot of money to go and see the game, and if they take their children with them it can be a very expensive day out.

'I also don't like sledging. Many older players say it adds a bit of spice to the game and that it doesn't matter, but I think it depends how far it goes. Some of the sledging you hear about is pretty relentless and pretty nasty. There is a line which ought not to be crossed and sometimes it is.

'In many ways, however, cricket has become much more entertaining. The run rate has increased – the Australians started that about 10 years ago – and now it is generally a good deal higher per over, even though the entertainment could be so much better if there were slightly more overs in the day. Other things have also improved tremendously. The fielding is infinitely better overall than when I first started watching. There were magnificent fielders then, of course – Tony Lock, for example, Micky Stewart, Stuart Surridge, all of whom I saw at The Oval, and many others beyond Surrey. But, as a general rule, the fielding, and particularly the outfielding, is probably better than ever before in the history of cricket.'

I remind Sir John that a typical example of outfielding in the 1940s or 1950s would have been Alec Bedser sticking out a size-12 boot in an attempt to stop the ball reaching the boundary. It prompts him to tell me of an occasion when he found himself sitting with Alec in the Surrey committee room. 'Steve Harmison ran round the boundary, threw himself full length and stopped the ball going for four, and the batsmen were only able to run three. A very distinguished guest, a senior military man, was sitting beside me, and said, "That was wonderful – what commitment! And he's going to have to bowl after tea, too." Alec turned to him and said, "He's a bloody fool! If he'd injured himself he couldn't have bowled after tea." It was a very different attitude in Alec's day.'

When I ask about players he has particularly admired, his list seems endless, and this is from a man who does not see himself as much of a hero-worshipper. But there have clearly been some that were extra special to him. 'Starting with batsmen, Peter May would be pre-eminent. I still think he's the greatest post-war English batsman, and I saw quite a lot of him in the 1950s. Tom Graveney was a delight to watch, and Denis Compton, of course. And from overseas, I don't think people quite realise how great a batsman Ricky Ponting is. When he retires, people will see him right up there in the top 10 batsmen of all time. Viv Richards was magical, as was Gordon Greenidge, and what an all-round player Richard Hadlee was. Amongst the bowlers, watching Laker and Lock in their different styles was wonderful, and Trueman at his best was a remarkable sight. The great West Indies fast bowlers were tremendous, and Lillee and Thomson were quite something. There have been some great fielders, like Derek Randall and Colin Bland – wonderful accuracy from mid-wicket or cover point, hitting the wicket time after time.'

Sir John gets great enjoyment from watching, listening to and reading about the game, and one particular favourite writer was *The Times'* Johnny Woodcock. 'I loved reading his reports. They were always of a very high standard. I also have quite an extensive cricket library, and in it is every book Jim Swanton ever wrote. Of the broadcasters, John Arlott was wonderful, but overall I think the standard is very good, and *Test Match Special* is unfailingly so. It's very rare you get someone who is boring to listen to. Sometimes they are irreverent, like Brian Johnston or Jonathan Agnew, but they are very good, and it is entertainment as well as a commentary on the game. I actually think the television coverage is good too. Richie Benaud was outstanding, and people like Geoff Boycott brought a new dimension. I know quite a lot about the game from the outside, but I've never played it at top level so, when you listen to a Boycott or an Atherton or any one of a number of others, you get a completely different insight. They are much more technical, too – going to the dug-out, where Simon Hughes points out what's happening. The commentaries now include how the ball is delivered, what the batsman is doing wrong. As an aficionado of cricket, I find all that absolutely fascinating. And for the young would-be cricketer, there is a huge amount to learn from listening to these former Test match players talking about the game.

'After all, cricket is probably as entertaining today as it has ever been, and I think the quality of the cricket is generally very high. People always hark back to the past as though it were a golden age, but – as in so many things – when you see it in the round, it often wasn't so. Many cricketers have made the point that cricket is played in the mind, but that is also true to a degree for the spectator. There are so many subtleties to the game that the real cricket lover understands, but which are a complete blank to anyone else. Every time I go to a cricket match I find it totally absorbing; it can wipe everything else out of my mind. That was always the great joy for me during my years in politics: I could go to any cricket ground, and whatever else was going on simply disappeared from my mind. The whole world narrowed to what was happening on that cricket pitch. That total absorption in the gladiatorial contest between batsman and bowler, with the fielders in attendance, just cleared the head. I was then ready to return to the fray. I can't imagine a time in which I wouldn't find my heart lifting a little when I walk into a cricket ground and see the green turf and the stumps in place, ready for the start of play.'

I have one last – albeit hypothetical – question to ask. Imagine that the young John Major is nearly 16 years old when the careers master says to him, 'I have a special gift that, every so often, allows me to tell one of my pupils that there are two exceptional options open to them when they leave school. In your case, you can either be Prime Minister or you can be England captain and win the Ashes back from Australia. Which is it to be?' Sir John's response is immediate. 'Well, I don't believe in preordination, so I would have taken the Ashes and still tried to be Prime Minister!'

He has seen the question coming and is comfortably in position to deal with it, as I imagine he would have been had he been given the opportunity to score the winning Ashes runs at his beloved Oval.

CHRISTOPHER MARTIN-JENKINS MBE

'ON 99, WITH THE BENEFIT OF HINDSIGHT AND
MORE EXPERIENCE, I MIGHT HAVE DONE THINGS
DIFFERENTLY, BUT I SUPPOSE ONE IS REMEMBERED
MORE FOR GETTING 99 AT LORD'S THAN
FOR GETTING 100 THERE!'

*Christopher Martin-Jenkins was born in Peterborough on 20
January 1945, and is a cricket journalist, commentator and author.
He joined* The Cricketer *magazine from university and has been
cricket correspondent for the BBC in two spells, for the* Daily
Telegraph *for 10 years and for* The Times *also for 10 years, and
where he was most recently chief cricket correspondent until 2008.
He has been a member of the BBC's Test Match Special team
since 1973 and has written numerous books, including several best
sellers. He was awarded an MBE in 2009 for services to sport
and was appointed president of MCC in 2010.*

It is the fifth and final day of the Test match at a packed
Newlands in Cape Town and a fascinating day's cricket is in
prospect, with every conceivable result possible. Christopher is
anchoring the first session of play for the BBC's *Test Match
Special* programme. I sit quietly in the wings, waiting for him to
come off air. The view from the media centre, flanked away to

the right by Table Mountain, is simply magnificent. As soon as he is free, we climb a flight of stairs and seat ourselves behind rows of journalists crouched over their laptops, not daring to miss a single delivery as the drama is acted out in front of them.

It is difficult for us not to be distracted at times, particularly when England wickets start to fall, but despite this Christopher talks enthusiastically about his life-long love of the wonderful game. He became interested as a small boy and as is often the case, his father was a big influence. 'He was a very keen cricketer and as long as I can remember I was passionate about the game. We played in the garden at home and I played as soon as I got to prep school in Eastbourne. As a small boy, I was quite good, I think, which always helps. I played whenever I could because I just loved it. I also had my first opportunity to watch county cricket when I was at prep school because we had a very good master, Reg Lord, who had played for Oxford University. He was an excellent cricket coach who loved the game, and took us at the end of the summer term to watch two Sussex matches, in the Eastbourne week at The Saffrons. It was enormous fun sitting on the edge of the boundary and then getting the chance to go and play with a tennis ball in the intervals.

'As I say, I was a bit of a star in prep school cricket and, in those days, I was quite a demon bowler. I could bowl until, at about the age of 14, I suddenly shot up and lost the control that had come naturally. I was never really a consistent bowler after that.

'But I was also a reasonable batsman, capable of going in at first wicket down, until I got in amongst better players. When I went to Marlborough, I should, in normal circumstances, have had three years in the team but in 1961 they had probably the best side they'd ever had. Mike Griffith, for example, was absolutely outstanding as a schoolboy, and I don't think he ever got better than he was at Marlborough. He did have his odd triumphs, such as the hundred against the Australian touring team at Hove in 1968. So he was still capable of brilliance, but his misfortune was not to keep wicket at Cambridge, because Deryck Murray, the West Indian, went there and then, later on at Sussex, Jim Parks was 'keeper.'

In 1963, Christopher played at Lord's in what was then an annual two-day school match between Marlborough and Rugby. He remembers it very clearly for an innings that might have had a happier ending than it did. 'It was one of those very good games of cricket, with Marlborough losing a game we should have won. We needed 200-ish to win the match in the fourth innings, but we lost early wickets and were in trouble at about 20 for three. I hadn't played for three weeks because of a broken finger that had not healed properly, but another batsman called Tim Halford and I had a stand and we got to a position where we were sailing to victory when he got out. I got close to my dream of making a hundred at Lord's, which probably temporarily took precedence over winning the match, instead of the other way round. We took a risky single, there was a moment's hesitation and a throw from cover hit the stumps directly. And then the same thing happened on the other side of the wicket: again a brilliant bit of fielding and another direct hit. Both were feasible singles, but a bit of hesitation, as I say, and two run-outs, with me on 99. Then I got hit on the damaged finger and holed out to mid on! But they bowled very well and we lost a good game of cricket by a handful of runs. On 99, with the benefit of hindsight and more experience, I might have done things differently, but I suppose one is remembered more for getting 99 at Lord's than for getting 100 there!'

After Marlborough, Christopher went up to Cambridge and the prospect of more opportunities on the cricketing front. 'I was probably a better cricketer as I grew a bit stronger. I was too much of a beanpole at Cambridge and although I was always there or thereabouts, I never got into the University side. I had one big opportunity in 1965, when I was pushing for a blue and was picked to play for the Quidnuncs [a club for leading Cambridge University players] against the University at Fenners. I think fate was against us because the three-day game started on a Saturday in beautiful weather, and the University made 350 or so and then declared. By close of play, I believe, we had lost Henry Blofeld, who had opened the batting, but must have made close to 70 in reply. There was a rest day on Sunday and then on Monday the weather completely changed. It was foggy, and it was unplayable – it really was. By the time the match was abandoned we were about 75 for 8, Mark Whittaker and Jonathan Harvey had four wickets apiece and I had been bowled for a duck. Peter May had been due to captain the Quidnuncs but wasn't able to. It was officially a first-class match at the time it was played, but then they had a look at it at an MCC meeting at Christmas and decided it didn't merit first-class status. So that was the start and finish of my first-class career!' The only small consolation that I could offer Christopher was that, had the match retained its first-class status, he would not have qualified for inclusion in *Cricket Wonderful Cricket*. I couldn't help but feel that he would have been prepared to make that sacrifice!

Over the years, he has made appearances for Surrey second XI at the Oval, in J P Getty's XI at Wormsley, for Marlborough Blues, the Lord's Taverners and others, but opportunities have been limited. 'Once I started working for the BBC in 1970 it became very difficult. Being a cricket journalist inevitably meant working on Saturdays so I was able to play in a few Cricketer Cup matches but not much more than that.'

At Lord's in May 2010, long after our meeting in Cape Town, it was announced at MCC's annual general meeting that Christopher had been appointed its next president. He started his term of office in October and quickly identified corruption within the game as an issue that has to be addressed, both as far as spot fixing and even more seriously, match fixing are concerned. 'The programmes of education, prevention and investigation appear not to have been entirely successful but this is clearly more the fault of the criminals and a few greedy cricketers than it is of the administrators. The corruption, which results from illegal bookmaking on the subcontinent, is more deeply entrenched than cricket itself and I feel that, in the main, it is Asia's responsibility to try to get rid of this corruption at its very source. In the final analysis, however, gamblers will only succeed if there are players who are prepared to be bought, so there is only one way of tackling this and that is zero tolerance.'

Another of Christopher's concerns, one that we initially discuss in Cape Town, is fixture congestion and how to deal with it. 'I think there is just too much professional cricket played, and too much international cricket, and I don't think it does anybody any good, really. The lack of principles amongst those who run cricket depresses me a bit. They just don't have any concern, it seems to me, other than making as much money from the game as they can. You just long for them to sit down and say, "OK, let's have a logical programme that keeps everybody wanting more." Subsequently, wearing his president's hat, he tells me, 'I think it is true to say that there is general agreement that we must have fewer domestic and international fixtures. Twenty20 cricket is in danger of expanding too fast and, hopefully, the need for a more sensible county programme working alongside the right level of international fixtures is in the process of being dealt with.

'I also want to see what I can do as far as over rates are concerned. I will try, with MCC's 450-odd matches played around the country and abroad, to persuade the match managers to attempt to get in 16 or 17 overs per hour. I remember when Hubert Doggart was president and I was a match manager in the early 1980s, that he pressed us all to try and bowl 20 overs an hour, because things were already slipping at that stage. That was hard enough, and now they're down to well below 14 at first-class level. I feel that if MCC can at least set an example at that sort of rate, it can teach the schoolboys how quickly the game can be played if there is not too much of the posing that goes on almost imperceptibly at first-class level. A lot of the problem seems to stem from what they see at matches and on television, and that is why the spirit of the game is so important and why first-class cricketers should observe it.'

Christopher would also like to try to help MCC to reach the right decision regarding the further development of the ground at Lord's. 'There is a lot of money at stake if it all goes ahead, and there could be a massive upheaval for very many years. Obviously, there needs to be a lot of careful thought before any move is made and I am sure that will be the case.'

Christopher's son Robin, the Sussex all-rounder, retired from the game in July 2010, to start a new career in teaching at Hurstpierpoint College. Had Christopher ever found it difficult reporting on a Sussex match in which Robin was playing? Had the family drawn up a set of rules to cover what could be an awkward situation? 'The only rules as such were self-imposed ones. I got a little less embarrassed about it as he established himself in the Sussex side. In the early days I did almost anything not to mention him at all unless I had to, and I think the first time I did, I referred to him as a "double-barrelled all-rounder"! But as time went on I decided I must treat him just like everyone else – reporting what he did only if I would have reported on it had it been John Smith. I couldn't say he was worth a place in the England squad, not publicly anyway, but it never brought about any friction, at least not that I'm aware of. He ploughed his own furrow with great determination and I tried not to offer advice unless it was asked for – and it wasn't often asked for! Of course, once he retired, it ceased to be a problem. He had such a good last season in 2010, and it shows you about the psychology of the game. He relaxed. He knew what his future was. If Sussex had realised his potential, as a one-day batsman in particular, he might have gone a bit further in that form of the game.'

When Christopher came down from university it was to join *The Cricketer* as assistant editor. E W 'Jim' Swanton, who was editorial director of the magazine for more than 20 years, helped him to develop both his writing skills and his knowledge of the game. 'I knew from a very early age that I wanted to be a sort of Swanton. He was probably the one I read most and he taught me some of the basics. He also made me read cricket history, which I hadn't done up to that point. He gave me a book by Robertson-Glasgow [R C 'Crusoe' Robertson-Glasgow, a cricketer and cricket writer] and wrote in it, "Christopher, in high expectation." Which was nice of him, because it was almost as soon as I started at *The Cricketer*. Despite being passionate about contemporary cricket and knowing everything about it, I didn't know much about the history of the game. A chap rang up in my first week at *The Cricketer* and said, "I just want to check the spelling of Kortright." I said, "Do you mean Cartwright?" and he said, "No, no – Kortright. Haven't you heard of Kortright?" I hadn't, but I swiftly put that right. In fact, he was one of the fastest bowlers of all time, and played for Cambridge and Essex in the late W G Grace's time. But I realised then that if I was going to be taken seriously, I needed to brush up on my history.'

Since those early years at *The Cricketer*, Christopher has watched and written and talked about masses of cricket, but how much has stuck? Does he have a very good memory or does he rely on a wonderful database? 'Yes, I have quite a good memory for cricket. But not for anything else…What's your name again?!

Increasingly, I find that the more cricket there is, tours fuse into one another. Once upon a time, you remembered years by who was touring in that summer, but not any more. So it is a case of jogging the memory, and even that's all changed. Once, it was by recourse to *Wisden*, to check the facts. Now you can do it instantly on the computer, or your telephone, on websites like Cricinfo and so on.

'Computers have changed it altogether for access of information, and also for speed of communication. When I started at *The Cricketer*, it was a case of typing out pieces. When someone like Neville Cardus produced something, which he did every month, I would get handwritten stuff which I would have to type out – and jolly tricky handwriting it was, too! Then it would go to the printer and you would get a galley [proof] back and correct it for any literals, and then you would paste it on to the page. Then it would go back to the printer again and you would get a page proof of what it looked like on the page. The whole thing was a very long process. Now they just do it all on a computer. So, from a production point of view, it has all changed.

'And from a writing point of view, too. Again, I started on typewriters and I suppose you fiddled with your copy much less than you do now. Now you can just rejig what you've written and it's done in no time at all, but you were much less inclined to do that when you had typed it out. It ought to be quicker to do it nowadays but because you've got this infinite capacity to make little changes, I'm never quite happy with the way I have phrased it, and have tended to stay rather late in the press box when others have already finished!'

In that context, it is sometimes said that Christopher is not the world's greatest timekeeper, a suggestion he finds quite amusing. 'It's absolutely true, but I do try to squeeze whatever I can into every minute. But I would claim to be last-minute as opposed to late!'

For journalists and commentators, with new technologies have come changes in relationships with and access to the players, who are now media-trained to toe the party line. 'In my early days of touring I was the same age as the players. We were probably in the same hotel and it was all very friendly and easy. There were no press officers to go through. Although, on one occasion when Geoff Boycott said something controversial – it was deemed that he had criticised Mike Denness's captaincy – it was blown up into tabloid headlines and Donald Carr, the tour manager, said, "Right, no more interviews with the press." This made me rather unpopular with the tabloid writers for a while, because it was my interview which had caused this decision. It was rather nice for me, because I didn't have to put a tape recorder in front of somebody at the end of every day's play for a while. But now everything seems to be much more controlled, through press conferences and so on, which is boring if you are reasonably independently minded and you have views of your own. I think, even now, the most interesting writers are the ones who don't feel they have to quote players all the time.'

In 2008, during the *Test Match Special* coverage of the New Zealand game at Lord's, Christopher, perhaps ill advisedly, used a fishing analogy: 'Vettori stays on the bank and keeps his rod down, so to speak.' The commentary team sniggered and giggled as Christopher battled to regain his composure, and Bill Frindall helpfully and audibly wished him good luck. But he admits it was not the first time that he had 'corpsed' during a commentary. 'There have been one or two others, actually, but in recent times that is the only one that has reduced everyone to giggles. Back in 1979, Brian Johnston and I once had uncontrollable giggles, but no one was listening then, because it was a Prudential Cup match between England and Canada. What set us off on this occasion was the unusual name of a Canadian substitute, Showkat Baksh. I had done a little bit of homework on the Canadian team and actually taken in what this chap looked like, but Johnners hadn't done any. I pointed to the name on the scorecard, but he just couldn't believe it and off he went in a fit of giggles, which, of course, was extremely contagious.'

In cricketing circles, it is very apparent that Christopher has a host of admirers, including the cricket-mad lyricist Tim Rice who says, 'I have always been a great fan and think he is my favourite commentator by quite a distance. I just like his use of the language. He's witty and he's obviously passionately committed to cricket. I like his voice, which is probably the kind of voice that's not very fashionable these days. He is just very good, and writes beautifully as well.'

Although Christopher has passed the role of chief cricket correspondent at *The Times* to Mike Atherton, he still writes regularly for the paper and elsewhere, and maintains his place securely as a long-term member of the *Test Match Special* team with as much enthusiasm for writing and broadcasting as ever. 'Well, perhaps not quite. I still love it but I am relieved not to have to write a piece at the end of every day – I really am. I have become a bit tired. It's worn me out, to be honest. I think I've got the same basic enthusiasm but not the same energy. I still enjoy the travel but inevitably you go to the same places over and over again, so it loses its novelty. There again, I have got wearier of the whole business of airports and hotels. But still I am not sure I can go through a winter without seeing cricket in the sun, somewhere, at some time.'

From playing and watching to writing and commentating, Christopher has been totally immersed in cricket for virtually his whole life. So what has he gained from it all? What has he most valued? 'Gosh. Infinite pleasure really – especially playing. Cricket people on the whole are nice people, and civilised people. So it is making a lot of friends, and seeing the world, and doing something I love for a profession. A lifetime's good fortune in doing something that I like doing, which so many people don't get from their work. I've been incredibly lucky, really.'

It is time for Christopher to start his second *TMS* session of the day, with England four down following the dismissal of night watchman James Anderson. I leave the media centre and head for my seat at the other end of the ground, reflecting on our chat and totally unaware that I am about to witness the climax of one of the most exciting drawn matches ever. The joy of cricket surely comes in many different and wonderful ways.

BARRY
NORMAN CBE

'THIS LITTLE BLOKE CAME OUT, WITH A FLOPPY
GREEN CAP, WALKING TO THE MIDDLE LIKE A
GIANT, MOBILE, GREEN MUSHROOM.'

*Barry Norman was born in London on 21 August 1933. He is
a film critic, writer and broadcaster. He presented the BBC's* Film
*programme from 1972 until 1998 when he moved to Sky, and
he has written and presented documentary series for the BBC.
He was a prominent journalist on national newspapers and still
writes a weekly column for the* Radio Times. *He was also a
regular broadcaster on radio and has written a number of novels
as well as a book on cricket. He was awarded the CBE for services
to broadcasting in 1998.*

Having arrived early for our meeting, I sit in the reception
area at the Groucho Club in London's Soho, turning the
pages of *The Independent* without taking in a single word. I am
waiting for a man who has interviewed every film star worthy
of the name, from George Clooney to Sophia Loren. I am
feeling a touch apprehensive. Barry Norman appears, very
apologetic, having suffered a train delay on his way into town.
We settle either side of a small table and order coffee as he
describes how his lifelong love of cricket began.

'It all started with my maternal grandfather, who had been a huge Surrey fan all his life, and was always telling me tales of men called 'Obbs and 'Ayward, because they were a very working class, south London family and aspirates were an unnecessary luxury as far as they were concerned. I was about 10 years old and my granddad just kept talking to me about cricket and I got more and more intrigued by the whole thing. Because it was wartime, there wasn't a lot of cricket being played, not even club or village cricket, or anything like that. So, never having seen it played, I went down to the public library and borrowed every book I could, and read avidly about the game.

'The first game I ever saw was the Victory International, when England played the Australian Services, at Lord's in 1945. I just fell in love with Lord's there and then. Since then it has been one of my favourite places in the whole world. Wonderful! There were some pretty amazing players in both teams: Wally Hammond, who scored 83, Cyril Washbrook, who made 112, and Bill Edrich, who got 73. That was a great introduction to cricket. I was amazed at the beauty and the power of Hammond's cover drives. I had read about cover drives and knew what they were, but when I saw Hammond batting – and that was the only time that I did – it was truly memorable.'

Barry's memory and knowledge of a match played nearly 65 years earlier is quite remarkable. When I returned home, I find details of the game in the 1946 *Wisden Cricketers' Almanack*. Each of the scores that he had quoted was spot on.

Barry was also a spectator at Don Bradman's last appearance at Lord's three years later. 'I still see it all so vividly in my mind. It wasn't a Test match; it was the Australians against the Gentlemen of England. It is unbelievable now that I got there at half past nine in the morning with my mates from school and the queue outside the Grace Gates went all the way round the corner to what was then the car park. Two men and a dog you would get in now. The place was absolutely packed and when

Bradman came in, the whole crowd rose to him and cheered him all the way to the wicket. I do remember feeling slightly disappointed, because I had read about Bradman and I knew about his incredible exploits, and I was expecting a giant! Instead of which this little bloke came out with a floppy green cap, walking to the middle like a giant, mobile, green mushroom. But then, when he got there, wow! You suddenly realised that this was something else again. And he scored all of his runs with not a single shot in the air – all along the ground. Then, when he reached 150, he just lobbed one up and Martin Donnelly caught it. Bradman simply tucked his bat under his arm and walked back to the pavilion to another standing ovation from the entire crowd. And people were weeping. I mean, I was weeping. It was a hugely emotional occasion and we all knew we were never going to see anything like it ever again. And I never have. I have seen some wonderful players since, but nobody quite like Bradman. I think Bradman is the kind of Shakespeare of cricket: just as Shakespeare bestrides the English language, so Bradman bestrides cricket. The number one player of all time.'

Two memorable matches at Lord's, but another particularly memorable match for Barry was played at Manchester in 1956. 'I think probably because I got to know him quite well, the match I would love to revisit would be Jim Laker taking 19 wickets at Old Trafford, because you wouldn't invent that. And the most amazing thing is that Tony Lock only got one wicket. Nevertheless, that is what happened. I think Jim is the greatest off-spinner that ever was. He was the second person, after Eric Morecambe, to describe me in public as a "cricket nut". Because of that, and because I was kind of an off-spinner myself – albeit not in Laker's class, of course – if I had a time machine and went back to a cricket match, that would be the one.'

Still looking back to those early days, Barry now talks about his active involvement in the game. 'I started playing a bit at prep school but I don't remember that very much. When I went to Highgate, which was my public school, that's when I started playing. I was already hooked on the game, so playing it was just sheer bliss. I loved it. I started off as a fast medium bowler and a bit of a batsman and then, in my mid-teens, I suddenly grew during the winter and when I tried bowling fast medium again the next summer, for some reason my body wouldn't let me. I had changed shape completely. So I switched to leg breaks and I bowled those for a number of years at school and then in club cricket, until I realised that being a leg spinner was not very sensible because you tend to be a bit too expensive for the captain. I had a couple of years off the game because I was working at weekends, and when I came back, I started to bowl off spin and stayed with that until the end of my playing career, such as it was.'

For 25 years, Barry enjoyed playing village cricket for Datchworth in Hertfordshire but towards the end it all started to get more serious. 'They entered a league and suddenly it was much more competitive. I figured that my daily life in the media was competitive enough and that I didn't want to carry that on into my weekend leisure activity, as it were. So I opted out of the first XI and went to play for the seconds instead, because they were still playing friendlies, which were great. Everybody is still trying their best but you are not treated as a pariah if you drop a catch or don't get any runs.'

Then he became involved with the Lord's Taverners, something that gave him another cricketing lease of life and a further interest in the game. 'The first time I was approached was in the 1970s, when I was presenting the *Today* programme on Radio 4. Just before we went on air, the guy I was about to interview, whose name I've now forgotten, said "Oh, I've got a message for you from Eric Morecambe," who at that time was

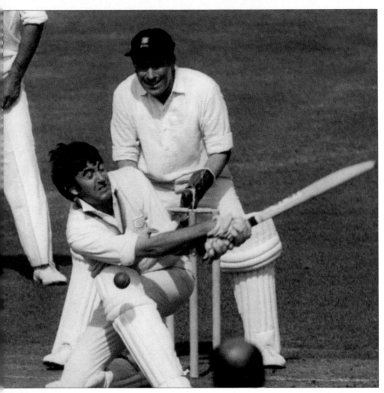

Above: John Alderton goes for the sweep against Warwicks in 1975.

© *Lord's Taverners*

Below: Sylvia and Victor Blank with Australian legend Shane Warne.

© *Victor Blank*

Above: Rory Bremner, a man of very many voices, entertains the crowd.

© *Keith Curtis*

Right: Lorraine Chase, kitted out and ready for play.

© *Lorraine Chase*

Left: Alan Davies –
proud of his county
and of his shirt!

© *Alan Davies*

Right: A few bowling tips from
Ainsley Harriott for Nick
Hancock's daughter, Dolores.

© *Lord's Taverners*

Above: The Duke of
Edinburgh on form
with both bat at
Arundel Castle, 1957…
Courtesy of Press Association

Right: …and ball at
Bournemouth, 1949.
*Collection of H.R.H. The
Duke of Edinburgh – By
kind permission*

Above: David English *(middle)* and John Major *(right)* enjoy Jeff Thomson's Aussie brand of humour.   © *Keith Curtis*

Below: Ian Maclaurin *(left)* with son Neil *(middle)* and Geoffrey Boycott.   © *Ian Maclaurin*

Left: A young Michael Parkinson prepares for action.

© *Michael Parkinson*

Right: Christopher Martin-Jenkins on the front foot.

© *Phillip Brown*

Left: Tim Rice hands over a Taverners cricket bag to a group of youngsters at Scarborough.

© *Lord's Taverners*

Right: Nicholas Parsons pauses in a typically elegant fashion outside Balmoral Castle.

© *Nicholas Parsons*

Sussex captain Tony Greig leads the attack against the Australians at Hove in 1975 and (*inset*) with John Duncan, enjoying a relaxed evening in the same town a few years later. © *Getty*

© *John Duncan*

Elite Taverners group on the steps of Leslie Thomas's home in Salisbury in 1992. *Back row left to right*: Dennis Whitehouse, unknown boy, Bill Frindall, Ian Botham, Jack Russell. *Middle Row (l to r)*: Leslie Crowther, Brian Johnston, Allan Lamb, Derek Pringle. *Front row (l to r)*: Micky Stewart, Leslie Thomas, Robin Smith, Rory Bremner, Richard Stilgoe.   © *Lord's Taverners*

Left: Martin Sorrell plays firmly and confidently off his legs. © *Martin Sorrell*

Below: Chris Tarrant on the chase to save a second run.

© *Lord's Taverners*

Above left: Graham Taylor in cricket whites for Watford
Football Club. © *Graham Taylor*

Above right: Barry Norman on the bench between umpiring
stints at Wormsley. © *Lord's Taverners*

Below: Richard Stilgoe delivers one of his accomplished
non-turning off-breaks. © *Lord's Taverners*

Above: Bill Wyman delivers under the eagle eye of fellow spinner, Phil Tufnell.

© *Keith Curtis*

Below (l to r): Allan Lamb, David English and Eric Clapton enjoying the company of Bill Wyman.

© *Keith Curtis*

President of the Taverners. And the message was, "Why isn't Barry Norman, the biggest cricket nut in the country, a member of the Lord's Taverners?" And I said, "Well, they've never asked me." I couldn't see any reason why they should because I thought that the Taverners members consisted mainly of people who had played for England. The kind of people who wouldn't normally let me in the same ground, let alone the same side. But nevertheless an invitation came through.'

I show Barry the scorecard for a match between the Lord's Taverners and a Scarborough Festival XI played in 1983. Amongst an impressive list of players is one BL Norman. 'Good Lord! Well, I'll be damned! I remember that. That was the start of the greatest weekend of my cricketing life, because it had started on the Saturday with a game in which I caught and bowled Mike Denness for six. But what that scorecard doesn't tell you is that if I hadn't caught that ball, I would have ended up with a navel the size of a Jaffa orange, because it came straight back out of the middle of Mike's bat. I put my hands down there for protection, and it stuck. What made it even better was that our skipper was Brian Close, the hardest man who ever played cricket. He came up to me afterwards and said, "I wouldn't have put my hands behind a ball like that on a cold day like this." I reckon that is the finest compliment ever paid by one man to another.

'Then it was down to Arundel on the Sunday and I got Colin Cowdrey caught at mid-off for about 13. I mean, totally misreading the vicious spin and cunning flight! Now, if Colin had got 53, he would have given me his wicket, but Colin didn't give his wicket away at 13 in any kind of game. That was a genuine wicket. I took four wickets in all but was just pipped for Man of the Match by Kevin Keegan, who had also taken a few wickets and scored a lot of runs.'

Barry played as often as he possibly could until he decided

to stop when he was 60. 'I was on the Taverners' Cricket Committee at the time and we were about to play our 40th Anniversary match at Lord's. Derek Ufton, chairman of the Cricket Committee, was picking the side and, out of courtesy, every playing member of the Committee was invited. I thought, "Wow, my God, playing at Lord's, wonderful." And then I thought, "Well, I don't know." The pitch would be the one nearest the Tavern stand, with the short boundary on that side and a huge, huge boundary on the other side. I just had this image of myself fielding on the furthest boundary, the ball coming to me and my not being able to throw it back anywhere near the wicket. I would just be lobbing it in. I thought, "Only humiliation awaits me here." So, because the batting had also pretty well gone, even though the bowling was still all right, I decided that this was probably a good time to bow out. So I said to Derek, "Thank you very much, but I won't play." He was terribly polite but I could see the look of intense relief in his eyes, as he could now get a proper cricketer to take my place!'

Films have been an everyday part of Barry's life, not only because of his own career, but also because of that of his father, Leslie, a director and producer. But cricket was not really part of his family life, because his father and brother weren't very interested. He also sees very little connection between the film world and cricket. 'There is a strong connection between acting and cricket, but that's mostly theatrical rather than film people. There is no real interplay between the two and consequently there aren't too many films about cricket. It's not a game that lends itself to films when you think about it. The most famous one was *The Final Test*, with Jack Warner, and that was made more than 50 years ago and was pretty absurd really. When you look at shots of Jack Warner trying to hook the ball, it is like a man with a newspaper trying to swat a fly. It's quite clear the man had never held a cricket bat in his life. And he was already in his fifties and too old to be playing Test cricket. There is a lovely moment – I think it is Warner himself who came into bat, with the opening fast bowler, Ray Lindwall, supposed to be in action for Australia. As he passes the outgoing batsman – one of the famous cricketers – Warner asks, "Is he turning it much?" *Turning it?!* Not quite Lindwall's type of bowling!

'Then, much more recently, there was a film called *Wondrous Oblivion*, starring Delroy Lindo. Cricket was very important within the plot of the film but wasn't the predominant part and the fact that nobody was very good was OK because they weren't supposed to be. So that worked, although I suppose the best of all cricket films was the Indian film *Lagaan*. It's not all about cricket, and the Indian team had never actually played cricket before. The British officers they were playing against were also not supposed to be all that good. So at that level it works rather well.

'I remember David Puttnam telling me once that he wanted to make a film about the Bodyline Tour but there were all kinds of reasons why it wouldn't really work. First of all, he would have to simplify the game for Americans – everyone would have to be caught or bowled. The intricacies of lbw would totally defeat the American audience. The actors who would play Douglas Jardine, Harold Larwood and the rest of the players would have to look like real cricketers when they were bowling and batting. He also wanted professional cricketers to stand in on the field for the actors. His main problem, the one that clinched it for him, was that the only bowler he could find whose accent seemed to resemble Larwood's was Norman Cowans, and he was a slightly different colour from the original! So the whole thing was abandoned.'

We turn from films to books. *Barry Norman's Book of Cricket* was published in 2009. 'I have never enjoyed writing a book so much in my life. I have written 20 books and I have enjoyed this one far more than any of the others. It was bliss to be able to do something I really love, looking up cricket statistics and the rest of it, and to have an excuse for doing it, not just out of interest but while working and earning money. That was marvellous. And it went on and on, because I delivered what I thought was the final version – and then cricket went nuts. There were the Mumbai bombings, England abandoning the one-day internationals and going back to India to play two Tests. Then there was South Africa beating Australia in Australia, followed by Australia going to South Africa and winning there. And then the attack on the Sri Lankan team bus. So, in the end, my publisher said, "For goodness sake, stop, or we will never get it published!"'

Despite his love of all things cricket, Barry is not a great fan of the Twenty20 form of the game, seeing it as 'text message cricket'. 'Sachin Tendulkar said that Twenty20 cricket was like a dessert: very nice, but you can't live on dessert – you have to have a main course. For me, the main course would always be Test cricket, because if all you know is Twenty20, you don't know very much about cricket at all. It is the Test match that really sorts out the sheep from the goats and the men from the boys.'

Nevertheless, I suggest to him that Test Cricket could easily become an endangered species. 'I suppose it is quite possible, because we have a generation coming up with the attention span of fruit flies! They don't seem to have the ability to concentrate that long on a game. I don't see where the problem is, frankly, because if you are watching a game it's like reading a novel: everything is unfolding in front of you and the characters are developing as you go along. So I think it is endangered. Graham Gooch, the Eeyore of cricket – a really gloomy man, said that he could envisage a time when Twenty20 became like the golf circuit, with people just flying around the world following the sun and playing Twenty20. But I don't think it would last long. If Test matches died out and the first-class game with it, so all you were left with was Twenty20, I think within 10 years cricket would be completely dead.'

But for the time being at least, it is very much at the forefront of his mind, conjuring up images of various games and players. 'Harold Pinter said that he thought cricket was even better than sex and I can see where he is coming from. I don't entirely agree with him. I think they are both very enjoyable activities with much to be said for them, but they are not exactly the same. But I think cricket is still marvellously English. There is a suggestion by some Australian that it was actually invented by the Flemish. There is no Belgian in the world who has ever had the kind of devious subtlety to invent a game like cricket and I think that is what I love about it. It is the subtlety, the deviousness, the complexity of it – the very perversity of it. It is quite the most ingenious game that was ever invented. Also, the finest way of wasting time that was ever invented!

'But even so, there are a few things that I might want to change. To start with, there is probably too much of it – there shouldn't be as much international cricket going on. I do think this is burning the players out too fast and it devalues the game. What is the point of Australia v Bangladesh, except that from the Australians' point of view they come back with greatly enhanced averages, which are meaningless? I think it might be a good idea to have a stern look at who is actually playing Test cricket, making the qualification for Test cricket a bit harder, so that countries like Zimbabwe and Bangladesh have to prove themselves elsewhere rather than in Test cricket.

'Or keep the statistics against Bangladesh and Zimbabwe separate. Look at the record of off-spinner, Muttiah Muralitharan, for example. More than one in five of his wickets were taken against Bangladesh and Zimbabwe. And they are saying he is a greater bowler than Shane Warne. Well, he's not. He's as big a spinner of an off–break as I have ever seen but to me his action is, and always has been, suspect. And then the laws seem to have been changed to accommodate him. If you remember, Muralitharan was called for throwing, very properly in my view, by an Australian umpire in 1995. There were big repercussions and I think that the ICC thought that Sri Lanka might say, "OK that's it – we are not going to play Test cricket any more" and there would have been a huge international incident. So all this tinkering went on. At the time this happened, a spinner was allowed to bend his elbow by five degrees at the time of delivery and I think fast bowlers could do it to ten degrees. Well, now look what happened. They discovered that Muralitharan was bending his elbow by 14 degrees when he bowled the doosra [off–spinner's delivery that turns the other way like a leg break]. So they said, "OK, tell you what – everybody can bend their elbow by 15 degrees now." What they appear to have done is look at Murali's action which, in my view hasn't really changed since day one, and said it's now okay, never mind what a few umpires might have thought. So what happens in the future? If another magical spinner turns up, who bends his elbow by 17 degrees, are they going to say that's fine, too? And where will it all end?'

Barry's lunch appointment beckons and we agree that he should end on a lighter note. And he succeeds – kind of… 'I associate playing cricket with having lots of laughs afterwards and in all the years of playing cricket, I only met two people that I really disliked in the game. I was playing for my village side and a friend of mine, the local headmaster, had opened the innings. He based his game on that of Geoffrey Boycott, so he was hitting the ball all right but not really much off the square. Even so, I came in and joined him and we had a decent partnership, in the course of which he made his very first 50 ever in any form of cricket. To get to that milestone, he hit a two. I ran back up to the bowler's end to complete the second, safely made my ground and then started walking down the pitch to congratulate him. The bowler picked up the ball, broke the wicket and asked, "How's that, Dad?" and the umpire said, "That's out, son." And I was given out. I will never forgive those two people. If I met them again, I would kill them, even now. I got 46 and I was run out. That was appalling. It really means something when we say, "It's not cricket." But not to those two bastards.'

And on that funny but sad note, we leave the Groucho. Barry pauses to light a cigarette and heads towards another more traditional club in St James's Square for lunch with some long-term journalist friends. I head home for a sandwich with *Wisden*.

SIR MICHAEL PARKINSON CBE

'I ONCE BATTED FOR THREE AND A HALF DAYS AND SCORED 1,792 NOT OUT!'

Sir Michael Parkinson was born in Cudworth, Yorkshire, on 28 March 1935. He is a broadcaster, journalist and author. His interview series, Parkinson, *ran on BBC TV from 1971 until 1992, returning in 1998 before switching to ITV, where it remained until 2007. He has presented several radio programmes, including* Desert Island Discs *and* Parkinson's Sunday Supplement. *He was a local journalist before writing for the* Manchester Guardian, Daily Express, Daily Telegraph *and* Sunday Times, *and has written several books, including* Parky: My Autobiography. *He was awarded the CBE for services to broadcasting in 2000 and knighted in 2008.*

We settle at a large table alongside the picture window in Michael's spacious study, part of an impressive neo-Gothic building with panoramic views across the Berkshire countryside. For many years, he has written impressively about a wide variety of sports, both for newspapers and in book form, and it comes as no surprise to find him immediately on the front foot, telling me about his cricket initiation.

'Cricket for me started in the womb because my father and

my mother both loved the game. In fact, all my family were cricket nuts. It's like the Welsh and rugby. You're not a proper Yorkshire lad unless you play cricket – and play it properly – so I never had any alternative, even if I'd wanted one. In those days Yorkshire County Cricket Club was *the* predominant club in the world, in the sense that it was the club with the most fearsome reputation. You had to be born in Yorkshire to play for Yorkshire and that was the aim of every Yorkshire child. It was the ultimate accolade to have the white rose of Yorkshire on your cap. I loved the game and wanted to be a professional but I wasn't good enough. So my father, who had had this great ambition for me, went to his grave believing I was a failure because I hadn't played for Yorkshire!

'It was my father who gave me my first cricket bat when I was about four, and from that point on I went through the club sides, often playing in teams skippered by him, and school. I played every minute of every day that God sent. We played in the street or on little patches of grass. I once batted for three and a half days and scored 1,792 not out! Initially, I played for Cudworth, the pit village where I was born, and stayed with them until I was 14, when Barnsley came in for me. Now that was serious cricket – a "leg up", that was an indication of whether you were any good or just an ordinary club player. Barnsley Grammar School – which had a beautiful batting track, the best I have ever played on – was next door to Barnsley Cricket Club, so you literally hopped over the fence if you were any good and played for Barnsley, and that's what happened to me.

'I made my first team debut at 15 or 16 with Dickie Bird, and later on played with Geoffrey Boycott. Even then Geoffrey knew he was going to play for England. Dickie had an idea he might play for Yorkshire. And I thought I'd play for both! I went to the Yorkshire nets where the coach – Arthur Mitchell, the old Yorkshire pro – was watching me bat. He turned to Dickie, who was standing next to him, and said, "Is he a mate of yours?" Dickie nodded. Arthur asked, "Has he got a job?" and Dickie said, "Yes, he's a reporter." Arthur said, "Tell him to keep on reporting." And that was the end of my cricket career!'

Michael left behind him not only his dream of playing for Yorkshire and England but also two interesting but very contrasting characters. 'Geoffrey Boycott had determined from a very young age that he would play cricket for Yorkshire and England and he went about it in a methodical way. He wasn't the most gifted player but he was a man prepared to work hard and, from that point of view, he is an object lesson to any young player. They won't all have David Gower's talent – the difference between those who really succeed and those who stay where they are is hard work. Boycott understood that better than anybody and turned himself into a very fine player. My only claim to fame came when I arrived home on leave from the Army and found him opening with Dickie. In my place! Much to his anger, they dropped him but I scored a century and made 50 the following week, so he couldn't complain about that. And he says in his book, ruefully, that at that point they thought I was a better player than he was. Mind you, he was only seven at the time!

'But Dickie Bird and I have been lifelong friends and he is a bit different. He's 77 and is still a true innocent. He's been round the world several times and seen nothing. He is one of my favourite men and he rings me about the most extraordinary things. The last time he called was about his statue, which was being unveiled in Barnsley. I confirmed that I couldn't be there for the ceremony because I was working. There was a long pause. Eventually he said, "I've got a problem – which way should the statue be pointing?" I was astounded. "What do you mean 'pointing'?" "Well," he said, "I've got me finger up like you'd expect. Well, they want to know where I'm to be pointing." I said, "Well you're pointing to heaven, aren't you? Which is where you'll end up, Dickie – there's no doubt about that." I didn't know what to suggest, so I said, "Tell you what, point it towards Shaw Lane" – which is towards Barnsley Cricket Club. "Oh," he said, "I'm glad I've got a friend like you to tell me these things" – and he put the phone down! He is a true, wonderful original – a total, utter innocent.'

There was one last brief flirtation with county cricket for Michael. 'While I was in the Army, in Southern Command in Salisbury, I was playing for a club side called South Wiltshire. I played against Hampshire Club and Ground side and scored 130, including three sixes off their captain, a left-arm bowler called Jim Bailey, who used to play for Hampshire. At the end of the game, he asked me whether I'd had a trial for Yorkshire. I said, "Yes, but it didn't come to anything." And he said, "Would you like a trial for Hampshire?" I played for their Club and Ground side and was bowled first ball by an off-spin bowler, C J Knott! But I made 90-odd in the next game, so they picked me for their southern tour. Then I got a telegram from the War Office, saying, "Report back to base immediately." Next thing I knew I was on the Suez operation so, instead of playing cricket for Hampshire Seconds, I was on a bloody landing craft landing at Port Said! I never went back to Hampshire and I reckon it wasn't a bad result. I would have been in charge of a sweet shop and retired when I was about 38!'

When he eventually moved south, Michael joined Maidenhead and Bray cricket club, where he skippered the Thirds with all three of his young sons in the team alongside him.

With his broadcasting, writing and travelling commitments, it has always been difficult for Michael to see as much cricket as he would have liked. 'I kept up with cricket, and listened and saw enough to know what was going on in the game. And not to approve of a lot of it! But I have always liked cricketers and I have always got on very well with them. I don't think I've met one cricketer I didn't really like. I met footballers I wasn't too keen on, and one or two boxers I could forget about meeting, but cricketers, generally speaking, I have found to be incredibly pleasant people.

'With regard to changes in the game, I think it's about the same in terms of skill, but undoubtedly the guys today are much fitter. One thing I don't like about modern sport is the emphasis on the coach. I think players play and coaches are what you go to matches in! I do think there is a kind of over-reliance on this mythical figure who sits on the sideline and makes a difference to a team. I think that's crap, quite frankly.

'But I think the worst aspect of modern cricket, from England's point of view, has been the way that we have pillaged the South African cricket scene to make up for our own lack of a system. There is no doubt in my mind that we have a system in England that doesn't work. If you want proof of that, then look at the fact that we have three or four South Africans in the team, who have been brought up under a different and a better system than ours. What we should be looking at is: what is the difference, and why? Why are they able to replenish all the time and we can't?'

By now, Michael has really got the bit between his teeth and the focus of his attention turns to cricket academies. 'It's no good having an academy if what you do at the academy isn't right. We are not producing the finished article. Look at the number of young cricketers that have been tried and found wanting for one reason or another. Look at how we are still reliant upon one or two old-stagers. We shouldn't be bemoaning the fact that Freddie Flintoff can't play – well, we should, because he's a fine player – but they need to find somebody else. What's wrong with our system, basically, is that we have too many counties playing. You've got to start by cutting back on the counties, you really do. There should be no sacred cows.

'I think the English county system also needs to look at the number of tournaments currently being played. I can't tell you what these games are called. Is it the Super Soap Twenty20 or the Kraft Cheese County Championship? I've got no idea. Also baffling is the points system; it seems to me you need a calculator in your mind. It's all got to be simplified in my view, too. The English system is too complicated at present and I would like to see a radical shake-up. Radical reform. I really would.

'In 2003 I was part of a cricket reform group with Michael Atherton, Bob Willis, Nigel Wray and a couple of other people, and we did this thing about the survival of cricket, including the organisation of the county system. All the pros were worried about what was happening and why we had this inadequate system that didn't produce quality players and meant we had to go elsewhere. Our group tried to get things shifted but it was like rolling a stone up a hill and we were blocked wherever we tried to go. Ian MacLaurin, the first chairman of the ECB, was seen as a great hope for reform, and they trounced him too. The problem with English cricket is that it is dominated by the chairmen of the county clubs, so it's turkeys and Christmas. Until you get rid of that fundamental problem and another body is running cricket, it will all stagnate – and that's what it's doing now. What this country needs is to find another Kerry Packer, which is something I never thought I'd hear myself say!

'I don't know what the ECB can do, because cricket is a product with an assembly line clogged by the club chairmen. It does a passable job in attracting people, although what they have that other countries don't is a captive audience. What is remarkable about England is that, in spite of having a team that on a regular basis doesn't fulfil its promise, and ticket prices that are frankly ludicrous, Test cricket still sells out wherever you go. This is the only place in the world where it does.

'That apart, the game is not being properly funded and promoted where it matters most of all: at grass roots level. It is left to organisations like Chance to Shine and the Taverners to try and fill that gap. But they can't. The Government must have a say. For God's sake, let's start playing games properly. Let's try having sport back in the curriculum at school as a proper subject, taken by proper teachers, not by some retired old duffer from down the road. Let's be as serious about this as they are in Australia and South Africa.'

One organisation that Michael has been beating up for years is MCC, or the Marylebone Clodpoles Club, as he used to delight in calling them. I ask him whether he feels that at long last he has knocked them into shape. 'Yes, I think I am responsible for the new reformed MCC! It has improved a great deal. They've got reformers in there, people who think about and understand the modern game. It's no longer this beehive of traditionalists, a retirement home for [long serving administrator] Gubby Allen. I think they can be very proud of what they have done. Lord's is a beautiful cricket ground now and I love it because it's daring architecturally. I also think that the way they have transformed the catering is terrific. It's the greatest cricket ground in the world, of that there is no doubt. The way they really have tried to adapt to a modern game is an object lesson, in many ways.

'My original ire with MCC was not based so much on traditional class warfare as it was on the fact that they were bloody incompetent. I mean, Gubby Allen and that lot used to sit there enjoying the lovely view, looking down on the peasants and deciding not to build a stand because it would obscure the trees.

'More seriously, they behaved appallingly over apartheid –

Basil D'Oliveira and South Africa. It was a very messy and nasty time in English cricket, which did itself no favours whatsoever and came out of it looking ugly. Sport is important in South Africa. I remember Nelson Mandela's masterstroke in the 1995 Rugby World Cup: first of all to convince the ANC to let the Springboks be the Springboks. Then, when they won, he was wearing a Springboks jersey and cap, and all of sudden you had the Rainbow Nation. It had a significant effect on the way that events developed and it probably stopped that country from tearing itself apart.

'But, in the days that I am talking about, MCC was run by some who simply didn't take on board the political significance of the South African situation. I remember doing a TV debate with Malcolm Muggeridge on a Sunday evening show called *Matter for Concern*, or something like that. Every week he had two people, one proposing and one opposing. They asked me if I would go and debate the apartheid thing with someone senior from cricket. I turned up and the guy opposite me was Wilfred Wooller. He was a very brave man, who had been captured by the Japanese in the war. He was also maybe the loudest and most boorish of all the advocates of supporting and playing against South Africa. Malcolm didn't know much about sport and, although he knew about the principles involved in the apartheid debate, I could see he didn't know the cricket situation. So I thought all I could do was let Wilfred go on and on about why we should play cricket with these appalling people, and I could see Malcolm looking at him with total horror on his face. In the end, Wilfred, mistaking Malcolm's silence for agreement, turned and asked Muggeridge, "What do you think?" Malcolm looked at him and said, in that wonderful voice, "I think you are a twerp!" A wonderful put-down!'

One other MCC issue that upset Michael for a long time was the ban on women membership. 'I just think that any organisation that excludes women is barmy, quite frankly. Why exclude half of the human race? Because they are a different sex from you? That's the best reason for bringing them in. I would rather look at ten women than ten men, quite frankly. I think that only makes me normal! Mary, my wife, and my mother too, are, and were, wonderful cricket fans and they loved the game. They would sit and watch all day. I'm like most men. I'll sit down for a couple of hours and then start wandering around chatting to people. Mary will still go to a five-day Test match – she absolutely adores the game and knows something about it. So are you going to exclude women? Why?'

I turn to the subject of world cricket and suggest that the Indians appear to be taking over. 'There is a problem in the power of the subcontinent because almost all their cricket is geared towards instantaneous satisfaction and Twenty20. I think we have to do what we can to protect the five-day game. With the West Indies becoming a much-reduced power and given the appeal of the easy money, you can see how quickly the traditional game, which I think is the finest game in the world to watch and play, could disappear. Whatever problems we have with the reduced influence of England, the ECB and MCC, one thing they have done is to make sure that the five-day Test match remains more or less unassailable, unaltered, and I think that is terribly important. I would not be interested in cricket if it comprised only one-day tournaments. I see Twenty20 as relevant only in its ability to attract the new generation of young people, as a kind of loss leader into the wider game. Unless it does that, it's not worth bothering about.'

We talk next about cricketing heroes. Michael's top three choices are not only clear-cut but are reinforced by photographs of each of them, hanging in a cluster on the wall. 'My first hero was Keith Miller, without a single shadow of a doubt. What I admire most in all sport, even though we are talking about cricketers now, is grace. I love style. And that means my runner-up is Tom Graveney, who was to me the epitome of grace and style. He was a wonderful cricketer and a remarkably nice man as well. My third hero, you will not be surprised to hear, was Fred Trueman, who I think was maybe the greatest fast bowler I ever saw. The thing about Fred, it's like a great actor. The difference between a star and an ordinary player is that with the star, you cannot take your eyes off them on the field. Ray Illingworth said to me, "The great thing for a skipper about Fred was that, at twenty past six, 110° in the shade and he's already bowled 30 overs, he has come back and gone flat out for you.'

I suppose it is inevitable that we should end by talking about what it is that makes this game so special. 'In my case there would be a mixture of things that really enchant. Being born in Yorkshire isn't the only reason for my inordinate love of cricket. For me it is the most English of games, a game that so easily defines our nature and our personality. I really love watching cricket in the traditional English setting; I think there is something romantic and reassuring about that. I also think it is the most social of games, and the intermingling of people of different classes and races in a cricket team is possible because people find a commonality. It attracts a certain kind of person. And of all the sports, apart from boxing, it has produced the best prose and some of the best poetry. No sport has produced the poetry that cricket has, because it is something that reacts deeply in a person's soul. There is a desire to express cricket in poetry, as Arlott did, and many better poets even. It was something in Arlott's voice that convinced you that he could only be talking about cricket. He reported on soccer as well but cricket was the game that really brought him out and made him into the fine writer that he was. He never wrote as well about football. What was it about cricket? He was romantically attached to the game.

'All these things, I think, add up to a reason why the game is special. The great thing about cricket is that the Americans don't understand it. A game invented by a group of shepherds in the 16th century and the most powerful nation can't bloody understand it. That's why we should love it! It is the complexity of the game. They can't work it out. We recognise that it is its complexity that attracts us.'

A splendid note on which to end, and one very close to my heart, particularly when I think of that nation's golf spectators who are so frequently heard to utter that charmless exhortation 'In the hole!' But now it is time for Michael to return to the nearby editing suite to work on his DVD collection *The Best of Parkinson,* having shared with me some of the very best of his cricketing moments.

NICHOLAS PARSONS OBE

'I BOWL ONE GOOD BALL IN A SEASON AND THAT GOOD BALL CAME OUT OF MY HAND THAT DAY, WENT DOWN THE PITCH TO DENNIS LILLEE AND GOT THROUGH HIS DEFENCES!'

Nicholas Parsons was born in Grantham, Lincolnshire on 10 October 1923. He is an actor, radio and TV presenter who started in repertory, before moving on to the London comedy circuit. On TV, he starred in The Arthur Haynes Show *and* The Benny Hill Show, *was host of* Sale of the Century *and has presented Radio 4's* Just a Minute *since 1967. He has featured in many films, including* Brothers in Law *and* Doctor in Love. *His West End theatre appearances include* The Rocky Horror Show *and* Boeing Boeing, *and his* Happy Hour *has been staged at the Edinburgh Festival Fringe since 2000. He was awarded the OBE in 2007 for services to drama and broadcasting.*

We meet at the Marriott Hotel in London's Regents Park. Nicholas arrives, immaculate as ever, in a blazer with a Water Rats badge, striped shirt and red–and–blue striped tie. After our chat he will be attending a lunch in the hotel, so the attire may not be entirely for my benefit. I have ordered coffee, which is served in a quiet corner just off the main lounge. Quiet, that is, apart from the inevitable muzak.

Reviewing our conversation later, I realise that by his own rules I should twice have stopped Nicholas in mid-sentence. The presenter of *Just a Minute* – in which panellists are required to speak for 60 seconds without hesitation, deviation or repetition – had alluded three times to the occasion when he knocked Dennis Lillee's middle stump out of the ground, and followed that up by stroking two effortless boundaries off the bowling of the great Australian 'quickie'. I make no apology, however, for not interrupting. The anecdote Nicholas understandably treasures not only sums up the magic of the Lord's Taverners, whose team he was captaining, but captures vividly that David and Goliath moment which all cricketers – indeed all sportsmen – relish, when a prize scalp is unexpectedly and joyously earned.

'The match took place at Stock Brook Park in Essex, against a team organised by Gestetner, the office equipment company and match sponsors. Basil Sellers, Gestetner's boss, was from Australia and a good friend of Dennis Lillee, whose participation in the match naturally made it a great occasion for everyone who was there. All the other celebrities in the Taverners side had had a bowl when I was reminded that it was my turn. So I put myself on, with Dennis Lillee batting at the other end. Well, I've said it before and I'll say it again, that I bowl one good ball in a season, and that good ball came out of my hand that day, went down the pitch to Dennis Lillee and got through his defences!'

Nicholas was so elated, he says, that he felt like retiring on the spot. When he came out to bat a little later in the day to find Lillee limbering up at the bowler's end, he must have wished he had. 'I could hear the crowd oohing and aahing a bit, thinking they were about to see some fireworks, but I've always thought that in the sort of charity cricket we were playing, I'd rather face a professional cricketer than a club cricketer. A club cricketer normally only appears in front of a few people, but when he's suddenly got a thousand or two watching him and someone like me at the crease, he's likely to bowl aggressively and try to get them out. Indeed, that's exactly what happened to me in another Taverners game, when I'd been rehearsing to take over a part in *The Rocky Horror Show*, hadn't had much batting practice beforehand and this fellow bowled a beamer, which I was only just able to duck out of the way of in time!

'Lillee, on the other hand, like all the professionals who take part in this sort of cricket, knew the ethos of the charity game, which is to make people like me look good. He could have removed my stumps with five out of the first six balls, I'm sure, but he put the first few nicely on the spot and I was able to get a couple of fours. Then I noticed something about the way he was walking back to the end of his run which made me think I wasn't going to see much of the next one. I didn't. My own middle stump came out of the ground! He had let me have my bit of fun, the public had enjoyed it, and it wasn't any skin off his nose to help me score a few runs.'

Nicholas's love of cricket and his support for Surrey had started many years earlier, when he was a young boy in Grantham and he and his older brother would pore over the previous day's county scores in the newspaper. 'I can remember, particularly on the camping holidays we went on, that we weren't allowed to look at the results until we had done our chores. My parents were very strict about this. Some time later, when I was about eight or nine, my brother announced that we both had to support a county team. He was going to take Sussex and I could have Surrey. I don't know why he said it, but he was my older brother and I looked up to him. I just said, "Right, Surrey" and that is how I became a Surrey supporter. It turned out very well because for a time after that we lived in south London, not far from the Oval.'

Nicholas has happy memories of trekking across Clapham Common with a little suitcase of sandwiches, boarding the

Tube, and spending whole days fascinated by what was going on in the middle. He reels off some of the old names, including Sandham, Gregory, Fishlock, and captain Errol Holmes. 'Freddie Brown was a regular before moving to captain Northants, H E Watts was a fast bowler, and Brooks was the wicketkeeper. The other fast bowler I remember well was Alf Gover, who later became a friend through the Taverners, and whose academy in Battersea Rise, south London, was well known to many generations of amateur cricketers. I went there myself once or twice in my twenties for a bit of coaching when I was starting out as an actor. Surrey continued to be my county through the glory days after the war, when players like Stuart Surridge – a good cricketer and a brilliant catcher, Alec Bedser, Tony Lock, Jim Laker and Peter May brought the team frequent success in the County Championship and achieved lasting international fame.'

Nicholas was keen on sport from the word go but his talents were more suited to rugby than cricket. 'I played a lot of sport at my school, St Paul's, where I got my colours for rugby, cricket and fives. I also did a bit of boxing because in those days St Paul's was a great boxing school, though they don't do it now. When I went to Glasgow University, I played rugby in the first team for three years and when I was 18, I had the distinction of playing at Murrayfield in what was called the East West game, tantamount to a Scottish trial. You have to remember, though, that these were the war years, and a lot of people who might have been playing had been called up. I was training to be an engineer at the time and was told that this was a reserved occupation.'

When I first saw Nicholas play cricket, around 15 years ago, he was perhaps a touch past his very best as a player, while still having the unmistakeable look of someone who was very comfortable with a bat in his hand. But how good was he in the early days? 'I actually have a pretty good eye for a ball, was reserve wicketkeeper at school, and was always quite agile in the field, in the covers or at mid-off. Bill Frindall once paid me one of the nicest compliments when he said he'd never seen me drop a catch! But all this said, cricket was not the sport at which I particularly excelled. I could put up a good show at school but was never one of the stars. In rugby, on the other hand, as a youngster I was one of the best.'

Nicholas's cricketing career did not really resume until the 1960s, when he made a couple of appearances in charity games, including for the Taverners. 'People found out that I could play a bit but I would mostly turn out for friends.' But even then a young family and a wife who wanted to spend Sundays at home, rather than by the side of a cricket ground, meant he only occasionally put on his whites. Nearer the end of the 1960s, however, he became a member of the Lord's Taverners, and began a happy association with the charity that has continued on and off the field for more than 45 years.

'I think I would describe myself primarily as a wicketkeeper-batsman, an aggressive hitter who relied more on instinct than technique, although I did try to improve this by going first to the Middlesex Indoor School, and then to the indoor school at Lord's. Indoor net practice certainly helped me follow the flight of the ball and to play each ball more on its merits, rather than trying to hit every one. I was a bit of a slogger, really. I could score quick runs but I could also be out quite quickly!'

Nicholas's bowling career – and the now well-documented Lillee dismissal! – owes much to the Taverners' tradition of getting the celebs to turn their arm over in mid-innings, often in order to give the other team a chance to get back into the match. 'You don't want teams back in the pavilion for only 40 or 50 runs when there are so many people watching. I am not a natural bowler at all, but everyone usually has to have a go.

The funny thing is, the day I bowled Dennis Lillee I got a wicket with the very next ball. Unfortunately, though, I dismissed Basil Sellers, the Gestetner chief executive, whose company was providing the sponsorship, and that was not something you were meant to do! I tried to call him back and if the umpire had been one of ours, he would have called a no ball or something. But the batsman, very properly, kept walking.'

Charity cricket has been an important part of Nicholas's sporting activities and his experiences on and off the field have matched many of the highs of a long and successful life in the entertainment business. 'Walking down the steps at Lord's, or the Oval, is as good as walking on to the stage at the London Palladium. It is a great thrill playing alongside giants such as Bill Edrich, Denis Compton and Godfrey Evans, men whose accomplishments I first followed as a boy. Men who I never dreamed I might meet and befriend one day, when they retired from the professional game and joined the Taverners circuit. I remember going on tour with Godfrey to Barbados and chatting to him for a whole week. It was absolutely fantastic. He was such a lovely, lovely man.'

Like many cricket fans, Nicholas also has a soft spot for certain commentators, including the *Test Match Special* team, from the late lamented Johnners (Brian Johnston) to the incumbent Aggers (Jonathan Agnew), and Sky Television's David Gower, Ian Botham, Michael Atherton and David Lloyd. 'All the *TMS* ones have their own personality and style, plus the late Bill Frindall's amazing statistics. One of my greatest thrills was being asked to be a guest on "View from the Boundary" during the luncheon interval. Jonathan Agnew talked to me about my interest in cricket and my love of the game, and it was meant to last for about 20 minutes. However, rain delayed proceedings after lunch and although I didn't know this until afterwards, we actually went on for 45 minutes. There was so much to talk about, so much reminiscing, so many names to drop in to the conversation. At the end, they said it was the longest "View from the Boundary" they had ever done.'

I am anxious, given the long and distinguished list of players Nicholas has known personally, to ask him to name his top three professionals and whose exploits he has witnessed. His first choice, Don Bradman, is shared by others, but his election to the Parsons Hall of Fame is all the more compelling given that Nicholas was actually witness to his final, anti-climactic act on English soil. 'I did actually see Don Bradman bowled by Hollies for nought at the Oval. I was just a youngster but I remember it vividly, sitting with my little bag of sandwiches. He was so loved and respected, and the crowd gave him such a wonderful standing reception when he went to the middle, that I reckon, while he wasn't a very emotional man, he was probably overwhelmed by the occasion. Knowing it was his last appearance and given the great rivalry between the Australians and the English, the reaction just got to him.

'I didn't realise I was watching history until much later. I went because, as a youngster, I just wanted to see him hit the ball. I wasn't sufficiently knowledgeable or mature enough to take in the enormity of the situation when Hollies bowled him for a duck. As we all know now, if he'd scored just four runs his Test average would have been 100, but as it was, he ended his career on 99 point something. I remember the atmosphere as he walked back to the pavilion. People wanted to clap him because it was his last time in England, but there was a huge sense of shock.'

So who would be Great Cricketer number two? Nicholas is almost stumped by this one, begging for time to consider, but then plumps for Denis Compton. 'You know it must be Denis, because he had such a wonderfully cavalier attitude towards cricket. He would go out and hit unbelievable shots. He was the most inspirational batsman you could ever watch. He was magic. You were always thinking, "What will he do next?" because he could be so unorthodox in some of his strokes and yet he had such brilliant timing.'

Number three, after another pause, turns out to be Ian Botham 'because Beefy could do it all. When he was on song, the way he smote the ball was fantastic. I will never forget that incredible occasion in 1981, when England were on a hiding to nothing, miles behind. Beefy, who had probably had a few beers the night before, went in when they were five wickets down. Godfrey Evans, who was adviser to one of the betting syndicates, put England's chances of surviving, let alone winning, at about 100 to 1. And Godfrey knew his cricket. It takes a great man to defy such incredible odds, against one of the finest teams in the world, and Australia had a very good team then. But Botham gave England enough runs, not only to stave off an innings defeat, but to force a win.'

Nicholas is now thinking about other candidates he might have chosen – Lara, Tendulkar, Gavaskar – as we move the conversation to the limited-over game and the benefits – or otherwise – of technology. 'As a traditionalist – and if you love something you want to preserve that tradition – I was hesitant when the one-day game came into existence. But then I began to realise it was a great form of cricket and terribly exciting. Similarly, when Twenty20 started up, I was sad about the way it was commercialising the sport, but I now think it is also very exciting and, in its own way, has perhaps helped the game become more popular. Those who don't understand the ethos and the technicalities of cricket can get bored by the four and five-day game with just 200 runs in a day, but can be absolutely captivated by Twenty20.'

Nicholas draws a parallel with stage and television performers. 'Some actors are better at plays with a four to five-week rehearsal build-up than they are at a film or television, where you just learn the part for a particular scene and you put it together bit by bit. Radio is a different technique, playing to an unseen audience. In the same way, cricketers have to adapt to the different formats of limited over and five-day games. As a performer myself, I understand the importance, and the challenge, of having to be an all-rounder.'

He is also a convert to umpiring technology. 'Even with the changes, I think the umpire still has enough responsibility. I think it's right that they use it for stumpings and lbws.'

We are getting to the end of the interview so I ask Nicholas what cricket means to him, what he finds so magical. 'It's all the little moments, the cameos, the things that people who have never played the game can't quite see, because they don't realise the amount of skill that goes into every ball that's bowled, the different delivery, the way the batsman has to decide how to play it, and the involvement of the fielders. If there's cricket on a village green I'll automatically want to stop and watch it – there's something about white flannels against a green background that I can't quite analyse.

'There's also something about the way it never gives you a second chance. In a game of squash, if you play a duff shot and you lose the point, you can still go on to win the game. In cricket, if you play a duff shot, you're back in the pavilion. The pressure is tremendous on all sides. If a batsman is dropped, he may go on to make a century, but if the catch is taken and he only had a few runs to his name, we would have been shaking our heads, saying he didn't do very well. By contrast, the bowler can be whacked through the covers one ball and take out somebody's middle stump with the next.'

Nicholas's only lament is that cricket is no longer quite the gentlemanly game it was when he first played and watched it. 'Golf is now the one really gentlemanly game left, because players do own up if they have done something wrong. I don't hear people saying, "Oh, that's not cricket, is it?" in the way they used to. I regret that sport is an activity in which you push your luck to win at all costs, even if you don't cheat.'

We return (briefly) to the triumph of Stock Brook Park, but there is another memory Nicholas is anxious to share – a game at his boyhood shrine, the Oval. 'It wasn't a particularly high-profile game, but Jack Rayfield, one of the early movers and shakers and a past chairman of the Taverners, was doing the commentary. I've even forgotten who the opposition was, but I do remember that I managed to get my eye well and truly in, and went on to make 67 not out. Raman Subba Row, who was there, always reminds me of that occasion, but what sticks in my mind are the words that came over the loudspeaker, in a voice that betrayed just a touch of surprise: "…and Nicholas Parsons has now got 67 runs."'

It's an achievement not to be sniffed at. Nicholas rises to his elegantly shod feet to make his way to lunch and we walk to the hotel lobby, pursued at an almost discreet distance by a waiter clutching the bill for the coffee. As I settle my dues, Nicholas exits to join his fellow lunchers. I cannot help but wonder if they will hear the name of Dennis Lillee…

SIR
TIM RICE

'I WAS PROBABLY THE WORST CRICKETER EVER TO BE PRESIDENT OF MCC.'

Sir Tim Rice was born in Amersham, Buckinghamshire, on 10 November 1944. He is an Academy, Golden Globe, Tony and Grammy Award–winning lyricist who has written songs for Jesus Christ Superstar, Evita, Aladdin, The Lion King and many more. He has published more than 30 books on British pop music and cricket, and appears frequently on radio and television. He has been inducted into the American Songwriters' Hall of Fame and was knighted in 1994 for his work in the arts and sports. He has established his own charitable trust and is a long-standing member of the Lord's Taverners.

When I arrive at Tim's beautiful home, close to the Thames, I am taken through his garden, where gardeners are busily and noisily at work pruning the trees, past the now covered swimming pool, to his office, tucked away in the far corner. It is here, in a bright, sunlit room, that we sit and talk cricket.

The depth of Tim's love of the game is evident in many ways: in his continuing involvement with MCC, his impressive collection of cricket books, his detailed knowledge of the game and, perhaps most of all, his very own cricket team. After he had started to play for the Lord's Taverners in the early 1970s, he thought it would be quite fun to play one or two purely social matches. 'In 1972 I organised my own team, to play just one game against a friend of mine called Bill Heath,' Tim recalls. 'He got a team together called Bill Heath's Gentlemen, and I think my team was called the Occasional Creamers – a rather strange name which one of the guys in my team suggested. The match was a great success – everybody enjoyed it – so we decided to do it again the following year. This time I called my team Heartaches after the company that I set up when the top rate of tax was 83 per cent and the only way you could avoid it was to form a company! That game was also very successful and led to five more that summer, and we now have anything between 10 and 20 games each year. I invite the odd celebrity who happens to be a friend, like David Essex, to play and a few serious cricketers. Then it is just friends and over the years it becomes friends of friends, so it is a social network really.

'We don't have a home ground and although it would be nice, I don't think it's going to happen now. I have often thought about moving out to the country and getting a pitch but we have access to a beautiful ground at Stonor Park in Oxfordshire, quite near the Getty ground at Wormsley. I am vice president at Stonor and I help them out occasionally on a few things, so we pay a hundred quid fee or something like that to play there against other wandering sides. We go to Cornwall, where I have a house, virtually every year, and we've been up to Yorkshire for a couple of tours in and around Scarborough. Those are the only tours we've done in England but we have also been to Berlin, Estonia and St Petersburg, which was great fun. We've even been to North Carolina in America two or three times and to South Africa some time ago, which was very successful.

'We much prefer the traditional form of the game but do

play a bit of limited overs, which some teams prefer even though it's a bit frustrating to lose a game by nine runs when you are 171 for 3. I quite like the concept of a drawn match: we have had some very good games with one side or the other battling to hold out for a draw. For example, in one match recently, we bowled the opposition out for 138 and thought, "Oh, we'll win this." But when we found ourselves at 50 for 7, we clearly weren't going to! Then some real old codgers down the bottom of the order had to bat out to save the day; my brother Jo and I survived the last four overs, which was very satisfying. Had it been limited overs, there would have been no point and the game, in effect, would have been over. I always say, rather pretentiously, it's a bit like life – at the end of their lives, most people will be happy to go away with a draw. Some things in life are good and some are bad; some work and some don't. I feel cricket mirrors life more than any other sport, much more. And one of the reasons is that you can go on a long time, and at the end of it, not much is resolved.'

At this stage I suggest to Tim that the Heartaches' colours – red, pink and green – might be regarded as somewhat bizarre, particularly when seen in all their glory in the blazer, for example. 'Well, let me tell you how it came about. One night, somebody suggested we had our own colours and one of the players' wives said that she would design a cap for us. She did, and the three colours were red, pink and purple – a combination that was frankly a bit "Yikes!" So I suggested that maybe we should change the purple to green – and the club's colours were born! They *are* quite bright but they are nice colours and I think ours are better than one or two that I can think of.'

I ask Tim if he has had any great achievements as a player with the Heartaches – possibly with his notorious slow left-arm deliveries? 'Well, strangely, I have twice completed a hat-trick. Only seven have been recorded in Heartaches history, which is pushing 600 games now, which means we are getting one hat-trick every 80 matches or so. And I've had two of them – which is obviously because I have played more than anybody else!'

This prompts me to take Tim back to his earliest involvement in cricket and to what had initially attracted him to the game. 'My first memory of watching cricket was the Ashes in 1953, when my parents bought a television set, as many people did, to watch the Coronation. The Ashes was a bonus and so the TV was on quite a bit, although I doubt if it was for every ball by any means. I was at prep school then and I was very keen on maths and numbers. One of my masters was a very enthusiastic cricketer as well as a mathematician. I remember we had one lesson in which he said, "Right, today we're not going to do maths. Instead we're going to teach you about cricket scoring. You'll find it very useful as you progress up your prep school and public school ladder if you can score." And he was right, because I did.'

Tim's mobile phone is sitting on the table and rings almost non-stop while we are talking. But he answers it just once, and then only after asking me if it is OK to do so. It is his young daughter, calling him from Cornwall. This brief interlude is typical of the man and I really warm to that. A couple of minutes later we are under way once more and I ask him about his early playing days.

'When I was nearly six I began to play at my prep school, a basic game with a soft ball, but by the time I was seven or eight we wore brown cricket boots and we definitely played with a hard ball.' I had to interject – brown boots? It all sounded rather like Stanley Holloway! 'It wasn't long after the war and it seemed to be just the way it was. We definitely had brown cricket boots; I remember that quite clearly. They had sort of spikes on and they were probably a bit cheaper than the proper white boots that the senior boys wore. Perhaps the reason was that children's feet grow so quickly!'

When Tim went to Lancing College he swam for his house and the school and this, coupled with a hip injury he suffered in his mid-teens, meant that he played very little cricket in his time there. 'After I left school I don't think I played any cricket at all until I was 24 or 25. I was still very keen on the game and used to watch it at Lord's, becoming a member of MCC in 1969. Then, when things like *Jesus Christ Superstar* took off, I remember getting invited to play for the Lord's Taverners for the first time.

'It was at Blenheim Palace. John Gorman of The Scaffold was playing and, I think, Michael Cox, who had a hit record with "Angela Jones", plus the usual regulars like John Price and John Snow, although they were still playing for England in those days. I remember playing with Bill Edrich, although I might be cobbling several early games together to make one memory! But I recall playing then, for the first time in many moons, and thinking, "Gosh, this is wonderful." Everything just came back to me – the smell of grass, the track, holding a bat, all these things I hadn't done for a long time. I'm not even sure I had any kit. As a result, I thought I would like to play more cricket so I continued to play for the Taverners and one or two other charity teams, and then started the Heartaches.'

With one notable exception, Tim has never seriously combined his award-winning talent and experience as a lyricist with his love of cricket. However, in 1986, he joined forces again with composer Andrew Lloyd Webber, eight years after they had parted company. 'Prince Edward, who was working with Andrew at the time, had asked him whether he would write something for the Queen's 60th birthday and Andrew very kindly asked me to work with him on a sort of mini operetta. I had had this idea for a long time – a little joke-ish thing – about a cricket scene where the best batsman has to choose between putting his team first and sorting out his love life. He has spotted his girlfriend with a caddish racing man but, of course, like every decent chap, he decides to bat on, with the result that his girlfriend has time to see the error of her ways. We expanded that into a Gilbert and Sullivan-type story about 25 or 30 minutes long and called it *Cricket*. We staged it at Windsor before a very small private audience, including the Queen and the Duke. The Queen Mum was also there, which was why we had deliberately included a racing theme. They all sat there and listened and seemed to enjoy it and got the jokes – and the tunes are very pretty.

'Subsequently, we performed it at a Taverners' Ball but it didn't really go down very well because people were chatting, as they do, and unless you have a really loud cabaret which people can dance to, they don't take any interest. It was a rather quiet, gentle and, in a way, quite sophisticated performance, and of course, people didn't really hear it. It was the wrong venue for it. We were also going to record it, but a lot of the tunes ended up going into other shows of Andrew's so that kind of put the kybosh on that. Some of them were in *Phantom of the Opera* and several others are in *Aspects of Love*. The hero's big song in *Cricket* is called "All I Ask of Life", which he sings as he is being battered by a vicious West Indian paceman! This became "All I Ask of You" in *Phantom of the Opera*.

'*Cricket* could easily be expanded to about an hour and done by schools and elsewhere – that would be quite funny. The whole script is published, I'm glad to say, because it is nice to feel it exists. It is in a book of cricket verse [*A Breathless Hush… The MCC Anthology of Cricket Verse*], which David Rayvern Allen put together, so if you find that, you will get the whole story there. But unfortunately most of the tunes have disappeared or are probably not able to be used.' Tim still seems disappointed about this, although he is careful not to say so. It was his last collaboration with Lloyd Webber.

Despite the outcome with *Cricket* I express surprise that he has never felt tempted to do a cricket musical on a grander scale. 'I'm sure there are exceptions but by and large any dramatisation – be it through a play, film, musical or a novel even – of any sort of made-up cricket, or any other sport, is never as exciting as the real thing. You've got the *Roy of the Rovers* sort of thing, I suppose, for kids but any sort of play or story that hinges on the sport itself, I think is difficult. Apart from anything else, cricket doesn't really have an absolutely international appeal. In America, it would mean nothing. I'm not saying it can't be done, but I have never particularly had the desire.'

Tim became president of MCC in 2002, following in the footsteps of a boyhood hero, Ted Dexter. 'I was very honoured to follow Ted, particularly because he made that marvellous 70 in 1963 against the then mighty West Indies – the first Test match that I had seen at Lord's. The appointment was also very special for me because, certainly in the last 20 to 25 years, they have tended to go for people who are actually quite good cricketers, whereas I was probably the worst cricketer ever to be president of MCC. My brother Jo did a book, a very good book, called *Presidents of MCC* and I think his research led him to the conclusion that there were one or two other candidates around the time that the Club was founded in 1787, but it couldn't really be proven! But it was a great honour and I enjoyed it.

'I was very lucky because it was great representing MCC during the Ashes series in Australia, when I saw quite a few of the Test matches and spoke at a lot of dinners. I went to Melbourne and Adelaide but by the time we reached Sydney, we were 4-0 down. Fortunately, we did win there, quite comfortably, Michael Vaughan making a big hundred and Andy Caddick taking seven Australian second innings wickets.'

During his presidential year Tim was heavily involved on the social side as the key representative of MCC, but what achievement had pleased him most, not only when he was president but also during his time on the committee? 'Getting women into the Club was probably the most important thing. There have been lots of improvements to the ground which, by and large, are very good but that is something which is always going to happen. In 100 years' time they will still be altering and improving it. But in the late 1990s, purely as a committee member, I was quite heavily involved in the membership for women issue with the then president, Colin Ingleby-Mackenzie. It was really his great achievement but I was helping to swing the mood of the members and acting as Rachel Heyhoe Flint's proposer. Getting that voted through was the most important thing, because we had to, for the general good of the Club and because it was beginning to harm its image. I did have some sympathy with the old buffers, because old buffers have rights as well, but all the same it was undoubtedly a time for change.'

This leads me to ask Tim whether there are things that he would really like to see change in cricket today? Anything that he finds particularly irritating? He is swiftly into Victor Meldrew mode. 'At the moment it is going through so many changes so quickly you feel like saying, "Hang on, enough already. Let's just take stock." However, my biggest complaint is the shambles of the English domestic fixtures list – it is a complete disaster. I don't know why it's always such a mess. There are different competitions going on at different times. One like the County Championship gets going, then it stops. Then another starts, then that one stops. There is no sort of real logic. You pick up the paper and you don't really know what you are going to read about. When I was a kid it was Saturday, Monday, Tuesday, Wednesday, Thursday, Friday – those were the days that your team was always playing and you knew it. Now you are not sure when your county are next going to be playing and when it does appear, it's usually got so many people in it who are only there for three weeks that it is simply hopeless. It is just that the whole structure of English cricket at the moment is a bit of a mess in my view. Obviously Twenty20 has a lot to do with that. I am not against Twenty20 particularly; I just hope it is not going to pull everything down around it.'

Tim has a fine collection of cricket books, including his beloved and valuable complete set of *Wisdens*. 'If I don't want to get stuck into some incredibly heavy work it is rather nice to pull a cricket book off the shelf and read about an old tour or Test match. As for the *Wisdens*, the first one I got was 1954, which was all about the 1953 season. A friend of mine at prep school had it and I just thought it was a wonderful book. I couldn't get enough of it and I was given a copy for my 10th birthday. After that, I began collecting them every year, while slowly moving backwards as well, looking for earlier editions. You could pick them up in second-hand bookshops and I gradually found one or two really obscure ones, like 1903, which I found in a book shop in Tottenham Court Road. I was trying to collect in sequence but there comes a point when you realise it is all but impossible to get a complete set by buying them one at a time. I suppose it might be possible but, as it happened, in 1973 a complete set came up for sale for £750. I bought it, even though that seemed rather expensive at the time. I suppose you could multiply that figure by at least 20 today to allow for inflation, so we are talking maybe £15,000. But I think a complete set now would be at least £100,000. You have also got to bear in mind that since 1974 there have been nearly another 40 *Wisdens*, so that in itself would make it more expensive. So it was a good purchase.'

Indeed it was and, as Tim has said, it is a way to relive past games and revisit cricketing giants. Not surprisingly, he has some particular favourites. 'Denis Compton and Bill Edrich, I suppose, are two of my initial heroes, from right back when I was a child, even though I didn't see them at their best. I would always think of Bradman as well and although I never saw him play, knowing a fair bit about the history of the game, I feel I know his career quite well. I did meet him once or twice, which was great. Of course, Ian Botham was quite fantastic, and Bob Willis was capable of incredible bowling spells. I was also a great fan of John Snow, who was a brilliant bowler. I just have so many memories of an awful lot of amazing players.'

Tim has put a great deal into cricket in many different ways, with his own team and with what he has done for charity, for MCC and for the Taverners, but I wonder what he feels he has gained from this deep involvement in the game. 'It's been a very good way to make friends, and to keep friends. It is difficult when you are running around in the modern busy world, but of all sports it is the one that gives you time, not only to enjoy yourself playing the game, but also to talk and reflect, and to get to know friends. I am sure that is true of a lot of sports but I am equally sure that people who are playing football sweat away for an hour and a half and have a great time but don't really have conversations. They might have a beer afterwards but that's it. With cricket, the fact that it is a full day means that unless you are a pretty useful batsman, half the time you're not actually on the field. So there is plenty of time to meet people and talk, and get to know people, and play with the kids. This is very important.'

By now, Tim is being badgered by his long-serving PA, Eileen. Having been more than generous with his time and his cricketing memories, he is now late for a lunch appointment. As he rushes off, I depart at a somewhat more leisurely pace, reflecting on my time with a man of many cricketing parts.

SIR MARTIN SORRELL

'I WAS BOWLING TO JOHN EDRICH AND I HAD HIM
PLUMB LBW. BUT THE ARCHBISHOP OF CANTERBURY
WAS UMPIRING, AND GAVE HIM NOT OUT!
I COULD HAVE KILLED HIM.'

Martin Sorrell was born in London on 14 February 1945. He is chief executive of WPP, the global advertising, marketing and communications group, which he has transformed since the mid-1980s into an industry world leader. Early in his career he worked for sports agent Mark McCormack, before joining the advertising agency Saatchi & Saatchi in 1975, where he was group finance director from 1977 until 1985. He is a non-executive director of Formula 1, a governor of the London Business School and a director of the Harvard Business School. He was knighted in 2000 for services to the communications industry.

My personal experiences, coupled with far too much exposure to television's *Mad Men*, had led me to expect WPP's headquarters to be loud, glitzy and over the top. In fact, the building is modest, subdued and tucked away in a quiet corner of central London, not far from Grosvenor Square. On arrival for my meeting with Martin, I am ushered into the boardroom, which is modestly furnished and functional – more IKEA than Chippendale.

When Martin appears he explains that he is very tight for time, although by the time he leaves we have been chatting for more than an hour. So I dive straight in and ask him where he first played the wonderful game. 'We had a lawn, with a triangular rose bed in it, but you couldn't get 22 yards of grass, so we used to put the wicket in front of the bird bath. Then I would disappear to the garage and run across a terrace, trying to imitate Fred Trueman, and bowl to a friend of mine, a guy called Alan Goulden. I used to drive my father crazy because when we were playing cricket, we would demolish flowers and bushes.

'I played at school, and for Middlesex Public Schools about half a dozen times and captained them one year. Then when I went up to Cambridge I played college cricket. I wasn't good enough to get into the Crusaders [the Cambridge University second XI] or into the Blues. I also played club cricket for Stanmore, when Reg Hayter [sports reporter and agent] was the captain – he kindly put me down for MCC membership. And I captained the Stanmore Colts. There were some very useful cricketers, many with first-class experience or potential, playing for and against us. One was the Middlesex fast bowler John Price, who played for Wembley and who everybody was terrified of. He was quick, but there were a few West Indies fast bowlers around as well.

'After university I went straight to Harvard Business School. There was no cricket there, except I played one game on the Smith College Open Day. Smith College was a very pukka girl's university, or college, and we were asked to play – I think it was the Americans against the English. We had no equipment, so I wasn't wearing spikes. I turned and slipped, and was run out for one. That was the last game I played until the fathers against sons match at Arnold House in 1987. So I had a gap, from about 1968 or 1969 when I didn't play, which I really regret, because I would love to have gone on and played for Stanmore.

'The trouble is, when you get married and have kids, playing Saturday and Sunday – or even just Saturday – every week is not on. Your wife and your kids don't always want to come and watch you play cricket all day. So I didn't play again until 1987, which, memorably, was in the middle of WPP's hostile bid for [advertising agency] JWT. I would be fielding at cover or square leg when a call would come through and I would have to go off to take it. But the important thing was that I played, and that gave me the taste again. I began to get a WPP side together, and then Victor Blank started to do his charity match, which I like to play in.'

Martin's WPP team started playing against a Fleet Street XI run by Mihir Bose, a sports writer and broadcaster, as well as against Ogilvy, part of the WPP group. 'We now also have a game against Cambridge Crusaders and that is probably our toughest fixture. On the last weekend in August we play at Wormsley, on Getty's ground in Buckinghamshire, against a local village called Ibstone, and it's just the perfect cricket ground. I think both the Oval and the Lord's groundsmen were responsible for the wicket and the ground. The outfield is as good as any wicket you would find. It's just perfect, and with the ground set in a natural bowl, you hit a four and it just rolls up to the boundary. When you look out from the pavilion, you can see the four hills, on which there are different sheep or Texas longhorn cattle, and the red kites are flying above you. Very special.'

The fixtures are quite challenging for a side that, relatively speaking, is a newcomer to the cricket circuit but likes to win. How many WPP people are in the team, I wonder. 'Well, you know, we have a pretty good mixture. Let's say 50/50 for public consumption. We do get ringers to play for us. You know, it's a question of whether our ringers are better than the other people's ringers! We get some pretty useful people turning out for us, from home and abroad, including some from New Zealand and South Africa.'

And what standard is set by Martin Sorrell, the captain and batsman? 'Mediocre. Mediocre! I only played three or four times last season. It's because of travel, which even in the summer is significant, so I don't play as much as I would like to. I love the game and I still like to play, even though I was never very good at it. I was dour. I was Huttonian, or Boycottian, or Bailey-ish. I idolised Hutton. Boycott, I think, was a good batsman, but as boring as hell. Hutton had a little bit more to offer. But I was not a Graveney or a May or a Cowdrey, or anything like that. Or a Dexter!'

It has been suggested that Martin's management style was comprehensible because of his love of cricket, but when I suggest this to him, he is not so sure. In fact, he finds the notion amusing to the degree that his response is interspersed with a series of chuckles. 'I have not been able to connect the two. I mean, "ponderous" might be a possibility. My cricket style is very much a head–down opening batsman, and no risk. I could comfortably be at the other end propping up someone else, and stay there for days. I am not a cover driver or a hit-it-over-the-top for a six or whatever. I am much more a pusher and a prodder – a nudger rather than a flamboyant stroke player.

'I did like bowling, but I've stopped now as my shoulder is not as good as it should be. I used to take a few wickets, and once actually bowled Clive Lloyd – on the second bounce! That was pathetic, but I did bowl him, even though his knees had gone by then. On the other hand, I did bowl Mike Procter out with a corker in Victor Blank's game. Mind you, even though he was certainly trying, I think his legs had gone as well! Michael Parkinson was umpiring and Etienne De Villiers [a senior business executive], who is a very good player, was keeping wicket. There were a couple of overs to go and they needed 15 or 20 to win. David Frost asked me to bowl, so I marked out my run, took the ball, and just put my finger on the seam and hoped that the application of a little downward motion would produce what was effectively a slow medium leg break. It was an absolute beauty, which pitched about middle and leg, and hit his off stump. Michael Parkinson was stupefied; he couldn't say anything. Etienne was hugging me. Mike Procter gave me his shirt afterwards, which I still wear, even though it's now frayed at the edges after so many years.

'In another match, I was bowling to John Edrich, and he was trying, and I had him plumb lbw. The Archbishop of Canterbury was umpiring, and gave him not out! I said, "Why didn't you give that out – that was plumb?" and he said, "It would have spoiled the game." I could have killed him.

'Then there was an encounter with Imran Khan, who used to play in Victor's games, although he did seem to take it all a bit seriously and try too hard. I open the batting and Imran's first ball comes in. It seems a full length to me, so I go to drive it and it bowls me between bat and pad. So off I went. I was about 10 yards away from the wicket when the umpire called, "No ball!" So I went back to the wicket, the second ball comes in and I manage to block it. The third ball comes in and it seems to me to be outside the off stump, and I pad up. It comes back sharply, hits me on the pad and I'm plumb lbw – but he stifles the appeal. The fourth ball is very similar to the first: a full and driveable range – or so I think. I go to drive it, it bowls me and I just said, "I've had enough of this" and walked off!

'The other great experience, albeit equally short lived, was facing Shane Warne. I lasted four or five balls, and was then caught and bowled. Mike Brearley was keeping wicket and he said to me, "I have never seen anybody turn the ball as much as Shane Warne, even on Victor's pudding." Because in those days Victor's wicket was a pudding, although it is now very good indeed.'

The earlier mention of Boycott has reminded Martin of when he worked for Mark McCormack, handling the commercial affairs of sports people such as the Yorkshire opener. 'I am the only person, the only 21 or 22-year-old, who has gone into a negotiation – it was with Gray-Nicolls, up in Nottingham – on behalf of Boycott and left the room with less than I went in! Geoffrey was being paid £150 a year and I came out with £100 a year. He was now getting less money with us than he had been before! He was the first cricketer, the first batsman that I can remember who used contact lenses and he negotiated a commercial contract himself as a result of wearing them.

'I remember he was very upset with me because we never got him anything and after a year he rang me up and said, "I want to go through everything." I said, "Geoffrey, you have to understand we have written to 150 people and we have had 150 rejections" – and he didn't believe me! It was a Saturday, I remember, and he said, "OK, I'll meet you tomorrow." So on the Sunday I went up to somewhere in Hertfordshire with the file and, I am not joking, it was enormous. In it was every letter we had sent and every rejection. I met him at the house where he was staying at about 9.30 and he was still saying, "I don't believe you!" We opened the file and I took him through the first letter. He could see the date and "Would you be interested etc." and then there was a rejection letter. By the time we got to the 15th letter, he was convinced!

'In 1994, Victor Blank and I went to Guyana and saw England lose by an innings to the West Indies, with both Lara and Atherton making big hundreds. The Queen had visited Guyana the month before and you would walk around in the hotel and tell where she had been because everywhere she'd gone had been freshly painted! And I remember that Geoffrey was extremely upset because Victor had the nicest room in the hotel and he didn't. We were walking back from the game one evening – it was just Geoffrey, Victor and I – when Geoffrey said to Victor, "That f*****g Sorrell, he is f*****g useless." And I'm there! Walking with them! He said, "He worked for me and did absolutely f*****g nothing." So I turned around to him and said, "You know what the trouble was, Geoffrey?" and he said, "No." I said, "You didn't have any f*****g charisma!" But to be fair, he's changed, maybe because of his illness. He is a very good commentator, very good.'

Mention of Gray-Nicolls reminds Martin of when, some 40 years ago, the cricket equipment manufacturer had been shocked by the ideas they were coming up with at McCormack. 'We walked in – this is late 1960s, early 1970s – and we said, "All your bats are white with black handles. Why don't you have blue handles, yellow handles, pink or green? Why don't you put advertising on the face of the bat, and on the back?" In a funny way we were in effect predicting the future, although it was some years before equipment advertising and colour came into the game. You were dressed in white with blue caps – I mean, you never had anything other than blue or black caps. That was all there was. It was a different time, a different place. I used to go and watch the Gentlemen and Players at Lord's. It was usually the first game of the season and there they were in different dressing rooms. I mean, it was archaic, but wonderful in its way. Typically English. Class-ridden.'

All this was somewhat different from Marcus Codrington Fernandez, a former creative director in the WPP group, who was recovering following a stroke when he created a bat called the Mongoose. It was ideal for the Twenty20 format, as Martin explains. 'He was thinking about cricket bats and that we don't use the top of the cricket bat, the shoulders, very much. When I was at school, I liked light bats, not heavy ones, because I haven't got very strong arms. Do you remember the old Gray-Nicolls bats with the sloping shoulders? They were devised in the 1950s or 1960s to be lighter than the traditional bats, which were square. I used to love those bats. They were called Supalite and they were fantastic. So here is this guy, who is sitting in bed and he's ill. He's had an operation and he still manages to create the Mongoose bat. Matthew Hayden was using it in the Twenty20 – we helped him with a bit of PR and these are the little things that happen.' An interesting little thing for sure is that while MCC did not object to the Mongoose, Stuart Law, the former Australian Test player, was calling it "a half-brick on a stick."'

The continuing corruption issue, and specifically the allegations of spot and match fixing bubbling to the surface, is a major concern for every cricketer and spectator around the world. Martin, who spends much of his time travelling, not least to the Indian subcontinent, is no exception. 'We don't know how deep the problem has become. You can't stop people betting on spot events, I guess, but bookies must be making a lot of money out of it and they just write off a few losses because of what happens. But why would you want to bet, and why would you want to accept a bet, on whether somebody was going to be no balled on the third ball of the sixth over after tea or whatever? It is just the most bizarre thing. When you look at some of the replays you wonder how anybody could be doing it. If you're watching WPP play on a Sunday you can imagine the wicketkeeper doing this or not doing that, but some of the stuff you see on television does make you think, "What the hell is going on?" One front-foot no ball that I saw on Sky was so far over the line that Mike Atherton was astonished, commenting, "Well, that was a big no ball."'

If and when someone gets caught, how should they be punished? Should the punishment fit the crime? Should there always be a lifetime ban? Martin considers the options. 'I have a little bit of sympathy with the argument that there are some crimes that are worse than others. There is some logic in taking a different view if it is a match result is being compromised rather than a no ball being called in the 33rd over. That doesn't mean you shouldn't punish, but whether it should be lifetime ban or not – well, there is something in my head that says maybe there is a difference. But other people will argue that it's the thin end of a very big wedge and, if I may mix my metaphors, it's also a slippery slope!'

With Cambridge and Harvard under his academic belt, I can't imagine that cricket had much left to teach Martin, but I put the question to him nevertheless. 'Graft! I learned graft. No, seriously, you learn a lot about people through cricket. When WPP played, we were always very competitive, we always wanted to win. Or I certainly always wanted to win. There are those who say that you should show mercy if you are in an advantageous position, and I say, "No, you certainly shouldn't do that." I think you learn a lot about human nature. You learn a lot about people by the way they play, the way they bowl or the way they bat – particularly about the way they bat. You learn a lot about character.

'Maybe the reason I liked Hutton so much is because he wasn't flamboyant. He had the shots but he was careful – he was a grafter. Denis Compton wasn't my idol; Hutton was. Maybe I didn't like Compton's Brylcreemed head! On the other hand, I did like Graveney. Graveney to me was classical elegance. I didn't like Peter May, maybe because he played for Surrey, and I didn't like Cowdrey, because he played for Kent. But to come back to the subject, you learn a lot about people and how they behave, and being captain of a side was always interesting. I think it's probably too grand to believe that cricket can give you leadership skills, even though there have been some outstanding captains.

'I think the best captain I have ever seen was Mike Brearley, but he is a psychoanalyst and psychotherapist. I think he was the best at getting things out of people. He wasn't a great player – he wasn't a great batsman. In fact, ordinarily he probably wouldn't have got in the England side, but as captain he was a tremendous inspiration and still has the best record for percentage of wins, ahead of Michael Vaughan and Peter May. I think Hutton was a good captain, but the guy I admire the most is Douglas Jardine, captain in the Bodyline series. He was going there to win against the Australians and didn't care how he got there or what he had to do. Bodyline and the leg-trap were all part of the game for him. I thought Douglas Jardine was a very interesting, much maligned guy. Richie Benaud was a fantastic captain, as well as being a great leg break bowler and a very nice man. I also thought Ricky Ponting was very good – someone who is open, very direct and very matter of fact and truthful. Gives honest reactions, doesn't cloak them in any bullshit.'

At school, Martin played cricket, football and rugby, and had the opportunity to become closely attached to one or all of the three games. But his choice is clear. 'I like football but I love cricket. I will watch football and if I am in a city and someone says, "Would you like to come to a game?" I will go. I went to a couple of games in the World Cup in South Africa. But I really love cricket. Cricket is the most illogical game, the most eccentric thing. It is about England – it is not even about the UK. It is all about England's nuttiness and its eccentricities and how, in a country where the weather is so bad, you can play on these outdoor grounds and exposed wickets. I think the game was more interesting when the wickets were uncovered, when the elements meant that you could get caught on a "turner". I just think cricket has a character and charm and Englishness about it which makes it totally different from any other game. What other game do you play for five days, and have lunch and tea, and yet you can get a pulsating draw? Whoever heard of anything so ridiculous?'

SIR MARTIN SORRELL

Martin has been generous with his time, despite the executive pressures, and has been far more relaxed than I had expected of a man who has been described as 'professorial' in conversation and as having 'balls of titanium'. When we part, he enquires after my transport arrangements, organises a supply of personal cricket pictures and wishes me well with the book. I suspect that under the Hutton persona, there may be more Compton to him than he cares to admit.

RICHARD STILGOE OBE

'DAVID GOWER ON FULL SONG, JUST LEANING BACK
AND SQUARE CUTTING... IS AS REMARKABLE AS
HEIFETZ, THE GREAT VIOLINIST, IN ITS WAY.'

Richard Stilgoe was born in Camberley, Surrey, on 28 March, 1943. A lyricist, musician and songwriter, he wrote the lyrics for such musicals as Starlight Express *and* Phantom of the Opera *and has toured frequently, often with Peter Skellern. He founded the Orpheus Trust, which offers performing arts experiences to disabled youngsters, and launched the Stilgoe Family Concerts series at the Royal Festival Hall, featuring young performers. He has been High Sheriff of Surrey and president of Surrey County Cricket Club and the Lord's Taverners. In 1998 he was awarded an OBE for services to music.*

This is my only home fixture. Richard and his wife Annabel are spending an hour at my house in Islington before heading off for dinner in nearby Camden. Richard begins by recalling a match in Liverpool between Lancashire and the West Indian tourists that, partly because of the pedestrian scoring rate, the seven-year-old Stilgoe had found really dull. This was despite a high-scoring display by Frank Worrell and wickets in abundance for slow left-armer, Alf Valentine. Three years later, however, Richard's experience was more enjoyable.

'The first match I remember was in 1953 when I was just 10. It was at Old Trafford and my nanny took me and my friend Geoffrey Morris to see England against Australia. We were there just for the morning and I saw Ray Lindwall and Keith Miller. We sat just outside the boundary rope so that we were really in touch with the cricket – somewhere, alas, you are no longer allowed to be, I think, anywhere in the world. I don't know why, because we weren't intending to do a pitch invasion and we didn't bother about health and safety very much, and we wore our school uniforms because back then you wore your best clothes to go to a sporting event. Certainly I remember that all around us in the crowd were guys in three-piece suits and trilby hats, dressed up even on a sweltering hot day because they were going out. We saw Len Hutton, who was out for 66 I think, and Denis Compton and Reg Simpson. And then at lunchtime we went home, because I had to get back in time for my tea.'

Moving on from spectator to player, Richard became interested in the game via his parents and his school teachers, who helped him to develop his enthusiasm for cricket. 'There was Mr Stott at school, who was good and encouraging, and my dad, and particularly my mum, who had played for the school. She was very funny and had been a wicketkeeper and one of her skills – actually, it is still there – is to tell loads and loads of really good jokes to put the batsman off. You can hear it nowadays in stump "cams" – the amount of chat going on all over the world by a wicketkeeper. It is one of the signature skills. You have to be able to catch, you have to be able to stump and you have to be able to bat, but you also have to be able to natter all the time to put the batsman off. My mum, bless her, was good at all of that.

'I played at school for the Second XI, which sounds grander than it was, because I think only 22 boys played cricket, so the Second XI was loads of us who were really fairly hopeless. Later on I went to a school in Somerset and I have still got the Second XI picture, with all of us sitting the special way that schoolboys sit, with arms really tightly squeezed together to make it look like you have biceps. If you really push hard enough, you could kind of look as if your skinny little sticks of arms have actually got muscles in them.'

By then Richard was trying to emulate the great off break bowlers of the 1950s. 'I was trying to be Jim Laker or Roy Tattersall, both off break bowlers. But my deliveries set off as off breaks but they always went straight on. I have two deliveries: basically the off break which doesn't turn from left to right and the leg break which doesn't turn from right to left.'

Richard never played club cricket. It was some years after leaving school that he eventually started again in social and charitable matches. 'I don't think I played for anybody ever until there was a Nationwide-sponsored match. I think it was broadcaster Michael Barratt's XI against Michael Parkinson's XI, and when I tell you that the highest scorer in that game was another broadcaster, Sue Lawley, you will get an idea of the quality of bowling.'

And then, of course, there were the Lord's Taverners games, with that lovely mix of celebrities, cricketers and other sportsmen. 'Yes, I've enjoyed them so much. We all have so much fun while we raise money for the kids. I remember one match, we had three Test fast bowlers in the side – they were regulars, namely John Price, Fred Rumsey and John Snow. Snowy had more than twice the number of England caps than the other two had between them. I remember him, one of those games, saying to Price and Rumsey, "Could I open the bowling for once? Because I used to!" And John Price said, "No, you're not on Warfarin. You can't open the bowling for the Taverners unless you're on Warfarin!" It is a very good qualification; unless you'd had a triple bypass, you weren't an opening bowler!'

CRICKET WONDERFUL CRICKET

Richard has been a lifelong supporter of Surrey County Cricket Club and became president in 2005. 'That year, we won the Ashes and we got the grandstand built, but all that is of little consequence because Surrey got relegated for the first time in its history. I am afraid I get blamed for that more than I get the credit for winning the Ashes, which I think is deeply unfair! But there is something about the Oval. I mean, there is something wonderful about Lord's but I never feel smart enough there – I never feel properly dressed and there is a feeling of having to be on your best behaviour all the time, and there is always somebody disapproving of you. The Oval is a much more welcoming, easy place and I hope it always stays like that. We have had women in the pavilion and families around for ages so there has never been a fuss about that sort of nonsense.'

Since the redevelopment of the Vauxhall end stand, you can't walk round the ground any more. At lunchtime you used to be able to walk round and have a drink with your mates behind the pavilion but not now. Richard empathises with my point of view. 'The members would like just to be able to go and sit where they like. I suppose, like a lot of aspects of English life now, we would like to be trusted more. If you have been a member of a county for years and years and suddenly they say to you, "You can't go and sit in that bit of the ground because of security," they are kind of saying, "We think you're a risk." People don't want to be thought a danger to somewhere they love and have been to for such a long time. They want to be able to go and sit wherever they like. In their favourite seat, the place they always used to sit.'

There has been an almost magical link between music, writing and cricket, ever since the game became a national sport. Richard believes there is an inherent beauty in cricket, particularly in relation to the unique sounds and tempo of the game. 'There are an awful lot of us who like these things, certainly, and cricket has always had people reflecting on it and writing about it, partly because nothing else goes on for five days. You have plenty of thinking time: an awful lot happens to the world in the length of time a Test match takes. There will be no great writing about Twenty20 cricket – it's really sad. I think Twenty20 cricket is an absolute blast, but nobody is going to get an award for writing about a Twenty20 game and all the commentators hate having to write about it.

'But the music and cricket thing, I don't know why they are not on the same side of the brain. Cricket is a left side of the brain activity on the whole: it is motor systems. Music is the right side of the brain, the imagination side, so it is not that. But there are a large number of people who like both. The greatest fan of all is George Shearing, the blind jazz pianist, who for years would come over to England from New York to sit at Lord's throughout a Test match. Whenever he had a spare moment, Brian Johnston would go and sit next to him and describe what was going on. Shearing said – and Peter White, a BBC journalist, who was also blind and a huge cricket fan, agreed – there is something about the atmosphere: cricket makes wonderful sounds. And it really does. If you leave the ground before close of play, you must know this. As you are walking round the back of the pavilion, or walking away up the street but can still hear the crowd, there is one noise for a four, another noise for an appeal, another noise for a wicket, and another noise for a six – they are quite distinct. You can actually tell whether the crowd is cheering or disapproving or what – you can tell pretty much what is happening. And although it would be a waste if you have sight to sit and watch a cricket match with your eyes shut, it would be quite salutary to see how much you get from it. After all, masses of us spend hours and hours listening to the radio in the car or anywhere.

CRICKET WONDERFUL CRICKET

I think the thing I like almost more than anything in the world, because it combines two of my great pleasures, is sailing on my boat during a Test match with a long wave radio on. Because you can go quite far out and still get long wave and still enjoy a Test match going on while you are sailing.'

Richard has written often about cricket and a particular favourite is the grace he said before the England captains' dinner, a marvellous event held at the Hilton in Park Lane in 2009:

> *Who would be a captain? Who would be that brave?*
> *To be chosen by committees with a lot of face to save?*
> *Who would be a captain, with a team that falls apart,*
> *Spraining ankles playing football half an hour before the start?*
> *Who would be a captain, from the moment you have tossed*
> *To bravely telling Nasser all the reasons why you lost?*
> *Who would be a captain, with the media on your back?*
> *"You're too timid in defence, and far too risky in attack!"*
> *Who would be a captain? For most that's just a dream;*
> *The young people we look after are not even in the team –*
> *Disadvantaged or disabled, people look at them askance.*
> *Taverners don't look away, but give them all a sporting chance.*
> *Help us all do that tonight – in the auction be good tippers.*
> *Eat wisely, 'cos for afters we are going to have grilled skippers!*
> *Give generously tonight, then when you roll back home again,*
> *Your wives will all forgive you, and smile and say "Ah – men!"*

Richard also wrote the 'Lillian Thomson' piece back in the 1970s. 'Yes, that was 1977, but five years before it was actually Lillian Massie to begin with. Because I heard John Arlott, after the first day of the Lord's Test, summarising it and saying that the English batting had collapsed, and the damage had been done by Lillee and Massie. So I had this picture straight away of this woman called Lillian Massie who could bowl at a 100 miles an hour. Eventually it became Lillian Thomson because Massie only had that one great match when he got squillions of wickets, and I think spent the rest of his life wondering how he had done it!' Indeed, there was talk at the time that the ball allegedly behaved in a peculiar fashion.

> *Lillian Thomson Australia's finest flower,*
> *A maiden bowling overs at a hundred miles an hour.*
> *She'd bowl 'em at your ankles,*
> *She'd bowl 'em at your forehead,*
> *If she bowled them in the middle*
> *She could hurt you something horrid.*

This humorous mixture of cricketing folklore and musical whimsy leads me to wonder whether Richard had ever considered writing a musical. 'Peter Skellern and I went off to India to do research for a musical about cricket in India. The thing that had intrigued us was that there had been an appalling custom in India called *suttee* where, when a man died, his wife was burned on the same funeral pyre as him. That had stopped. But suddenly in the mid-1980s, in one particular part of India, it started happening again. There was a lot of outrage and a lot of cover-up and a lot of talk about it. Peter and I had this idea of placing these events just down the road from where a Test match was being played, so you had these two dramas, one apparently unimportant and one really, really important, going on at the same time. We thought it might be interesting theatre.

'The mockers was really put on that when we went to India, did the research and saw Mark Tully, the great BBC broadcaster who lives in Delhi, and he basically said, "Don't do it, because it will be misunderstood and it will look like the English pointing fingers at the Indians. It won't be seen as a piece of drama or a piece of comment; it will invoke exactly the same reaction as the *Satanic Verses*." It was very wise advice. If you have a long, long imperial past, you can't then talk about things without being accused of sort of trading on that imperial past. So it never happened and I am not sure that the world lost a great work as a result. Nevertheless, there is always something terribly exciting about a fire on a stage because straight away the audience always knows this is bloody dangerous. But that is not a good enough reason to have a race riot outside!'

It's not surprising to hear that Richard tried to emulate the great off break bowlers such as Roy Tattersall. But who else did he like to watch or admire the most? 'Oh gosh. Jim Laker, partly for that wonderful sort of "stiff upper lip" thing of getting 19 wickets in a Test match and not telling anybody. I think he stopped at the pub for a half of bitter on the way home, but didn't tell anybody in the pub what had happened. Incidentally, when Jim Laker got nine wickets in the first innings, I bet David Oliver, a school friend, two shillings that he would get all 10 wickets in the second innings. At evens, this is. And David Oliver was furious at having to hand over two shillings, which was a lot of money. But at Ladbrokes I would have got a thousand to one. That's the only bit of real prescience that I can claim. I thought that on the wicket there is that patch and that patch is going to be there for the second innings as well. It was days later before you saw it on Pathé News, and Test match footage was quite bad then. You didn't even see very much of it – the radio commentary was so important. So, Jim Laker, a modest, very talented man.

'I am also a great admirer of David Gower. Quite embarrassing, really, because I know David. I have a scorecard at home with 'caught Gower bowled Stilgoe' on it, which I am as proud of as anything I own. Lazy devil as well. Absolutely brilliant catch: sort of down, one hand on the floor, when he was at mid-off and he strolled forward and picked it just off the grass.' Richard can't resist a forward lunge towards the appropriately green carpet before continuing. 'If he had just set off a bit earlier, the way anyone else would have done, it would have been quite an easy catch but he couldn't be bothered. So he had to make it brilliant. It is quite embarrassing, knowing somebody who has that kind of touch and skill. There are times when, in any game, it suddenly gets beautiful. George Best playing football, David Beckham taking a free kick – both had a kind of art to it. David Gower on full song, just leaning back and square cutting... is as remarkable as Heifetz, the great violinist, in its way.

'The one who fascinates me at the moment is Pietersen, because I am sure he fascinates everybody. Not as one of my favourite players, but just this strange thing of having a talent that you are not really in control of and you don't really understand. I mean he works hard – he really, really practises – but still he can do things that he doesn't know how he does them. Famously, it was Olivier, after the first night of *Richard III* when everybody came round and found him in a terrible state in the dressing room, and they all said, "You were wonderful, you were amazing" – he said, "I have no idea how I did that. I don't know what to do tomorrow night to do that again." Being in the grip of a talent like that, where you think, "All I can do is go out on the stage again and hope that the magic happens again." It is so exciting to watch a talent that is not quite under the control of the owner of that talent.

'The rise of Ian Bell actually gives me a great deal of pleasure because he is somebody who has had to find an awful lot, having been a glorious 18 or 19-year-old player and doing absolutely brilliantly and then being promoted to the higher level and everybody thinking, "He's a bit small, he's not very glamorous," and having a really tough time. He is growing all the time now and he is a lovely player to watch. There is a real touch there. He is my size as well – I like that.' The diminutive Richard chortles and when, at my six foot plus, I feel it safe to do so, I join in. Then he continues, comfortably perched on the edge of his seat.

'I mean, there are certain people we all love. We all loved Denis Compton partly because the... oh, just the attitude thing. You know, it's supposed to be a game and Denis Compton played it as if it was a game. Len Hutton was wonderful as well. I was a great Boycott admirer because he is not an athlete but somebody who turned himself into a fantastically successful player. I think there wasn't an enormous talent there. It was a fantastic amount of graft to make the very most out of what he had.' Which is difficult to criticise, I suggest, but it made for a very selfish cricketer. 'Yes, the words "team game" don't really fit in there, do they?'

Richard has been a cricket fan and amateur player for the majority of his life, and feels there is much to gain from the game. 'Oh, you do actually get a set of lifelong friends. In cricket, you spend a lot of time fielding, standing next to people and chatting. There is a lot of chatting that goes on during a match. You're all there for the same reason, you all like the game in the same way, you all have views on it and it is wonderfully easy, non-hierarchical, chummy and unpressured. It is terribly different, coming from showbiz to standing around in the slips knowing that nothing much is going to happen. As opposed to going out onto a stage all by yourself in the hope that the first joke will go well and then if it doesn't you tell another one. I suppose that is the difference as well. In cricket, when you're batting, if you miss the first one, that's it – you don't get another two hours of having to try and get the next bit right. But no – it is a trite thing to say, but the camaraderie of being in a not very important cricket team is terrific. My pride is in being part of that every now and then.'

An amusing and laughter-filled hour with a delightful man has flown by. As he prepares to leave, we are still talking cricket. That is, until Annabel tells him that they are already running somewhat late for his thoroughly well-earned dinner.

CHRIS
TARRANT
OBE

'HE HIT ME FOR 24 OFF THE FIRST FOUR BALLS. I CAN'T REMEMBER WHAT HAPPENED AFTER THAT.'

Chris Tarrant was born in Reading, Berkshire, on 10 October 1946. He has featured prominently on both radio and television since the early 1970s and has hosted the ITV quiz show Who Wants to be a Millionaire? *since 1998. Early in his career he co-hosted the children's programme* Tiswas *and then fronted Capital Radio's highly successful* Breakfast Show *from 1987 to 2004. He is heavily committed to a number of charities, including Centrepoint, Milly's Fund and the Lord's Taverners, for which he was awarded the OBE in 2004.*

Chris has invited me to meet him at the Club at the Ivy in London's Covent Garden. To gain access, I go up in the giant, glass-sided lift that almost engulfs the ground floor entrance lobby. When I emerge, I find him deep in conversation with a previous guest but he breaks off to make introductions and order me a drink. Quite soon afterwards, his business chat is over and it is time to talk cricket.

'I remember, when I was about five, having the most strange cut-down bat, which my dad had made for me. It was an adult bat and although he had the blade and the handle shortened, it was still a massive thing. We used to play in the garden and that was the bat I used for years. Dad used to bowl at me with one of those balls that had holes in it. You could bowl it quite fast but it had almost stopped when it got to you, and you could hit it quite hard without it going too far.

'I went to this very strange school, called the Number Nine School – basically because it was number nine in the road – in one of those big, tall Edwardian buildings which they used to turn into little posh private schools. They had a very good maths master who taught me to bowl line and length, how to bowl the perfect ball, absolutely on the spot. So I did quite well at that and I just loved it. I was playing for the school at that time where I became captain. Then I went to the big bad school in Worcester [The King's School], where I was suddenly a little oik again, among all the 18-year-olds. I was in the school team for rugby and for hockey but my main thing was definitely cricket. It was what I was best at and it was also what I loved.

'When I wasn't playing cricket, I would listen whenever I could to Test matches on the BBC. I was at a boarding school where you were certainly not allowed to have your radio on in the middle of the night but I would be under the bed covers, listening to commentary coming from Australia. They had weird, old school commentators in those days, including Peter West, who was a very strange man – a very nice man, but he was very sort of BBC. He must be the only person who covered rugby and dancing, which I always thought was quite bizarre. West would do his summing up at close of play and Jim Swanton would then come on and tell you what England had done wrong and what they had done right. Often when I came home from school and there was a Test match being played, the black-and-white television would be switched on and dad would say, "Homework can wait. See the end of play at 6.30 and then you can do it."'

Chris's first encounter with the Lord's Taverners was a little unusual, to say the least. 'I worked in the Midlands and Fred Rumsey – a young, slim, athletic man in those days – rang me up and asked, "Is there any way you could get a *Tiswas* cricket team together? We can get Trent Bridge on a Sunday." *Tiswas*, the children's programme on ATV, was huge in the Midlands, and he said, "We'll get a big crowd and you'll be playing against this load of actors and TV presenters called the Lord's Taverners." So I got Sally James, Lenny Henry and a few other people who had been in *Tiswas*, plus one or two pop stars, and we produced a team. We didn't really know who we were playing against, or anything about them, and in those days none of us cared very much.

'On the Taverners side there was John Alderton, Robert Powell, I am pretty sure Nicholas Parsons, the late, splendid Leslie Crowther and, I think, Kenneth Wolstenholme, and various much-respected actors. They were all really looking forward to a lovely Sunday, with a chance to play on the main pitch at Trent Bridge in their immaculate whites, against some other bunch of cricketers. They did not expect to be blown up or covered in soot or green gunge. Because we did what we were best at, which was basically throwing custard pies, buckets of water and soot bombs, and exploding stumps. When I think about it now, I go bloody pale. But the crowd loved it. I remember the stumps going; they just burst into flames. It was fantastic. In terms of commercial success, it made a fortune. It was really packed, with 20,000 people. So the Taverners, bless them, grinned and smiled, but clearly they were not happy. I think the dry-cleaning bill cost Fred Rumsey half the national debt. When I think about it now I think, "My God, I can't believe we did that." We had no idea.

'Despite that, they must have eventually forgiven me, because about three months later whoever was then in charge of the Taverners wrote to me and said, "Dear Chris, would you think of joining the Lord's Taverners?" And I remember writing back saying, "Are you really sure you want me, because I think there was a lot of bad blood at Trent Bridge?" "No, no," came the reply from the Taverners, "it was just a bit of a misunderstanding."

'My fondest memories after I joined were playing with the likes of Willy Rushton, bless him, and Ted Moult. Ted was certainly our most successful bowler and probably took more wickets per season than anybody else – by bowling utter rubbish! We had John Price, when he was young, pretty and athletic, and had only just finished playing for Middlesex, and Butch White, who was bloody quick. He would put his pipe out on the sightscreen and then come in and bowl at 90 miles an hour. Fred Rumsey and John Snow were also still very quick, and sometimes Derek Underwood would play. These guys were still pretty damn good and would come on and bowl about four overs each and maybe take a couple of wickets. Then we would bring on Ted, who would bowl absolute drivel and get wickets! He would bowl donkey drops, then huge deliveries that bounced about eight times, appallingly short balls, wide balls, and he would get wicket after wicket. I remember him once getting a hat trick with three of the worst balls I have ever seen bowled anywhere on an English cricket field. I mean, they were appalling.

'Ever since I first began playing for the Taverners, with and against first-class cricketers, I remember thinking, "God, fancy being that good." You actually see the gap between the people we think are reasonable cricketers and the professionals, like Allan Donald, Andy Caddick, Mike Gatting, Gordon Greenidge, Mike Denness and loads more. The gap is massive. For example, we play this team of dentists every year at Lord's. A very nice guy called James Hull, who is a keen cricket nut, generously sponsors the match and brings a team called The Drillers. This is, supposedly, a collection of dentists but one year we are looking at their team sheet and one of the names is B Lara. I say to my son Toby, "It wouldn't be, would it?" He shook his head. "No, it will just be some dentist called Barry Lara." We are in the field and I am about to bowl, just as a wicket falls at the other end. And the PA commentator says, "Coming in to bat at number seven is B Lara" and out comes, unmistakeably, one of the greatest batsmen in the history of cricket, Brian Lara. So I bowled him one of my Tarrant trundlers, full of guile and cunning! He played a classic block and said, "No, wait there." And did so for the rest of the over. So I was very proud that I had bowled to the man who scored 400 in a Test innings – I bowled a maiden to Brian Lara! He clearly couldn't read me.

'So I am thinking, "Blimey, that's a bit good." Toby is fielding at mid-on and as he hands me the ball, he says, "He doesn't know how crap you are." And I say, "I know, and let's not tell him, shall we?" Then I bowl to Lara again what I think are pretty much the same deliveries as I had done in the unplayable first over! He'd obviously had time to think about it and the first ball he hit so hard, it is probably still going up now. He hit me for 24 off the first four balls. I can't remember what happened after that; I prefer not to. Toby sidled up to me at the end of the over. "He sussed you!"

'Such is the gap in class. I remember, many years ago, when he was in his absolute prime, Ken Barrington came to Reading Cricket Club. It was just a fun game, just an afternoon on a Sunday, rather like we do now. Somebody interviewed him on the PA – somebody like you, JD – and asked, "Well, Ken, what are you going to do this afternoon? What can we expect?" He replied, "In the first over I am going to hit one of the balls straight into the press box up there." It was a very long way and obviously very difficult to hit from any angle. Sure enough, the third ball he faced, Ken hit straight into the press box, and there were beer glasses and typewriters flying all over the place. The professionals are different class.'

For many years, the Taverners played at Penn Street in Buckinghamshire, in a match organised by Ian Jones, a headhunter and president of the village cricket club. The ground is flanked on two sides by woodland. On one memorable occasion, Chris was fielding on the boundary. 'One of the batsmen hit a four, which disappeared into the trees. I went scuttling after it and ran into the woods, and there was a man with bare buttocks. I swear this is true. And underneath the bare buttocks were the spread-eagled legs of a woman. She turned her head round in the throes of passion and said, "Oooh, it's Chris Tarrant." And I said politely, "I'm terribly sorry, I'm looking for my ball." I went bright red, still managed to find the ball and scampered back onto the field. I just couldn't believe it!'

As he comes to the end of a committed and strenuous stint as president of the Lord's Taverners, Chris continues to do an enormous amount for a wide range of charities, as do many others, such as Michael Parkinson. 'Parky's annual cricket matches were really good fun. The crowds were huge, he always got some sort of sponsor and we raised a lot of money for charity. People like George Best, Billy Connolly, Rolf Harris, Gary Lineker and Jimmy Tarbuck used to turn out, and Parky himself, obviously. He used to get a sponsor – all sorts of people put money in to pay for the marquee, the wine, the food and everything else, and we were all well looked after. So one year I saw him on about a Wednesday and he said [Chris adopts a Parky voice], "Are you still playing Sunday?" and I said, "Yes I'm playing, but have you got a sponsor?" I knew that he was struggling to get one with only a few days to go. But he just said, "It'll be alright. Don't worry, we'll have a sponsor. The game is going ahead; it's all advertised now. We'll have a sponsor on Sunday." Sponsors provide the kit and want to have their logos on display. Now, you can imagine. Michael is a real old Yorkshire cricket traditionalist who believes in cream flannels, the five-day game, red balls and no floodlights. So we all arrive and he says, "Hello lads, come and have drink. The kit's upstairs in the dressing room and yes, we've got a sponsor." So we went up and we all said, "Bloody hell!" There is our kit: royal blue outfits with Potterton's Boilers written across the front!'

At this stage, the club pianist starts his evening stint and I suggest to Chris that not many interviews get set to music. 'Well, my plan was to find a nice quiet place, which this is at about four o'clock in the afternoon, but round about six it gets loud. I hadn't thought about that.' And as the pianist warms to his task, he pumps up the volume – a rousing version of 'Downtown'!

Chris is an enthusiastic fisherman and I suggest to him that it is a rather strange pursuit for someone like him, and a million miles away from a game like cricket. 'They are incredibly different and because what I do for a living involves me being very up front and talking a lot, and being very outgoing and loud and extrovert and larger than life, you would never associate me with cricket or fishing. For so many people they seem the dullest ways of spending a day off. And also the quietest – that's why I fish, often entirely on my own. I don't want to think about anything to do with television or radio, I just want to fish.'

I mention that there are a number of cricketers and performers who are keen anglers, such as John Barclay, who has the apt middle name of Troutbeck. 'Yes, I know. Which is a bit of a clue, I think! But the most unlikely people go fishing – guys such as Jim Davidson. Can you imagine anyone louder than Jim? He is an obsessive and loves to fish. I've fished with Billy Connolly – he is a very keen fisherman. Frank Carson is a fisherman, but still a very loud man. And, of course, Ian Botham. I had a weekend with Beefy, fishing on the Tyne.'

195

In what little remains of his free time Chris is a keen cricket spectator, either at a match or in front of a television. He particularly relished the One Day International between South Africa and Australia in Johannesburg in 2006, when Australia amassed 434 for 4. South Africa, astonishingly, won the match with one ball remaining. 'They call it the greatest escape ever. Australia, for the first time ever, scored over 400 in their 50 overs, when even now 250 is not a bad score and 300 is pretty damn good. Four hundred! That's never been done before. You think, "What did Graeme Smith say to his team between innings to somehow motivate them? To get them to come out and then not only give the Aussies a game, but to beat them?" It was almost unbelievable, the most fantastic game of cricket. I was watching it, glued to the chair, and the phone kept ringing, and I kept screaming, "Not now! Not now!" I couldn't miss a ball.'

And the previous year, when England won back the Ashes from Australia, there were many nerve-jangling moments for Chris, not least at Edgbaston, where England beat the visitors by just two runs. 'There was that amazing last wicket stand between Brett Lee and Mike Kasprowicz, who put on close to 60 together before Steve Harmison won it for England. But the moment that really sticks in my mind came at the end of that match, when the England team were going bananas. Apart from Andrew Flintoff, that is, who put a hand on Lee's shoulder as he commiserated with him; that was very special indeed.'

So, reflecting on those two games, one a 50-over match, the other a Test lasting a full five days, does Chris favour any one particular format? Not forgetting the ubiquitous Twenty20, of course. 'I love Tests and hope that they never, ever fall away. I am sure they won't, because there has always got to be a market for full-on, great Test cricket. The different skills, the changing pace of the game, the stroke play that is required – they are all part of the attraction of Test cricket. Plus there can be great draws. Americans ask, "How can you guys play for five days and then it all ends up as a draw?" Well, yes, you can, and it can be incredibly exciting. Thinking out loud, maybe the 50-over game will disappear, which I am not sure would be the end of the world. If it threatened Test cricket I would be appalled, but I think there is only so much fast cricket, one-day cricket you can play. I think Twenty20 is pretty damn good. It seems to me that, among the fours and sixes, it is a very exact science. I mean, they really are into every ball and how they play it. But in all forms of the game, there have been absolute nail-biters, right down to the last bloody ball.'

One of the few things in cricket that really sticks in Chris's craw is sledging, which he feels has got almost out of control. 'Sadly, day-to-day sledging on the pitch has become part of the sport. What I hate is the way you go to almost any school match and all these kids are doing it all the time. The babble is ridiculous and you think the teachers should go, "Kids, just shut up." It is too much; they are all at it. "Come on, we've got him, he's out, he's a pansy, he's no good, he can't hold his bat for anything." These are 12-year-olds! What's the matter with them? We never did that stuff at school and I think it's deplorable. I think teachers should stamp it out, because it is nothing to do with the game. The kids are aping TV, I'm afraid, as they do in all sports. I go along to my kid's school and you see 11-year-olds diving in the penalty area and screaming at the referee, and you think, "Oh, come on. It's pathetic!" But they watch Drogba every week, and I think that is quite sad, and I don't like to see it in school cricket. It is not part of the game we know and love.'

Nevertheless, Chris talks enthusiastically about some of the big matches he has watched and particularly about several of the players that he admires. 'Ponting is just a fantastic batsman. If he has to score quickly, he scores quickly. If he has to score slowly and dig in for four hours, he will dig in. That's the measure of a great cricketer. He is a fantastic cricketer and a great captain, and when he was booed in England in 2009, I thought it was appalling. It was outrageous and I felt quite ashamed to be English. He is a tough guy – a tough Australian captain. Ian Chappell was once asked about Ponting as a captain and he said, "Ponting's terrific, the best captain ever." When it was suggested that he lacks a bit of charisma, is a bit surly and is quite aggressive, Chappell argued he was really aggressive and extremely unpleasant to everybody, and that was his job. He said being captain of the Australian cricket team is not a PR contest, and said, "If I have to be really tough on everybody, if I am outrageous with journalists, it is what I need to do." Steve Waugh wasn't very nice to people, either. He was another tough captain. Off the pitch he is a lovely guy but when he is out there, that's what you have got to do. Chappell also said the last thing you need is a nice Etonian guy as the leader of the team. "You show me a nice Etonian captain," he said, "and I'll show you a side that is going to lose the Ashes."

'I was talking to an old England umpire once, up at Trent Bridge, and I asked him who was the most unpleasant person he had ever been on the field with, and he said Glenn McGrath. He is the most difficult, cantankerous, whingeing cricketer this English umpire had ever had the misfortune to stand with. Every time he bowled, if the umpire gave someone not out, McGrath was so bloody stroppy. Every ball must get a wicket – he used to drive him mad. He used to hate bloody umpiring McGrath, because he was constantly in his ear. Off the field, though, McGrath's one of the loveliest blokes he had ever met.'

And without being too sycophantic, that is how I, and many others, view the man who has shared his cricketing thoughts and experiences to the accompaniment of a seemingly inexhaustible pianist!

GRAHAM TAYLOR OBE

"HE WAS THERE LOOKING LIKE SOMEBODY FROM THE MAFIA..."

Graham Taylor was born in Worksop, Nottinghamshire, on 15 September, 1944. He is a former footballer who played for Grimsby Town before moving to Lincoln City where, in 1972, he switched into management. His time in club management, particularly at Watford, where he was in charge three times, and in his first spell at Aston Villa, was very successful. He also managed Wolverhampton Wanderers after a testing time as manager of England. He is now chairman of Watford FC, a football pundit and was awarded the OBE in 2001 for services to football.

Graham and I meet at the five-star Grove Hotel in Watford, which is set in 300 acres containing, among many other facilities, a championship golf course. Tiger Woods has won a major tournament here and Graham tells me that it is where the England footballers stay before internationals. It is necessary, from time to time, to drag him away from football, such is his deep and continuing involvement in the game, and back to cricket. I soon learn that his father, who'd come up from Westerham in Kent, was the local sports reporter for the

Scunthorpe Evening Telegraph and that his first sporting love was cricket and Kent.

'At the end of the road where we lived there was a piece of grass which was Wembley in the winter and Lord's in the summer, and we played "dads and lads" games on it. The dads were batting and I was bowling to my father. I wanted to bowl leg breaks. I was going to pitch the ball outside his leg stump for it to spin in – but the ball never moved! Next ball, the same thing happens. So he's giving me the "Come on son, you can do better than that" look. Third ball, he ignores completely because I've done nothing so far, but this one turns in and takes his leg stump. He surveys the wreckage, then looks across at the other dads and says, "I've been teaching him how to do that for the last fortnight."

'He was a big cricket man and a very inventive one. I remember that we used to play Subbuteo, the table football game, but he also created a table-top game of cricket. He cut out little fielders from thickish paper and we would write the name of a player on each piece, all the famous cricketers that I knew then. Then he made wickets and a bat and would roll up the silver paper from a cigarette packet to make a little cricket ball. I suppose we made up the rules as we went along; one was that if the batsman hit the ball and it stopped on a fielder, then he was caught. So many dark winter evenings were spent around the dining room table and it was just another way that my father helped me to develop my love of cricket.'

Having played cricket at Scunthorpe Grammar School, Graham turned out for the local steel works team, Lysaghts, although by then he had abandoned leg spin and become a batsman. 'I had had no coaching whatsoever but I had got an eye for the ball and I could hit it and get a few runs, so I don't think I was a bad batter. Nevertheless, it was decided that I should have some coaching and all of a sudden I was taught how to play myself in, whereas previously I had gone in, asked for my guard and if the first ball needed hitting, I hit it. Now I was told by the coach, "No, no, leave that alone, don't hit that. You could be out. You might not get it right. Leave it, it's going wide, leave it. Now play yourself in, get the feeling of the pace of the ball, feel of the wicket." So after that, when I went in, usually first wicket down, I scored 9 or 10 runs and got out. Previously I would have had around 30 runs on the board before getting out. After all this coaching, I was in longer getting my 10 than I had been getting my 30!'

In his first spell as manager at Watford Football Club, Graham started a cricket side that, as part of pre-season training, played against some of the villages around the town. 'It helped to build a good team spirit – a family ethos – and involved the players and management in the local community.' And there were some talented performers on the cricket field, not least John Barnes, who played for Watford before moving on to Liverpool. 'He was a left-handed Garfield Sobers and I was a left-handed Geoffrey Boycott. We used to open the batting and while I was carefully playing myself in, he would hit the ball that needed hitting. Inevitably, when I was on four, he'd be on 40!

'One game, I was fielding at first slip when the ball rockets towards me off the edge of the bat, comes whoosh and hits me. There were shouts of "Hold on to it!" then "Oh, great catch, boss!"' Graham clutches his ribs as he re-lives the moment. 'When it's our turn to bat, I am opening with John Barnes and the pain suddenly hits me, and I think, "I've cracked my rib! Can't say anything to the footballers, you'll never live it down." So I am not going to say a word. But then I make the worst mistake of my life. I walk up to Barnes: "Barnesy, I think I have cracked my rib," I grimace, "so there are no quick runs today. Not one." At the start of the second over, he strokes the ball a short way on the off side and straight away he's running. There's no time to shout so, instead of saying "No!" I react. I've got to run – and, of course, I get run out. To this day I tell him that's why I sold him to Liverpool. "You ran me out at cricket – I don't want people like you in my club!"'

When Graham was manager of Lincoln City, he signed a young player called Phil Neale, who was also playing cricket for Worcestershire. He had been to university and had a degree – a 2:2 in Russian. 'Quite soon after he joined, I had to give him a bit of advice,' Graham explains. '"Now look, Phil, don't take this the wrong way, but in order for you to make your mark in that dressing room, not only have you got to think like a peasant, you've got to act like a peasant and you've got to speak like a peasant. Do you get my meaning?" At that time Phil didn't swear, so I added, "Not one of them speaks Russian unless it's when they are swearing at you."'

Neale's current role is as the England cricket team's operations manager. 'We have kept in touch and sometimes I'll leave a message on his mobile phone while the team are warming up, saying, "Neale, what the hell are you doing? Your old boss is watching you. You've got this wrong or you're not doing that properly. Look at Strauss over there – he's taking no notice of you whatsoever, so what the hell are you doing in this set-up?"'

Graham continued playing cricket until August 2007, when he turned out for David English's charity fund-raising side, The Bunburys. 'I bowled a bit until the ball was hit back at me and I stupidly used my foot to stop it. That hurt! I had broken one of my metatarsals, a fashionable footballer's injury as it happens. I was following in the footsteps, if that is the right expression in the circumstances, of players such as Wayne Rooney, Steven Gerrard and David Beckham. While doing the rounds of doctors, specialist and surgeons I was also diagnosed as having damaged my Achilles, so that was the end of my time playing cricket.'

Now he keeps fit by cycling, including taking part in a charity ride from London to Paris. On the cricket front he is happy to continue his enjoyment of the game as a spectator. 'Although I was originally a Kent man, my county team since I first went to manage Aston Villa in 1987 has been Warwickshire, where I am an executive club member. My only problem used to be that spectators wanted to talk to me about Aston Villa. I don't blame people for wanting to talk about football but I don't like discussing it when I've gone to watch cricket. When I watch football I'm always a critic. When I watch cricket I'm just a fan. So, for certain games, like Test matches, I get invited in to the Committee Room, where nobody is talking football to you.'

Graham has been an MCC member since the mid–1980s and is an ambassador for Chance to Shine, a charitable organisation that is bringing competitive cricket – and its educational benefits – back to the country's state schools. 'I was asked to become involved. I liked what they are doing and what they have achieved. I've already been to three or four schools, talking to the youngsters about football as well as cricket.' At one such school visit he was described as being as boisterous and excitable as any of the children with whom he was playing cricket and had a word – and a smile – for everyone.

On television, Graham watches more cricket than football, mainly because he still sees so much football 'live'. He also listens to the BBC's *Test Match Special* when he is on the move. 'I like listening to Geoffrey Boycott. He does have an opinion, and it is overstated now and again, and sometimes he says things that are obviously wrong. I don't dislike him for that because I have a laugh and I think, "Yeah, go on Geoffrey – pull the other leg." Jonathan Agnew is another man I like to listen to. He is opinionated as well but I think you probably have to be opinionated and to have your views. And in the past I so enjoyed Brian Johnston, who was part and parcel of everybody's cricketing life and brought so much warmth and humour to the game.

'I've always liked the Sky team,' he adds, 'particularly commentator David Lloyd.' The respect, it seems, is mutual. Lloyd once remarked, 'Graham Taylor loves his cricket, but he was there looking like somebody from the Mafia. He was all in black, with a yellow tie and dark glasses, as if he was on his way to do an audition for the Blues Brothers. *Do I not like that!'* Upon hearing this Graham says gleefully, 'He's got me! And that's what I like about him, he's capable of bringing himself down as well as other people, and I like to think I am the same. So I like the Sky team generally; they do a good job. Certain people take to broadcasting naturally. David Gower has got it and so has Gary Lineker. They have great delivery and cheeky grins. They have everything.'

Graham is a big fan of Test cricket, despite feeling that there is too much of it played all over the world. 'It's 12 months of the year now. Players are exhausted and likely to pick up more injuries. People who have "proper" jobs may not understand the stresses and strains involved; it is difficult to relate to when you have a full-time job. Take Andrew Strauss, the England captain. He decided to miss the Bangladesh tour early in 2010, for which he was heavily criticised by some commentators. But he came back refreshed to lead the side and it also gave valuable experience to Alistair Cook, who took over as captain. It is such an easy thing for people of my age to question how you can ever pull out when you are the England captain. It is like me saying, "Could I have said no to the England manager's job?" Well, realistically, if I had known it would have come up 10 years later, I probably would have said no at that time, because I think I would have been better at it later on.'

Graham has quite a problem with standards of behaviour in all sports, not just cricket, and feels that there are far too many attempts, often successful, to simply cheat. Despite this, he has a confession to make. 'I have cheated at cricket once in my life. Once when I was batting, a delivery flew off the edge of my bat and was caught by the wicketkeeper. I just stood there and rubbed the side of my face and was given not out, and to this day I know I cheated. I have not done anything like that since and I am not trying to make myself out to be anything special. I just think you should walk. I don't blame the umpire for not seeing it, for not giving you out, and sometimes he will give you out when you are not. I think his job will steadily be made easier through the use of technology but in principle, it starts with you playing the game.

'I have no time for footballers who deliberately cheat. I have no time for cricketers who deliberately cheat. And all these wonderful rugby players who play the game and are good to the referees, I have no time for them either when they are in the scrum and they can do whatever they like and still think they are gentlemen. I love it when we beat the Australians. Although I love the way they approach the game and their desire to win, I also know they will cheat on you because they take it to the nth degree. That is why I like to beat them. But not by cheating on them – it has got to be fair and square.'

As well as indulging in his love of Test cricket whenever possible, Graham also enjoys watching the Twenty20 format. 'It's the other end of the spectrum from Test cricket and is a great attraction for those people who want to come in and see a match from start to finish in the space of just a few hours. It's what the younger people want; they want a result. And if it attracts some of the non-cricket people that you want to introduce into the game, then perhaps some of them will go on to watch Test and county cricket.'

I ask Graham to name his three favourite players, which soon gets him reminiscing. 'Miss Parkinson, who was my teacher when I was at Infants School, knew I loved cricket and she had a television, which we didn't. In 1953, when I was just eight, she invited me round after school – you just imagine this today – to watch the final Test match at the Oval between England and Australia. I was in her front room, watching Denis Compton hit the boundary that won England the Test match and the Ashes, and I have had him as my number one ever since.

'When I was England manager I met Colin Cowdrey, something my Kent-loving father would have envied me for. I remember Colin telling me how to bat against the West Indian fast bowlers. What you have to remember, he told me, when you go out against them, is that initially 80 to 90 per cent of your runs will be behind the wicket, because they are that fast. And they take one fast bowler off and another one replaces him. You just hope that, eventually, they will get tired and that there will be a bad ball that you will be able to hook for the occasional boundary. Colin was a marvellous man and a marvellous batsman.

'And there are so many more to choose from. I look at Kevin Pietersen in the present day and think, "What a batsman." I go back to Bill Edrich: what a batsman he was. But Ricky Ponting has got to be in my top three in the world. I think he is such a competitive batsman and he delivers when he has to deliver. When I see him coming in, I always assume that the chances are he will get a century.'

Graham is also a huge fan of Alan Knott – but was he better than Godfrey Evans? – 'Probably not as a wicketkeeper but certainly as a batsman. But should he be in my top three? This is very difficult. I need to think about bowlers now. I got to know Fred Trueman very well. He had this personality and character about him, you know. He was like one of the old-fashioned footballers. They got fit by playing football; he got fit by playing cricket. He had a few pints of beer, because he needed them after he had been bowling all day!

'I think Brian Statham was very underrated. He was a much quieter man in many respects and probably a bit more of a gentleman as well. I think that the combination of Trueman and Statham was formidable. But then you've got Glenn McGrath, who was probably the best bowler in the world.' He pauses, as if considering every single bowler he has ever seen, before adding, 'I have to go for McGrath. As I said before, whether I like it or not and I can't particularly say that I do, I think Australians at times are out of order in the way that they behave but boy, do they know how to win. So I am going to go for Compton, Ponting and McGrath. I am going for two Australians and people will dislike me for it but I've simply got to.'

As our time is nearly over I ask Graham for a final thought on the game. 'There is one thing I have said to myself I want to do before I die. I want to hit a cover drive along the ground for four. I just want to do that again, even if I go out on my own and get my grandson to toss a ball so I can just do that. I want to have that feel of having my feet in the right position, of the bat coming through in the right way, going through the ball, not slogging it, with the bat finishing in the right position, just holding my stance and watching the ball as it crosses the boundary. Then I will drop dead. That would suit me. I will have ended my life perfectly.'

On that interesting albeit somewhat sombre note, we have to finish our chat, one that leaves me feeling a touch concerned for his grandson when the time comes. Meanwhile Graham, totally unperturbed, leaves to prepare himself for Watford's match that evening at Vicarage Road against Crystal Palace.

BILL
WYMAN

'I HAD HIM CAUGHT FIRST BALL BY CHRIS COWDREY AND THAT WAS MY HAT-TRICK.'

Bill Wyman was born in Lewisham on 24 October 1936. A talented musician, he was a founder member of the Rolling Stones, playing bass guitar with the band for 30 years. Since 1997, he has recorded and toured with his own band, Bill Wyman's Rhythm Kings. He has produced records and films, scored music for movies and television and written seven books, selling two million copies. His photographs have hung in galleries around the world. He designed and markets a patented metal detector and owns several establishments, including the Sticky Fingers Café.

I wait for Bill at Sticky Fingers, just off High Street Kensington in west London, and take in the posters, cartoons, caricatures, photographs that cover the walls, along with an impressive array of platinum and gold discs marking his time with the Rolling Stones. When he arrives it is with Caroline, his PA, who has organised our meeting. Once Bill has specified his precise tea requirements, we all move to a quiet table at the rear of the restaurant, the music is turned down and we prepare to talk cricket. Then the stories, anecdotes, memories and encounters begin to flow, as he provides enough to fill three or four chapters.

Bill's earliest chance to play cricket came at Beckenham Grammar School, but it was far from a happy start in the game he came to love. 'All the rich kids and families came from Orpington, Petts Wood, Bromley and all round there. I was now living in a slummy area of Kent – really bad streets there, kids in borstals and that sort of stuff. So I was ignored because I didn't have the money to buy the gear, and I didn't get into any of the teams. It was very much like that because they only coached the kids who had the right clothes, which was very annoying. My family just couldn't afford that – it took them all they could scrape together to buy me the little blazer and cap, and the tie and all that. Even so, I started to bowl leg breaks and googlies with a tennis ball in the street and I went on doing it when I used to go to the recreation ground, or Cator Park in Beckenham, when I was 12 or 13.

'About the same time, I watched the Test matches on my gran's little six-inch television, because in the 1950s we didn't have one. We didn't even have electricity – just gas lighting, and a toilet in the garden. But my gran was a mad cricket fan and we used to watch it together. She taught me quite a lot about the game because, when she was a little girl, she went into service in Wells Park Road in Sydenham, at the house next door to where W G Grace was living at the time. He was retired by then but I suppose she was impressed and she became interested in cricket. Mind you, I hope he didn't bonk her or anything – he was said to be a randy bugger! There's a possibility that there was something going on there. But too late to ask her now…

'I forgot about actually playing cricket for a long time, until my son was at a private school in East Anglia and I was asked to play for the fathers against the sons. I remember that we played with a shaved-down bat, which was only about an inch and a half wide, to balance it out against the boys. And I did really well. I was still able to bowl leg breaks and googlies and was taking wickets and getting runs with this silly little bat. Then Eric Clapton asked me if I would play a game for the Bunburys and I took a few wickets, got some runs and became really involved in the game again. Phil Collins was playing, Mike Rutherford, I think, a whole bunch of musicians. Then we started to have people from all areas. We had snooker players, jockeys, footballers and a whole mixture of celebrities, right across the board.

'I was soon playing 12 to 15 games a year and every time I played for the Bunburys, something happened that was special and different and good. I was doing well because I always got people out. They didn't expect me to bowl googlies. I bowled Graham Hick once, round his legs, and he was really pissed off with me! That's what happened with Ramps [Mark Ramprakash] – bowled middle stump by a leg break that I don't think he expected to spin that much. He came running out to smash it and completely missed it! But when I bowled Michael Holding, well, that's a very different story...

'I bowled a couple of leg breaks to him, then a googly, then I bowled one wide on the leg side. He decided to leave it and it hit his leg stump behind him. He came up the pitch, stopped about six inches from my nose and said, "You wait till you bat, man. I'm gonna get you." And I thought, "Oh yeah, funny ha, ha" – thinking that he was joking. After we got them out, we went in for lunch, and David English and Eric Clapton are saying, "He's going mad in the dressing room. He's ranting and raving about how he is going to get you when you bat," and I said, "Get out of it, stop winding me up." Then Michael came out of the dressing room, came round to where I was sitting and muttered in my ear, "I am gonna get you, man, make you smell leather." I was due in second wicket down and a couple of wickets went quite quickly. As I made my way out of the pavilion and walked to the middle, an ambulance drove into the other side of the ground with its light flashing, going "de, do, de, do." I thought it was a bit funny that it should arrive at just that moment. Normally it would have been there right from the start, because there were a lot of professionals and international players and they had to be on duty in case someone got injured.

'So, as I took guard, they changed the bowling. Michael Holding just took the ball from the other bowler half way through the over and started walking almost to the sightscreen. I'm still thinking, "Yeah, he's winding me up." I decide that I had better look round the field and there's no one in front of me, not one fielder. I look behind me, and they are all 30 yards back – wicketkeeper, about seven slips and two gullies – they were all miles back. By now he's at the sightscreen. I'm still thinking, "No, he's having me on" and then he comes thundering towards me. He gets about 10 yards or so from the wicket and I think, "No, I'm wrong, he's serious." His arm swings over like lightning, and there's a massive appeal. I looked round: I hadn't even seen the ball. The fielders are all leaping up and down, the wicketkeeper is throwing the ball in the air, and the umpire is going, "Out!" Michael by now has come walking down towards me. I said, "Out? Out? I didn't see it, let alone touch it – how can I be out?" and he came right up to me and said "'Course you didn't see it, man, because the wicketkeeper had it all the time!" Totally wound me up – it was fantastic.'

In 1995 the Bunburys played a match against a former England XI at the Oval to mark the 50th anniversary of the end of the Second World War. Denis Compton was watching from the pavilion, the umpires were David Gower and Bob Willis, and the match was live on Sky Sports. It was a memorable day for Bill as he took the first televised hat-trick at the Oval. 'Gary Lineker was first to go and I think it was Rory Bremner who caught him. Gary was really pissed off because he had travelled a long way to play and was used to making 60s and 80s on a regular basis. Then I got Trevor McDonald next ball and in came the Sky cricket bloke, Charles Colville, who had been slagging us off saying, "Bloody Bunburys, load of rubbish, we'll slaughter you, you're a load of wankers." He was so full of himself and came out to bat with a live mike clipped on his shirt and was talking about what he was going to do during his knock. But I had him caught first ball by Chris Cowdrey and that was my hat-trick. Apparently phone calls were coming in from all over the country saying, "Well done, Bill — we hate him!" Charlie Watts rang me and I asked him where he was calling from. "I think somewhere like Bonus Airs," he replied, "I think it's in Argentina, isn't it? Or is it Brazil? Anyway I just heard you took a hat-trick at the Oval and they said you were smoking at the time you were bowling. I hope that you didn't put your cigarette out on the hallowed turf."

'Apart from the Bunburys, I sometimes played in friendly matches for county sides, such as Surrey and Northants, as their token celebrity. In one game they had Muralitharan playing, and I am batting and I've got about 20 runs. Before the next ball is bowled, he comes and stands about three feet away. I said, "What are you doing?" He smiled. "Oh, you're out next ball. You've got enough runs, so we are getting you out next ball. I'm going to catch you." I couldn't believe it. "You don't think I'm just going to give you a catch. I know you're there. I'm not going to give you a catch." He just repeated, "You are, you're out next ball." Nick Cook, the spin bowler from Northants, comes up and bowls, right on my legs, exactly where I want it. I go to sweep. It spins in, catches the top edge of my bat and goes straight into Muralitharan's hands. It was then that I realised the pros are so far up there that they can get you out whenever they feel like it. They are just a bit nice to you because you are a celeb!

'I was reminded of that when I played against a South African fast bowler, Richard Snell, in the 1980s. I opened with a professional cricketer – one of the Yorkshire players, I can't remember his name – but he is the pro and I am the amateur. I take first ball and this bloody fast bowler comes tearing in and knocks my middle stump out of the ground at 90 miles an hour. I never saw it. I went back to the pavilion and said to David English, "Well, that's f*****g nice, isn't it? I come all the way up here to play and first ball he does that to me." But when they came in for lunch Snell came over and apologised, saying, "Sorry – I thought you were the pro and he was the celeb!"'

Bill's stream of anecdotes is endless and his ability to remember so many of the matches he has played in, along with the players and incidents, is impressive. When he talks about his personal achievements, it is all very matter of fact rather than boastful in any way. He recalls his one appearance in a *Wisden Almanack*, back in 1991, when it reported that he had caught Brian Close one-handed while the other hand held on to his lit cigarette! Next, in graphically colourful language, he goes on to describe boxer Gary Mason dropping the same batsman five times in one over. Then the name of Eric Clapton crops up again. 'Sometimes, when it was raining, me and Eric would go out in sou'westers into the slips and whenever the ball came near us, Eric just dodged out of the way. I said, "Eric you can't do that all the time. You've got to try to stop 'em – that's what we're here for." But he was having none of it. "No way, man. The fingers, the fingers – got to look after the fingers!" He just used to go, "Whoops – four, whoops – four." It was just hilarious. It was always fun, everybody always having a good time, always having a laugh.

'I didn't play for about eight years and then they asked me to turn out on a Sunday, at Ripley. A lot of big names were there because there was no Test match going on – all the England players, Freddie Flintoff, Ashley Giles and so on, as well as the older players like Beefy [Sir Ian Botham] and Viv Richards. It was a Sunday – the hottest day of the year – a hundred degrees! We batted first. I opened with David English and carried my bat – was out there throughout the innings – something I had never done before. We had lunch and then I fielded for the whole of their innings. I was the only one on the field for the entire match, despite being the oldest person there! In my innings, I hit Giles for three fours and he was not a happy man. He sort of smiled and got a bit friendly afterwards when we had a drink at the pub, but he wasn't very pleased with me. But it was amazing that I was able to play quite well, to achieve those things. I don't know why it happens; I'm a bit blessed in that way somehow. I have always been lucky in my life, in all ways, not just in cricket.'

Whether it was through luck, timing, talent or a blessing, Bill spent 30 years with the Rolling Stones. But not one of all the tours abroad, even those to Australia, allowed him the opportunity to watch any Test matches. 'We were down under in 1965, 1966 and 1973, but you are just moving from town to town the whole time, so there was never the chance. If there were matches on, of course we would try and get the latest news and find out what was going on, which was not always easy when we were in bloody America. In different ways the three of us – Mick, Charlie and me – were very keen on the game. I'm the only one who played; they just watched. I still talk cricket with Charlie and he still buys memorabilia. He's got one of Don Bradman's caps, as well as one of his blazers. He's bought so much stuff, it's just amazing. So he is avid, while I think Mick just likes the social side of it, which is the way he is with everything! He's not devoted like Charlie, who will have a bad night if England are not doing very well, and won't be able to sleep. He'll sit in front of the TV the whole day, like I do, but I am usually working on something whereas he'll just be watching it. Yes, he's crazy about cricket is Charlie.'

Bill loves reading up on cricket's history, the great players and significant matches, and is a veritable mine of statistical information. He also has an eye for the unusual tales that are an intrinsic part of cricket. A particular favourite dates back to England's first tour of Canada, in 1859. 'During the trip the players, among them a spin bowler who was also a farmer and quite rural and raw, went sightseeing by coach to the Niagara Falls. They all got out to look and the guide was telling them when they were first discovered, that millions of people had been there over the years, that every hour 27 million tons or gallons of water fell 278 feet and landed right there, close to where they were watching. The farming spin bowler thought for a moment, and then went, "Aye, well, there's nowt to stop it!" and, completely unimpressed, climbed back into the coach!

'Then there was the story about the Notts batsman, George Gunn, when he played at Canterbury. He was batting and it came to one o'clock. So he played the last ball of the over, put his bat under his arm and started to walk to the pavilion, until one of the umpires stopped him and asked him where he was going. And he said, "Lunch. It's one o'clock." The umpire said, "No, no, we have lunch at 1.30 here." So the next ball Gunn had to face, he just walked away, the ball knocked his middle stump out and he put his bat under his arm and said, "I always have my lunch at one o'clock!" That would never happen in this day and age. There was another time when Gunn had hit about 30 runs and his bat just split in half – one bit went flying away and he was left with the handle and half a bat. He called for a replacement and they came out with an assortment of bats, but he didn't like any of them. So he batted on with the remains of his bat and got about another 30 runs. Extraordinary!'

Bill talks lovingly about his earliest visits to Test matches at Lord's and The Oval in the 1950s, seeing players such as Godfrey Evans, Denis Compton, Len Hutton and the Australians Keith Miller, Ray Lindwall and Neil Harvey. From those days and those players onwards, he has built an impressive list of personal favourites. 'Viv Richards, Jim Laker and Graham Thorpe were fantastic for me. So were people like Derek Randall, who did extraordinary things in the field. I love Paul Collingwood; I think he is great, and what a fielder. And what about some of the West Indians, like the three Ws – Weekes, Worrell and Walcott – and the spinners Ramadhin and Valentine. That West Indian team in the 1950s was extraordinary. Don Bradman, of course, was averaging 99 point something over a whole Test career. Then there's Hobbs and Sutcliffe. I always thought Sutcliffe, if I had ever seen him, would have probably been one of my favourites, because he was pure class. What I have read about him and heard about him and seen on very brief little bits of film, he is like a David Gower. The way he off drove – it was just one classic beautiful movement. I have batted a lot with Gower and to be 20 yards away and watch what he does, is amazing. There are so many, I could go on forever.'

Which makes me wonder what for Bill, as a player, spectator and student of the game, is foremost in his mind when he reflects on his involvement in cricket over so many years? 'I love the quietness and slowness of the game. It's a relaxing thing, aided by the social drinking. I like the people you meet through cricket, particularly the players. They all seem to be nice and I really don't think I have met a horrible one. I have always found everybody that I have ever crossed paths with as cricketers to be charming. From Mike Atherton to Henry VIII.' Henry VIII is a cricketer? 'Haven't you ever noticed, John? He's Mike Gatting's double!

Another fine batsman. But I have enjoyed it all so much; playing and being with all your idols is really special. There are players who you idolise from afar and then suddenly you are chatting to them, and fielding and batting with them, and you find that they are all lovely guys. All the celebs try to be a little bit like them, to play well, maybe get a good score, take a few wickets or hold a good catch. Then they say, "Well done, Wyman." And when you are batting, to have David Gower come down and say, "Well played!" – it is kind of lovely. Then, to go to a cricket event at Grosvenor House or wherever and talk to Shane Warne, who I had never met before, and then meet Neil Harvey again and give him a hug, and then it's Dennis Lillee and Jeff Thomson and they go, "Hey, how are you, man?" To have those people all come up to you and give you a hug and say, "Good to see you again," is just a nice, emotional experience.'

We have been talking cricket for more than an hour and a half and might still be doing so now had nature not called. "I need a wee," Bill announces, as our bladders finally succumb to Sticky Fingers' constant supply of tea and coffee. And so we adjourn, although as we make our way down the stairs to the Gents, there's still barely a break in the cricket conversation.

GLOSSARY
OF PLAYERS

Acfield, David
Off-spinner for Cambridge University and Essex between 1966 and 1986 who took 950 first-class wickets and more than 150 in one-day matches. Was also an Olympic fencer who won a gold medal in the Commonwealth Games.

Agnew, Jonathan
A fast bowler for Leicestershire, widely known as Aggers, who played three Test matches and three One Day Internationals during a career which lasted from 1978 to 1992. Took over 800 wickets in all matches before becoming the BBC's cricket correspondent and a leading member of the BBC *Test Match Special* team.

Allen, Sir Gubby
Cambridge University and Middlesex all-rounder who played 25 Test matches for England during which he took 81 wickets and scored 750 runs. He captained England in 11 of his Test matches and following retirement became a powerful figure in

MCC and Chairman of the England selectors. He was knighted in 1986 for services to cricket.

Ames, Les

Outstanding Kent wicketkeeper–batsman who played 47 Tests for England, averaging over 40 and taking nearly 100 victims behind the stumps. In his first-class career between 1926 and 1951 he scored 37,248 runs with 102 centuries, including a highest score of 295 against Gloucester.

Amiss, Dennis

Warwickshire opening batsman between 1960 and 1987 who played exactly 50 Test matches for England as well as 18 One Day Internationals. He averaged over 46 at the highest level and among his 11 centuries was an undefeated 262 against the West Indies at Kingston, Jamaica in 1974 to save the Test. Since retirement he has been actively involved in a range of senior roles in the cricket world.

Anderson, James

Lancashire fast bowler since 2000 who by the end of the 2010/11 Ashes tour had taken around 200 wickets for England in both Test matches and the shorter forms of the game. With his ability to swing the ball at a good pace he can be a devastating leader of the England bowling attack. With over 700 wickets in all forms of the game he is an impressive performer and more than useful fielder, not least in the recent Ashes series.

Atherton, Michael

England and Lancashire opening batsman who played 115 Test matches between 1989 and 2001, scoring more than 7,700 runs with 16 centuries. His top score of 185 not out came against South Africa in Johannesburg in 1995 when, as captain, he batted for more than 10 hours to save the match. Also played 54 One Day Internationals and in his first-class career scored nearly 22,000 runs with 54 centuries. Now a respected commentator, journalist and author.

Bailey, James (Jim)
Left-handed Hampshire all-rounder between 1927 and 1952 who scored 9,500 first-class runs and took 473 wickets. In May 1932 playing against Notts, he had the astonishing figures of seven overs, three maidens, seven runs and seven wickets.

Baksh, Showkat
Also known as Charles, he played a single One Day International for Canada in 1979 as a right-hand batsman but failed to trouble the scorer.

Barclay, John
Affectionately known as Trout, a Sussex batsman, off break bowler and captain who in a career that ran from 1970 to 1986 played 274 first-class matches and 236 limited-over games. In total, he scored more than 12,000 runs and took nearly 500 wickets. He made his Sussex debut at the age of 16 and since retirement has remained closely involved in the game as an author, directing and coaching at the Arundel Castle Cricket Foundation, as an England tour manager and as a recent President of MCC.

Barrington, Ken
Much admired Surrey and England batsman who played 82 Test matches, making 20 centuries in a Test career lasting from 1955 to 1968. An immensely talented batsman whose Test average of 58.67 is the third highest by an England player. Died of a heart

attack at the age of 50 while assistant tour manager for England in Barbados.

Bedser, Alec

Twin brother of Eric and fast medium right-arm bowler who played for Surrey and England. In 51 Test matches he took 236 wickets and was the mainstay of the England bowling attack. In 1953, at the age of 35, he took 39 wickets in the series to spearhead England's Ashes victory. Bedser played first-class cricket from 1939 to 1960 and died at the age of 91 in 2010.

Bell, Ian

Right-handed batsman and fine close to the wicket fielder who has matured into an excellent batsman for England and Warwickshire in a career which started in 1999. By the end of 2010 he had scored well over 12,000 first-class runs and has played many fine innings for his country, including 199 against South Africa in 2008 at Durban.

Benaud, Richard

Australian leg break and googly bowler between 1948 and 1964, who became a highly respected journalist, author and broadcaster. In 63 Test matches he scored over 2,000 runs and took 248 wickets. An inspirational and charismatic captain of his country, he is widely regarded as one of the most influential cricketing individuals since the Second World War.

Bennett, Don

Middlesex all-rounder between 1950 and 1969, who played more than 400 matches, scored 10,656 runs and took 780 wickets. Subsequently a highly regarded coach for his county.

Bird, Dickie
A right-hand batsman who played for Leicester and Yorkshire, he is best known as a mildly eccentric first-class umpire. He played 93 first-class matches between 1956 and 1964. As a batsman he scored over 3,300 first-class runs and as an umpire was widely admired and respected by both players and the public.

Bland, Colin
South African right-handed batsman who played 21 Test matches between 1961 and 1966. He was one of the greatest ever cover fielders, combining a gazelle-like athletic presence with the ability to throw with extreme accuracy.

Blofeld, Henry
An old Etonion, he played 17 first-class matches for Cambridge University before his cricketing career was curtailed by a cycling accident. He is best known as a journalist, author and one of the most familiar voices on the BBC's *Test Match Special*. His commentaries are dotted with references to London buses and pigeons.

Border, Allan
Left-handed batsman who, as captain, played a major part in the revival of Australian Test cricket from the mid-1980s. He played 156 Test matches, scoring 11,174 runs including 27 centuries, with an average in excess of 50. He also played in 273 One Day Internationals and since his retirement in 1996 has been a Test selector and television pundit.

Botham, Sir Ian
Played 102 Test matches and 116 One Day Internationals for England between 1976 and 1992. The Durham, Somerset and

Worcestershire all-rounder is best remembered for his unbeaten 149 in 1981 to set up victory over Australia against all the odds. In Tests he scored 5,200 runs with 14 centuries and in One Day Internationals more than 2,000 runs. He took 383 Test wickets, more than any other English bowler. He was knighted in 2007, partly for his efforts in raising money for leukaemia research. He is now a cricket pundit.

Boycott, Geoffrey

A right-handed opening batsman and occasional bowler whose first-class career lasted from 1962 to 1986, during which time he played 108 Test matches for his country, making over 8,000 runs, scoring 22 centuries and averaging over 47. As a batsman he was no cavalier and his run-making could be pedestrian. Nevertheless, he was one of England's most productive postwar batsmen and since his retirement has become a well-established pundit.

Bradman, Sir Don

The greatest batsman the game has ever known. He played 52 Test matches for Australia between 1928 and 1948, averaging an incredible 99.94. At the highest level, 'the Don' scored nearly 7,000 runs with 29 centuries and was a consistently successfully captain of his country. After his retirement he was knighted in 1949 and continued his involvement in the game in a statesman-like fashion until he died in 2001 at the age of 92.

Bradshaw, Keith

Tasmanian batsman between 1984 and 1988 who made a top score of 121 during his 25 first-class matches before his appointment as secretary and chief executive of MCC in 2006.

GLOSSARY OF PLAYERS

Brearley, Mike
Played for England, Cambridge University and Middlesex between 1961 and 1982, appearing in 39 Test matches. He was widely regarded as one of the best post-war captains. He is the author of *The Art of Captaincy* which was published in 1985 and is now a psychoanalyst and psychotherapist.

Brennan, Don
Played 232 first-class matches after debuting in 1947 for his native Yorkshire and appeared in two Test matches. He retired in 1964, having taken 318 catches and stumped 122 victims during his first-class career.

Brocklehurst, Ben
Somerset batsman between 1952 and 1954 who went on to become publisher of *The Cricketer* in 1970 and helped to set up The Cricketer Cup for leading public schools.

Brooks, Ted
A Surrey wicketkeeper between 1925 and 1939 whose 810 dismissals for the county have only been exceeded by one other player. Remembered for his acrobatic movements and keen sense of humour.

Brown, Freddy
An all-rounder for Cambridge University, Northants and Surrey between 1930 and 1953. He played 22 Test matches and in his first-class career scored over 13,000 runs and took 1,200 wickets with his mixture of medium pacers, leg breaks and googlies. He was a popular player who captained his country before going on to be chairman of selectors, a manager of touring sides and president of MCC.

Caddick, Andy

Opening bowler for Somerset who played 62 Test matches for England between 1993 and 2003, taking 234 wickets for his country. He also appeared in 54 One Day Internationals despite being plagued by injuries in the mid-1990s. In his career he took 1,180 first-class wickets and a further 356 in limited-over matches.

Cairns, Chris

Lively, talented but injury-prone New Zealand all-rounder between 1988 and 2008. He played in 62 Test matches, scoring 3,320 runs and taking 218 wickets. He also played 215 One Day Internationals, making nearly 5,000 runs and taking a further 201 wickets. He was only the sixth man to achieve the double of 200 wickets and 3,000 runs in Test cricket and at one stage held the record for the most sixes in Test matches.

Carr, Donald

Oxford University and Derbyshire left-arm bowler and useful right-hand bat who appeared in two Test matches for England, and scored nearly 20,000 runs and took 328 wickets in 446 first-class matches from 1945 to 1968. After retiring from the game he held a number of senior positions including tour manager, assistant secretary of MCC and secretary of TCCB.

Chester, Frank

Worcestershire all-rounder between 1912 and 1914 who became one of the most respected umpires in the first-class game. He stood in more than 1,000 matches including 48 Tests and is credited with having raised the standard of umpiring to a new level. He counted the number of balls in an over by using six small pebbles from his mother's garden.

GLOSSARY OF PLAYERS

Close, Brian

Was the youngest man ever to play Test cricket for England when he was capped in 1949 at the age of 18. In his 22 Test appearances he scored 887 runs and was briefly England captain. He played first-class cricket for Yorkshire and Somerset for 30 years, scoring nearly 35,000 runs and more than 50 centuries. Regarded as one of the toughest, bravest and most charismatic of all cricketers. A legend.

Collingwood, Paul

Durham all-rounder who first represented his country in 2003. His double century against Australia in 2006 was the first for England in the Ashes for 78 years. One of the very best fielders, particularly close to the wicket, he has captained England in One Day Internationals and the Twenty20 form of the game.

Compton, Denis

A cavalier batsman for Middlesex and England, for whom he played 78 Test matches averaging over 50 with a top score of 278. His career lasted from 1936 to 1958, the pinnacle being in 1947, when he scored a record-breaking 3,816 runs in a season with 18 centuries. Also played football as a winger for Arsenal and represented England in 12 war-time Internationals. An advertising contract earned him the label of The Brylcreem Boy.

Connor, Cardigan

A rare cricketing product from the island of Anguilla who took more than 1,000 wickets for Hampshire in a combined total of 521 matches from 1984 to 1998. His best bowling figures were 9-38 against Gloucester in 1996 as a mature 35-year-old.

Constant, David

Played 61 matches for Kent and Leicestershire between 1961

and 1968. Became an umpire at the age of 27 and remained on the first-class list for 38 years, during which time he stood in 36 Test matches and 33 One Day Internationals.

Cook, Alastair

Essex opening left-handed batsman who by the end of the 2010/11 Ashes tour had played 65 Test matches and 26 One Day Internationals following his Test debut in 2006. Has an average of over 47, has scored 16 centuries at the highest level and enjoyed a highly successful Ashes series in 2010/11. Already has more than 10,000 runs to his credit in all first-class matches as well as substantially more than 3,000 in the shorter forms of the game.

Cook, Nick

A slow left-arm bowler for Leicester and Northants between 1978 and 1994. He played 15 Test matches and in his first-class career took 879 wickets and a further 200 in one-day matches. After his retirement he became a first-class umpire.

Cowans, Norman

Jamaica-born Hampshire and Middlesex fast bowler who played 19 Test matches and 23 One Day Internationals for England between 1982 and 1985. In 239 first-class matches he took 662 wickets with a further 263 victims in 224 limited-over matches. His only first-class 50 came off just 19 deliveries.

Cowdrey, Colin (Lord Cowdrey of Tonbridge)

A highly talented batsman for Kent, Oxford University and England. Played in 114 Test matches between 1954 and 1975, scoring over 7,600 runs with 22 centuries. He captained England 27 times and is particularly remembered for the 1963 Test against the West Indies when he came in to bat with a broken wrist in plaster. In his first-class career he scored 42,719 runs with 107 centuries. He was made a life peer in 1997 for services to cricket.

Daft, Richard
Right-handed batsman for Notts between 1858 and 1891 who captained the county between 1871 and 1880. Scored nearly 10,000 runs in his career and was regarded as one of the finest batsmen of his era.

Denness, Mike
Scottish opening batsman who played for Essex and was an outstanding captain of Kent. Played in 28 matches for England, captaining the side in 19 of these, as well as in 12 One Day Internationals. In 1975 at Melbourne he led from the front, making top score of 188 as England beat Australia by an innings. In a first-class career lasting 501 matches between 1959 and 1980 he scored well over 25,000 runs and also played in 232 limited-over games, making close to 5,400 runs.

Dexter, Ted
A right-hand batsman and medium pace bowler for England, Cambridge University and Sussex, he was an elegant and exciting batsman throughout his first-class career between 1956 and 1968. He played 62 Test matches, scoring more than 4,500 runs. Probably his most famous innings was in 1963 at Lord's against the West Indies when he made 70 from 73 deliveries off the bowling of Wes Hall and Charlie Griffith. Also a very fine golfer.

D'Oliveira, Basil
South Africa-born Worcestershire all-rounder who averaged

over 40 for England in his 44 Test matches. In a first-class career stretching from 1964 to 1980 he played 367 matches scoring nearly 20,000 runs and taking more than 550 wickets. A much loved cricketer who was at the centre of the controversial 'D'Oliveira affair' when the England tour of South Africa was cancelled in 1968.

Donald, Allan

Highly respected right-arm fast bowler for South Africa, Warwicks and Worcester. Known as White Lightning, he took 330 wickets at a cost of little over 22 apiece in 72 Test matches between 1982 and 2002. He also played in 164 One Day Internationals in which he took 272 wickets. Since his retirement he has been both cricket pundit and bowling coach.

Donnelly, Martin

Left-handed New Zealand batsman who played seven Test matches for his country between 1937 and 1949, making 206 against England at Lord's in 1949. In his brief career, he also played in England for Oxford University, Middlesex and Warwickshire and in a total of 131 matches scored more than 9,000 runs and made 23 centuries.

Dujon, Jeffrey

Athletic West Indian wicketkeeper-batsman who played 81 Test matches and 169 One Day Internationals between 1974 and 1993. He made 3,322 runs in Tests and nearly 2,000 in the shorter form of the game. At the highest level he took 450 catches and made 26 stumpings and claimed a total of more than 700 victims in his first-class career.

GLOSSARY OF PLAYERS

East, Ray
Essex left-arm bowler between 1965 and 1993 who played 410 first-class matches and 280 one day games. He took more than 1,000 wickets with a best of 8-30, and was one of the most likeable, funny and entertaining men ever to play the game.

Edrich, Bill
Right-handed batsman and fast bowler for Middlesex and England who played in 39 Test matches between 1938 and 1955. In his first-class career he scored nearly 40,000 runs and took 479 wickets. After leaving the RAF, where he had won a DFC as a bomber pilot, in 1947 he scored 3,539 runs averaging over 80, only to be outdone by his batting partner, Denis Compton.

Edrich, John
Left-handed opening batsman for Surrey and England who played 77 Test matches, scoring over 5,000 runs with 12 centuries and a top score of 310 not out against New Zealand in 1965. Nephew of Bill, he came from a cricketing family, his four cousins all having played first-class cricket. During a career that lasted from 1956 to 1978, he scored nearly 40,000 first-class runs and 103 centuries.

Edwards, Charlotte
Right-handed bat and leg break bowler who, by the end of January, 2011 had played 19 Test matches and 145 One Day Internationals for England. She has made four Test centuries with a best of 117 and has scored over 4,000 runs in the shorter form of the game. At one time she was the youngest woman to have played for England and at the age of 17 made a score of 173 not out in the World Cup. She became England captain in 2005.

Emburey, John

Off break bowler and useful batsman for Middlesex and Northants between 1973 and 2000 who played in 64 Test matches for England taking 147 wickets. Also played 61 One Day Internationals for his country and in his first-class career took 1,608 wickets alongside 647 in one-day matches. Since retirement he has been both cricket coach and commentator.

Evans, Godfrey

Kent and England wicketkeeper, often described as the best the game has ever seen, who played in 91 Test matches achieving 219 dismissals. An energetic, inspirational and charismatic character, in his later years he sported huge mutton-chop whiskers. In a career lasting from 1939 to 1969, he scored nearly 15,000 runs, took 816 catches and made 250 stumpings.

Fishlock, Laurie

Left-handed batsman for Surrey, who also played four Test matches for England. During his career between 1931 and 1952 he scored over 25,000 runs with a top score of 253 against Leicester in 1948 and averaged nearly 40. A useful winger, he played football for Crystal Palace and Southampton.

Fletcher, Keith

Nicknamed 'the Gnome', during a career lasting from 1962 to 1988 he captained and subsequently coached England, led Essex to three County Championships and scored well over 37,000 first-class runs. He played 59 Test matches and 24 One Day Internationals, averaging a shade under 40 in both forms of the game at the highest level.

GLOSSARY OF PLAYERS

Flintoff, Andrew

A 6ft 4in all-rounder who was also an outstanding slip fielder for Lancashire and England during a career that lasted from 1998 to 2009, when a series of injuries finally brought it to an end. Universally known as Freddie, he was an exciting batsman who played 79 Test matches, taking 226 wickets and scoring nearly 4,000 runs. He played a significant part in the memorable Ashes victory over Australia in 2005 when he was named Man of the Series.

Flower, Andy

Highly regarded Zimbabwe-born England coach, who was a fine batsman and excellent wicketkeeper in his first-class career between 1986 and 2006. As probably his country's finest ever player, he appeared in 63 Test matches averaging 51.54 and making 12 centuries while also appearing in 213 One Day Internationals. He took more than 300 victims behind the stumps at the highest level and since his retirement has played a significant part in England's improving fortunes as their coach.

Fowler, Graeme

Left-handed opening batsman for Durham and Lancashire who played in 21 Test matches and 26 One Day Internationals for England in a career that lasted from 1979 to 1994. Scored more than 25,000 runs in all forms of the game, made 45 centuries and after retirement 'Foxy' has become a lively summariser, not least for the BBC's *Test Match Special*.

Garner, Joel

Known as 'the Big Bird', this 6ft 8in right-arm fast bowler took 259 wickets in 58 Test matches for the West Indies at a cost of less than 21. A formidable proposition with the ball in his hand, he took 881 first-class wickets and close to a further 400 in the shorter form of the game between 1975 and 1992. His ability to achieve steep bounce or deliver an awesome yorker made him one of the most highly regarded bowlers ever to play for his country.

Gatting, Mike
Right-handed batsman for Middlesex and England, who captained his country in 23 of his 79 Test matches. Led the country to a significant victory in the 1986/7 Ashes series. Played 92 One Day Internationals and in his first-class career scored over 36,500 runs and took 158 wickets with his medium-paced bowling. Since retirement, he has worked as a coach, commentator and as a managing director for the ECB. Renowned for his hearty appetite and his many contributions to the game.

Gavaskar, Sunil
Quite outstanding Indian right-handed bat, who made more than 10,000 runs in his 125 Test matches, averaging over 50 and scoring 34 centuries. He also played 108 One Day Internationals scoring more than 3,000 runs in a career that stretched from 1966 to 1988. His ability to concentrate and his excellent technique made him one of the most successful opening batsmen in the history of the game.

Gibbs, Lance
Played 79 Test matches for the West Indies between 1958 and 1976, taking 309 wickets with his notably accurate off-breaks. He took five wickets in an innings in 18 Test matches and amassed more than 1,000 wickets in his first-class career. Against India in Barbados he once returned the astonishing figures of 53.3 overs, 37 maidens, 38 runs, 8 wickets.

GLOSSARY OF PLAYERS

Gilchrist, Adam

Australian wicketkeeper-batsman between 1999 and 2008, who scored over 5,500 runs in his 96 Test matches and nearly a further 10,000 in One Day Internationals, usually at the top of the order. He normally scored his runs at an astonishing rate and this respected cricketer unusually would walk when he knew that he was out, regardless of the umpire's decision.

Giles, Ashley

Slow left-arm Warwicks bowler and useful batsman who played 54 Test matches taking 143 wickets and also appeared in 62 One Day Internationals between 1997 and 2006. He took 539 wickets and scored more than 5,000 runs in his first-class career and made many significant contributions with both bat and ball for his country. Now his county's director of cricket and an England selector.

Gooch, Graham

Played 118 Test matches for England scoring 8,900 runs on top of the 4,290 he made in 125 One Day Internationals. His 333 was the highest of his 20 Test centuries while his medium-paced bowling earned him close on 250 first-class wickets. He was the most prolific run scorer ever in top class cricket with 44,841 first-class runs and 21,087 in the one-day game. His Test career lasted over 20 years from his debut in 1975. As England captain, he was dedicated to fitness and a high work ethic.

Gover, Alf

A fast bowler for Surrey and England between 1928 and 1948. He played in four Test matches and took 1,550 wickets during his first-class career before becoming for over 40 years one of the most respected and best-known coaches. He died in 2001 at the age of 93.

Gower, David

One of England's most graceful and elegant left-handed batsmen, he played 117 Test matches and 114 One Day Internationals between 1978 and 1992. He made more than 11,000 runs for his country in both forms of the game with a top Test score of 215 amongst his 18 centuries. He captained England before moving into broadcasting and journalism where he quickly made his mark as a fluent and confident performer.

Grace, W.G.

Bearded batsman of the greatest possible renown during his first-class career, which lasted from 1865 to 1908. He played 22 Test matches for England, scoring over 1,000 runs with two centuries. But these figures in no way represent the awesome influence he had on the development of the game of cricket and his achievement in scoring well over 50,000 runs in nearly 900 matches during his first-class career.

Graveney, Tom

One of the most graceful, gifted and much loved batsmen in post-war cricket, he played 79 Test matches for England, scoring nearly 5,000 runs with 11 centuries. In his first-class career he also played for Gloucester and Worcester between 1948 and 1972, scoring 47,793 runs at an average of nearly 45 with 122 centuries. He passed 1,000 runs in a season 20 times, making more than 2,000 in six of them.

Greenidge, Gordon

Right-handed West Indian opening batsman who played 108 Test matches and 128 One Day Internationals for his country between 1974 and 1991. He made 19 centuries at the highest level of the game, averaging just over 44. With his powerful stroke play he formed an imposing opening partnership with

Desmond Haynes, which produced 16 century stands of which four were more than 200.

Gregory, Robert
Right-handed batsman and leg break bowler for Surrey between 1925 and 1947 who scored approaching 20,000 runs and took 437 wickets for the county.

Greig, Tony
South Africa-born Sussex and England all-rounder who played 58 Test matches scoring nearly 3,600 runs and taking more than 140 wickets. Between 1965 and 1978 he was a charismatic, competitive and towering figure at 6ft 6in, but his first-class career ended in controversial fashion when he helped Kerry Packer launch World Series Cricket, an event that changed the cricketing world. For the better. Now an accomplished commentator based in Australia.

Griffith, Charlie
Right-arm fast bowler for the West Indies between 1960 and 1969, who took 94 wickets in 28 Test matches. He formed a formidable fast bowling partnership with Wes Hall and in 1963 took 119 wickets during the tour of England at just over 12 runs apiece, 32 of these in Tests. He was twice no-balled for throwing during his career.

Griffith, Mike
Right-handed bat and wicketkeeper for Cambridge University and Sussex between 1962 and 1974 who played 276 first-class matches and 121 one-day games. He captained his county in the late 1960s and early 1970s and played hockey for Cambridge University and England.

Gunn, George

Generally regarded as the greatest batsman to have ever played for Notts, scoring more than 35,000 runs with 62 centuries during a first-class career from 1902 to 1932. His approach to batting was such that he could be the complete master of the bowling when he felt minded to do so. Made 15 Test match appearances for England and was a first class slip fielder who took nearly 500 catches.

Hadlee, Sir Richard

New Zealand's greatest ever cricketer who scored more than 3,000 runs and took 431 wickets in 86 Test matches at a cost of little over 22 apiece. He also played for his country in 115 One Day Internationals in his career between 1971 and 1990. He was the first bowler to reach 400 Test wickets, including 9-52 against Australia in Brisbane in 1985. He was knighted for services to cricket in 1990.

Hall, Wesley

West Indian fast bowler who took 192 wickets in 48 Test matches, often in partnership with Charlie Griffith, between 1958 and 1969. He was a formidable, well-built man who could easily intimidate the opposition: in the momentous Test at Lord's against England in 1963 he broke Colin Cowdrey's arm and bowled unchanged for three and a half hours.

Hammond, Wally

One of the greatest batsmen ever – certainly in the top four or five in a career that stretched from 1920 to 1951. He played 85 Test matches for England, scoring 7,249 runs at an average of 58.45 with 22 centuries. His top score, an undefeated 336, was made against New Zealand at Auckland in 1933 at better than a run a minute and included 34 fours and 10 sixes. In all first-class matches he scored more than 50,000 runs and made 167 centuries.

Harmison, Steve
6ft 4in right-arm fast bowler for England and Durham who made his first-class debut in 1996. In 63 Test matches he took 226 wickets with best figures of seven for 12 against the West Indies in 2004. He also made 58 appearances for England in One Day Internationals and on his day could be a formidable proposition for any batsman.

Harvey, Jonathan
Played for Cambridge University from 1963 to 1965, taking 17 wickets with a best of 5-28 with his fast medium bowling.

Harvey, Neil
Australian left-handed batsman who played in 79 Test matches between 1948 and 1963. He scored more than 6,000 runs at the highest level through a combination of impressive stroke play and an excellent technique. He scored 21,699 first-class runs with 67 centuries in his career.

Hayden, Matthew
Australian left-handed opening batsman in 103 Test matches and 161 One Day Internationals. He made over 8,600 runs in Tests, averaging more than 50 and scoring 30 centuries in a career that lasted from 1991 to 2009. Made a top score of 380 in 2003 against Zimbabwe at Perth, at that time a record for Test cricket.

Heyhoe Flint, Rachael
An England player from 1960 to 1982. As captain from 1966 she was unbeaten in six series and led England to victory in the 1973 World Cup. In 22 Test matches she scored nearly 1,600

runs at an average of 45.54 and in 23 One Day Internationals she averaged over 58. Her highest Test score of 179 was made against Australia at the Oval in 1976. She was one of the first women members of MCC.

Hick, Graham
Prolific right-hand batsman and off break bowler who played 65 Test matches and 120 One Day Internationals without ever completely establishing himself at international level. He scored heavily throughout his county career – more than 41,000 first-class runs at an average in excess of 52 with 136 centuries – before retiring from the game in 2008.

Hobbs, Sir Jack
The most prolific of batsman, he scored 61,760 runs, made 199 centuries and averaged over 50 in his first-class career between 1905 and 1934. This outstanding Surrey batsman made 61 Test appearances for England, averaging nearly 57 and making 15 centuries. His astonishing total of runs might have been far higher but for the First World War and his inclination to be dismissed after making a century to allow a team-mate to bat. A man of great charm who became the first professional cricketer to be knighted.

Holding, Michael
Jamaican fast bowler who played for Derbyshire and Lancashire and in 60 Test matches and 102 One Day Internationals for the West Indies. His smooth, rhythmic run-up earned him the nickname of Whispering Death and he took 249 Test wickets at a cost of less than 24 apiece during a Test career that lasted from 1975 to 1987. His best bowling figures of 8-92 were against England at the Oval in 1976. Now a fine performer in the commentary box.

GLOSSARY OF PLAYERS

Hollies, Eric
Bowled Don Bradman in his last Test innings for a duck, denying him an average of 100. The Warwickshire leg break bowler played from 1932 to 1957, appearing in 13 Test matches and taking 44 wickets, while in his first-class career he took 2,323 wickets at a cost of less than 21 runs apiece. His best bowling was 10-49 against Notts at Edgbaston in 1946.

Holmes, Erroll
Oxford University and Surrey all-rounder between 1924 and 1955 who played five Test matches for England. A talented amateur cricketer and captain.

Hussain, Nasser
Essex and England batsman between 1987 and 2004 who played 96 Test matches and 88 One Day Internationals. He scored more than 31,000 runs in the first-class and one-day game with a top score of 207 achieved at Test level. He captained England with considerable success winning four Test series in a row and was arguably one of his country's finest captains. He now commentates with some authority on the game.

Hutton, Sir Len
A fine technically correct and prolific batsman for Yorkshire and England who also became England's first professional captain in 1952. During his first-class career between 1934 and 1955 he made 79 Test appearances, averaging over 56 with 19 centuries. In his career he scored more than 40,000 runs and made 129 centuries. Under his captaincy England won the Ashes in 1953 for the first time in 19 years. He was knighted in 1956.

Ikin, Jack

Played 365 matches, scoring nearly 18,000 runs and taking 339 wickets, in his first-class Lancashire career between 1938 and 1964. He played 18 Test matches for England over a ten-year period without ever becoming a regular selection.

Illingworth, Ray

A supremely accurate off-spin bowler and more than useful batsman whose career with Leicestershire and Yorkshire stretched from 1951 to 1983. He played 61 Test matches for England, taking 122 wickets, and collected more than 2,000 victims in his 787 first-class matches. He was an outstanding captain of England and led his country in 20 Tests before losing one. He was less well regarded as chairman of selectors.

Imran Khan

Outstanding Pakistani all-rounder, who also played for Sussex and Worcester between 1969 and 1992. In 88 Test matches he scored more than 3,800 runs and took 362 wickets with best figures of 8-58 against Sri Lanka at Lahore in 1982. A handsome and talented individual, he led Pakistan to victory in the 1992 World Cup and enjoyed the social scene for many years before entering into Pakistani politics.

Ingleby-MacKenzie, Colin

One of the most liked, happiest, amusing and enthusiastic of men, he played for Hampshire from 1951 to 1966, scoring nearly 12,500 runs with 11 centuries in 343 matches. As Hampshire's last amateur captain he led the county to the Championship in 1961. He was president of MCC when women were allowed to become members for the first time.

GLOSSARY OF PLAYERS

Insole, Doug
Cambridge University and Essex batsman and medium pacer who was a useful wicketkeeper. He played nine Test matches for England spread over seven years and 450 first-class games, scoring over 25,000 runs and making 54 centuries. Since his retirement in 1969 he has remained heavily involved in the game as a MCC committee member, an England selector and chairman of the Test and County Cricket Board.

Irani, Ronnie
All-rounder for Essex, Lancashire and England who played three Test matches and 31 One Day Internationals. He scored approaching 13,500 runs with 28 centuries and took 339 first-class wickets in a career that lasted from 1990 to 2007.

Jackman, Robin
Fast medium bowler who played four Test matches and 15 One Day Internationals for England in the early 1980s. He took over 1,400 first-class wickets at less than 23 apiece and a further 439 in the one-day game. A lively and competitive cricketer, he is now a cricket commentator.

Jardine, Douglas
Captained England in 15 of his 22 Test matches, including the 1932/33 Ashes tour in Australia during which bodyline bowling earned him a controversial and unpopular reputation. He averaged 48 in Tests and made nearly 15,000 runs at first-class level. He retired in 1934 and died at the age of only 57.

Jones, Dean
Australian batsman who played in 52 Test matches between 1984 and 1992, scoring 3,631 runs at an average of 46.55. Also

played in 164 One Day Internationals, in which he introduced a new level of attack with both the bat and in the field. He scored more than 6,000 runs in the shorter form of the game, including seven centuries.

Kanhai, Rohan
West Indian right-hand batsman, who played 79 Test matches and made 15 centuries for his country with a top score of 256 against India in Calcutta in 1959. In his long career between 1954 and 1982 he played 421 first-class matches and scored more than 29,000 runs with 86 centuries.

Kasprowicz, Mike
Right-arm fast medium bowler for Australia between 1996 and 2006 who played 38 Test matches and took 113 wickets. In 43 One Day Internationals he took 67 wickets and claimed more than 950 victims in his first-class career.

Kenyon, Don
Worcestershire batsman, who played eight Test matches between 1951 and 1955. In 643 first-class matches he scored more than 37,000 runs with 74 centuries and was Worcestershire captain when they won the County Championship for the first time in 1964, a title they retained the following year. Widely regarded as the most influential figure in the county's history.

Key, Robert
Kent batsman and captain who played 15 Test matches and five One Day Internationals for England in a career which started in 1998. Scored 221 for his country against the West Indies at Lord's in 2004 but despite this has never been able to establish himself as a regular member of the England side.

GLOSSARY OF PLAYERS

Knott, Alan

Outstanding Kent wicketkeeper-batsman who played 95 Test matches for England, scoring 4,389 runs and claiming 269 victims behind the stumps. He made more than 18,000 first-class runs, 1,211 catches and 133 stumpings. Between 1964 and 1985 he became a player of great dedication who was a quiet but much liked member of both the county and England team.

Knott, C.J.

Hampshire off-spin bowler whose cunning deliveries earned him 676 first-class wickets at a little over 23 each during a first-class career between 1938 and 1957.

Kortright, Charles

Has the reputation of being the fastest bowler of his generation. Played for Essex between 1893 and 1907 taking 489 wickets at a shade over 21 runs apiece. Also a useful right-handed batsman with more 4,400 runs and two centuries to his credit.

Laker, Jim

Took 19 Australian wickets in the 1956 Old Trafford Test match, including 10-53 in the second innings, an achievement that is unlikely ever to be matched. He was a superb off-spin bowler who took 193 Test wickets in 46 appearances, 1,944 wickets in a 450-match career at a cost of only 18.41 apiece, and five wickets in an innings on 127 occasions. He was a crucial part of the Surrey side that won seven consecutive County Championship titles between 1952 and 1958.

Lamb, Allan

South Africa-born batsman, who played for Northants and for England in 79 Test matches and 122 One Day Internationals.

He scored more than 32,000 first-class runs with 89 centuries and more than 15,000 in the one-day game. His first-class career lasted from 1972 to 1995, during which time this stocky, punchy character made a lasting impact on the game.

Lamb, Tim

Played for Middlesex, Northants and Oxford University between 1973 and 1983, taking 361 wickets in 160 matches and a further 190 in 166 limited-over games. He was chief executive of the ECB from 1996 to 2004.

Lara, Brian

Phenomenal batsman whose undefeated 400 against England in Antigua in 2004 is the highest score ever made in Test match cricket. He played 131 times for the West Indies, scoring nearly 12,000 runs and averaging close to 53 with 34 centuries. He also played 299 One Day Internationals, scoring over 10,000 runs, and holds the record for the highest score in first-class cricket, 501 not out, for Warwickshire against Durham in 1994.

Larwood, Harold

A fast bowler of considerable stature, who left a lasting impression on the game and on the Australians. In 21 Test matches for England, this Notts cricketer took 78 wickets, most memorably during the 'bodyline' series in 1932/1933 when he was ordered by captain Douglas Jardine to bowl 'leg theory'. This involved short-pitched bowling at the opposition batsman and earned him 33 wickets and a 4-1 series win for England. Ironically, in 1950 he emigrated to Australia, where he died in 1995 at the age of 90.

Law, Stuart

Australian batsman who played 54 One Day Internationals and

one Test match for his country in a career that started in 1988. To date he has scored more than 27,000 runs in first-class matches and approaching 12,000 runs in the one-day game.

Lawrence, David
A promising England Test career, which lasted only five matches, was ruined by the fracture of his left kneecap. The Gloucestershire fast bowler, best known as Syd, played 185 first-class matches, taking 515 wickets and 113 one-day games before his 10-year career ended in 1991.

Lee, Brett
Formidable Australian right-arm fast bowler who, by the end of 2010, had taken 310 wickets in 76 Test matches since 1999. Still prominent in One Day Internationals he has already taken more than 330 wickets and is Australia's fourth most successful bowler. In first-class matches he has taken 487 wickets, despite injury problems later in his career.

Lewis, Tony
Cambridge University and Glamorgan batsman, who led the county to the Championship in 1969 and played nine Test matches for England, the first of these as captain. He played more than 400 first-class matches between 1955 and 1974, scoring 20,495 runs with 30 centuries. After retirement he became a writer and broadcaster, particularly with the BBC and was president of MCC.

Lillee, Dennis
In 70 Test matches for Australia, this outstanding fast bowler took 355 wickets at under 24 runs apiece with best figures of 7-83 against the West Indies at Melbourne in 1981. In 63 One Day Internationals he collected a further 103 victims and between

1971 and 1983 was the leader of the Australian bowling attack. His partnership with Jeff Thomson, backed up by wicketkeeper Rod Marsh, can only be described as awesome.

Lindwall, Ray

One of the greatest new ball bowlers of all time, he played in 61 Test matches for Australia between 1946 and 1960, taking 228 wickets at an average of just over 23 apiece. His best bowling figures of 7-38 were achieved against India at Adelaide in 1948. His bowling partnership with all-rounder Keith Miller was a sight to behold. In 228 first-class matches he took 794 wickets at a cost of only 21.35 and captured five wickets in an innings on 34 occasions.

Lloyd, Clive

Left-handed West Indian batsman, impressive striker of the ball and talented captain. In 110 Test matches he scored more than 7,500 runs with a top score of 242 not out, against India in Bombay in 1975. He also played 87 One Day Internationals and scored more than 31,000 runs in a first-class career stretching from 1963 to 1986. His record as captain included a spell of 26 undefeated Test matches including 11 wins in succession.

Lloyd, David

With the nickname of Bumble, this Lancastrian played nine Test matches and eight One Day Internationals for England and in a career stretching from 1965 to 1985 played more than 400 first-class matches, scoring over 19,000 runs and taking 237 wickets. When he retired from the game he was a first-class umpire for a short while as well as England coach but is now best known as an amusing, entertaining and knowledgeable member of the Sky Sports team.

GLOSSARY OF PLAYERS

Lock, Tony
Left-arm spinner for Leicester, Surrey and England who played 49 Test matches, taking 174 wickets between 1952 and 1968. He took 2,844 first-class wickets at just over 19 each and was Jim Laker's partner, not only for England but also for Surrey's County Championship winning side in the 1950s. He was a brilliant close to the wicket fielder and took 831 catches in his career.

Long, Arnold
Sussex and Surrey wicketkeeper who played 452 first-class matches and 232 one-dayers, taking 922 catches and making 124 stumpings. He captained Sussex between 1978 and 1980 and was predictably nicknamed Ob.

Lord, Reg
Played three matches for Oxford University in the mid-1920s, following which he became a coach. He died in 1997 at the ripe old age of 92.

Malcolm, Devon
Jamaica-born fast bowler for Derby, Leicester and Northants who played 40 Test matches and 10 One Day Internationals for England. Of his 128 Test wickets and 1,054 in first-class games, the best remembered by far are the nine he took against South Africa at the Oval in 1994 when, having been struck on the helmet when batting, he destroyed the visitors' second innings.

Marsh, Rod
Played for Australia between 1970 and 1984 as wicketkeeper-batsman, scoring 3,633 runs and claiming 355 victims behind the stumps. Made more than 11,000 runs in over 250 first-class

matches with 12 centuries. Since retirement he has run the Cricket Academies in both Australia and England.

Marshall, Malcolm

Born in Barbados, he developed into one of the great fast bowlers, taking 376 wickets at less than 21 apiece in 81 Test matches for the West Indies and five wickets in an innings on 22 occasions. He could swing the ball both ways and unleash a bouncer with the best of them. A highly intelligent bowler, he took more than 1,650 wickets in his first-class career at under 20 each but tragically died of cancer when only 41 years old.

Martin-Jenkins, Robin

Sussex all-rounder between 1995 and 2010, who scored nearly 7,500 first-class runs and took 384 wickets. Also scored more than 2,000 one-day runs and took 234 wickets. A talented member of a successful Sussex side, he never quite made it to international level.

May, Peter

Cambridge University and Surrey batsman who played 66 Test matches for England between 1951 and 1961, making a top score of 285 not out and scoring 13 centuries. A classic and effortless looking batsman, he scored 27,592 runs in his first-class career at an average of exactly 51. He captained England 41 times, winning 20 of these matches and losing only 10. He also captained Surrey from 1957 to 1962, winning the County Championship in the first two of these seasons.

McGrath, Glenn

Australian fast-medium bowler with the ability to bowl with gun-barrel accuracy. Played 104 Test matches, taking 563 wickets at 21.64 each. He claimed five wickets in an innings on 29 occasions at Test level with a best analysis of 8-24 in bowling out Pakistan for only 72 at Perth in 2004. He also played 250 One Day Internationals, taking 381 wickets, and amassed 835 wickets in his first-class career between 1992 and 2009.

Miller, Keith
A magnificent cavalier all-rounder for Australia between 1946 and 1956, during which time he played 55 Test matches, scored nearly 3,000 runs and took 170 wickets. At the time he retired from Test cricket he had the best figures for any all-rounder and was an outstanding fielder, particularly in the slips. One of cricket's greatest ever characters, he was also a Royal Australian Air Force pilot during the Second World War.

Mitchell, Arthur
A somewhat dour Yorkshire batsman who played six Test matches and 426 at first-class level between 1922 and 1947. In total he scored more than 19,500 runs with 44 centuries. He became the Yorkshire coach in 1945, a position he held for 25 years.

Moody, Tom
Tall Australian all-rounder who played eight Test matches and 76 One Day Internationals and was a significant contributor to Australia's success in the 1999 World Cup. In 300 first-class matches between 1985 and 2001 he scored over 11,000 runs and following his retirement became a successful coach with Worcester, Sri Lanka and Western Australia.

Morgan, Eoin
Dublin-born, left-handed batsman, whose effective and inventive style has established him as a regular member of England's one-day side. Averaging around 40 in One Day

Internationals with an impressive strike rate in excess of 80, the Middlesex player has also appeared in six Test matches during a career that started in 2004.

Morrison, Danny

Played 48 Test matches for New Zealand between 1987 and 1996, taking 160 wickets with a best of 7-89 on his debut against Australia at Wellington. He took 126 wickets in 96 One Day Internationals and 440 wickets in his first-class career before becoming a television commentator.

Muncer, Len

Glamorgan and Middlesex all-rounder between 1933 and 1957. He played 317 first-class matches, scoring 8,646 runs and taking 755 wickets. In an unusual development for a spinner, he switched from leg breaks and googlies to off breaks in mid-career.

Muralitharan, Muttiah

Controversial and record-breaking off-spin bowler who took 800 wickets in 133 Test matches for Pakistan between 1992 and 2010. He also took 517 wickets in 339 One Day Internationals and was particularly effective with the doosra, a delivery that turned the 'wrong' way. He was no-balled for throwing on more than one occasion but finished his career with well over 2,000 wickets in all forms of the game.

Murray, Deryck

West Indian wicketkeeper who claimed 189 victims in 62 Test matches behind the stumps and also played 26 One Day Internationals for his country between 1963 and 1980. In a total of 511 first-class and one-day matches he took over 900 catches and made 122 stumpings.

GLOSSARY OF PLAYERS

Mushtaq Ahmed
Pakistani leg break and googly bowler who inspired Sussex to their first ever County Championship in 2003. His first-class career stretched from 1986 to 2008 during which time he played in 52 Test matches and 144 One Day Internationals. He took over 1,400 first-class wickets with best figures of 9-48 against Notts in 2006. Since his retirement he has been England's spin bowling coach.

Nash, Brendan
Australian-born batsman who made his first-class debut in 2000 and moved to Jamaica, following which he appeared at both Test match and one-day level for the West Indies. Has made centuries at the highest level against England and South Africa.

Neale, Phil
Worcestershire batsman and captain between 1975 and 1992, who played more than 350 first-class matches scoring 17,445 runs, including 28 centuries. Also made more than 7,000 runs in 339 limited-over matches. Since retirement has been a successful coach and manager at county and international level.

Nicholas, Mark
Hampshire batsman and captain, who was one of the most talented players never to play for England. During his first-class career from 1978 to 1995 he scored more than 18,000 runs with a top score of 206 not out, as well as a further 7,000 in one-day cricket. Suave and urbane, he is now a cricket writer and commentator.

Parks, Jim
A wicketkeeper-batsman for Sussex, Somerset and England who took over 1,200 catches, made 112 stumpings and scored 36,673 runs with 51 centuries in his first-class career. In 46 Test matches between 1954 and 1968 he scored nearly 2,000 runs. He captained Sussex during the 1960s and joined Somerset before retiring in 1975.

Pietersen, Kevin
Notts, Hampshire and Surrey batsman with more than 70 appearances in Tests for England and well over 100 One Day Internationals. Born in South Africa, he quickly established himself in English cricket to become the quickest batsman to reach 1,000 and 2,000 runs in One Day Internationals, and 5,000 runs in Test cricket. Somewhat unconventional and sometimes controversial, he is simply an enormously impressive batsman on his day.

Pocock, Pat
Surrey off-spinner who played 25 Test matches for England between 1968 and 1985, taking 67 wickets. Known as Percy, he took over 1,600 first-class wickets in 554 appearances, as well as 327 in the one-day game. A man who enjoyed his cricket, he took four wickets in four balls, five in six, six in nine and seven in 11 against Sussex in 1972, hence the enjoyment.

Pont, Keith
Played a significant part in the Essex side between 1970 and 1986, with 198 first-class matches and 249 one-day games. In total he scored nearly 10,000 runs for the county at a time when it was winning its first trophies.

GLOSSARY OF PLAYERS

Ponting, Ricky

Australian batsman and captain, whose career started in 1992. By the end of the 2010/11 Ashes series he had played more than 150 Test matches and over 350 One Day Internationals and is one of Australia's most successful post-war batsmen. His top score of 257 came against India at Melbourne in 2003 and he has made approaching 40,000 runs in all forms of the game, including 39 centuries in Tests. He has captained the Australian Test side since 2004.

Price, John

Middlesex fast bowler, universally known as Sport, with a quirky, crescent-shaped run-up, at the end of which he bowled out-swingers at a lively pace. Played 15 Test matches for England between 1964 and 1972 in which he took 40 wickets. Took 817 wickets in his first-class career, including five wickets in an innings on 26 occasions.

Procter, Mike

An outstandingly talented South African all-rounder who played in only seven Test matches as a result of his country being excluded from world cricket in the 1970s and 1980s. In his 401-match first-class career he scored nearly 22,000 runs and took more than 1,400 wickets at a cost of less than 20. He was an impressive performer for Gloucester and when his first-class career ended in 2008 he became a coach, match referee and Test selector.

Radley, Clive

Middlesex right-hand batsman who played for England in eight Test matches, in which he averaged over 48, and four One Day Internationals, in which he averaged 83.33. Scored well over

26,000 runs in his first-class career and over 10,000 in one-day matches. When he retired in 1987 he succeeded Don Wilson as MCC's head coach and has spent more than 50 years working at Lord's.

Ramadhin, Sonny

West Indian off-spin bowler who took 158 wickets in his 42 Test matches alongside his 'spin twin' Alf Valentine. In 1950 at Lord's he took 11 wickets in the match at a cost of 152 runs in 115 overs as West Indies won at Headquarters for the first time. In his career between 1949 and 1971 he took 758 wickets in 184 matches.

Ramprakash, Mark

Right-handed batsman of considerable talent for Middlesex and Surrey who, despite 52 Test matches for England has never been able to establish himself at the highest level, where he averages only 27. However, at first-class level since his debut in 1991, his average comfortably exceeds 50 and 113 centuries are testimony to the quality of his batting.

Randall, Derek

One of cricket's great characters and a brilliant and entertaining cover fieldsman, he was known as Arkle and played for Notts between 1972 and 2000. He made 47 Test match appearances for England scoring 2,470 runs and played in two One Day Internationals. In his career he scored nearly 28,500 runs and more than 12,000 in one-day matches.

Reid, John

Immensely powerful batsman for New Zealand who appeared in 58 Test matches between 1949 and 1965. He scored more than 16,000 first-class runs and was a useful bowler who took

85 Test wickets. As captain of his country in 34 Tests, he was the first to lead them to victory both at home and away in 1956 and 1962 respectively.

Richards, Barry
A magnificent South African batsman who could also bowl a useful off break but played only four Test matches due to his country's absence from the Test arena in the 1970s and 1980s. At Test level he averaged over 72 and in first-class matches made more than 28,000 runs with 80 centuries. Such was the quality of his batting that he made hundreds before lunch nine times and had the ability to take any attack apart.

Richards, Sir Vivian
A dominating and destructive West Indian batsman who played 121 Test matches, averaging over 50 and scoring 24 centuries. Also played in 187 One Day Internationals and such was his confidence that, exceptionally, he never wore a helmet. Made a top score of 291 against England at the Oval in 1976, led the West Indies to victory in 27 of the 50 matches that he captained and scored 114 centuries in his career between 1971 and 1993.

Richardson, Peter
Kent and Worcestershire left-handed batsman between 1949 and 1965. He made 34 Test appearances for England, scoring over 2,000 runs with five centuries. In all first-class matches he scored over 26,000 runs. Scored 100 against Australia at Old Trafford in 1956 in the match better remembered for Jim Laker's 19 wickets.

Robertson, Jack
Middlesex opening batsman between 1937 and 1959 who played 11 Test matches for England and scored nearly 32,000 runs at first-class level, with a best of 331 in 1949 against

Worcester. A modest man with a superb and elegant style, he was also an occasional off-spin bowler with a creditable 73 wickets to his name at first-class level, including two in Tests.

Robertson-Glasgow, R.C. 'Crusoe'

All-rounder for Oxford University and Somerset who played 144 first-class matches between 1920 and 1937, scoring over 2,000 runs and taking 464 wickets. After retirement he became a highly regarded writer and author, primarily on cricket.

Roope, Graham

A talkative and charismatic all-rounder who played for Surrey between 1964 and 1988, and made 21 Test appearances for England. He was a brilliant fielder who took close to 750 catches in all versions of the game and scored more than 19,000 first-class runs. When he died suddenly in 2006, aged only 60, he left a lot of people wanting more.

Rumsey, Fred

Derby, Somerset and Worcester opening bowler who made five Test appearances for England in 1964 and 1965. In his first-class career, he took 580 wickets, including five wickets in an innings on 30 occasions. His best figures came in 1965 when he took 8-26 against Hampshire but in his whole career he never once managed to pass the 50 mark with a bat in his hands.

Sandham, Andy

Surrey batsman between 1911 and 1937 who played 14 Test matches for England, in one of which he made 325 in Jamaica against the West Indies at the age of 40. In 643 first-class matches he scored more than 41,000 runs with 107 centuries. He died in 1982 at the age of 91.

GLOSSARY OF PLAYERS

Sehwag, Virender

One of the most outrageously fast run scorers of all time, whose strike rate in Test matches exceeds 80 and is well over 100 in the one-day game. Since his debut in 1997 he has made more than 7,000 runs for India in both forms of the game, with a top Test score of 319 against South Africa at Chennai in 2008 off only 304 deliveries.

Simpson, Reg

Notts opening bat who made over 30,500 first-class runs in nearly 500 appearances. He was 26 before he made his first-class debut as a result of the Second World War but was a stylish batsman and fine fielder throughout his career, which ended in 1963. Played 27 Test matches for England making four centuries, a notable performance being an unbeaten 156 against Australia during England's first Test victory over the country for 13 years in 1951.

Smith, Graeme

South African left-handed opening batsman since 2002 who has made well over 7,000 Test runs at an average of over 50, with a top score of 277 against England at Edgbaston in 2003. Has scored well over 20,000 in all forms of cricket and has proved to be an effective Test captain since his appointment at the age of 22, his country's youngest skipper.

Smith, Robin

Between 1988 and 1996 the right-hand batsman played 62 Test matches for England, scoring 4,236 runs, and 71 One Day Internationals, in which he made 2,419. In first-class and one-day matches, he scored more than 41,000 runs and made 88 centuries in all, at international level, for Hampshire and for his native Natal.

Snell, Richard
South African fast bowler who played five Test matches for his country between 1992 and 1994 and took over 400 wickets in his first-class career.

Snow, John
Apart from being a published poet, he was also a legendary and menacing fast bowler for Sussex, Warwickshire and in 49 Test matches for England, in which he took 202 wickets. His best Test figures of 7-40 in Australia's second innings at Sydney in 1971 came in a magnificent bowling performance as England won by 299 runs. After a career that lasted from 1961 to 1980 he became a successful travel agent.

Sobers, Sir Garfield
Arguably the finest all-rounder the game has ever seen, he played 93 Test matches for the West Indies between 1954 and 1974, scoring more than 8,000 runs. These included a highest of 365 not out against Pakistan at Kingston, Jamaica in 1958, which remained a Test record until overtaken by Brian Lara. He could bowl left-arm fast medium, orthodox or chinaman, which brought him 235 Test wickets and more than 1,000 in his first-class career. This remarkable cricketer was also an excellent fielder, a creative captain and once hit six sixes in one over. He was knighted for his services to cricket in 1975.

Statham, Brian
Lancashire opening bowler between 1950 and 1968 who played 70 Test matches for England, taking 252 wickets at a cost of less than 25 runs apiece. Opened the bowling with Freddie Trueman in half of these matches, during which he was one of the most accurate bowlers of all time. Known by many as George, he was also a superb fielder in the deep.

GLOSSARY OF PLAYERS

Stewart, Alec
Surrey wicketkeeper-batsman who made 133 Test match and 170 One Day International appearances for England between 1989 and 2003. He made nearly 8,500 runs in Tests with 15 centuries and more than 4,500 runs in One Day Internationals. He dismissed more than 450 batsmen behind the wicket and was an outstanding performer in all levels of the first-class game for more than 20 years. He also captained England notably to win its first series of any consequence for 12 years, in 1998 against South Africa.

Stewart, Micky
Opening batsman for Surrey and England and father of Alec, he played eight Test matches for England and made approaching 26,500 runs with 49 centuries in a first-class career between 1954 and 1972. He was an outstanding fielder, a successful Surrey captain and after his retirement became manager of the England side. He was also a talented professional footballer.

Subba Row, Raman
Left-handed batsman and leg spin bowler for Cambridge University, Northants and Surrey who played 13 Test matches for England between 1958 and 1961, scoring three centuries and close to 1,000 runs. He retired from the game before he was 30 but was subsequently chairman of the TCCB and an ICC referee in 41 Tests and 119 One Day Internationals.

Surridge, Stuart
A highly successful captain of Surrey, leading the side to championship success in five successive seasons in the 1950s. He took over 500 first-class wickets with his fast-medium bowling. After retirement in 1956, he returned to the family cricket bat making business.

Sutcliffe, Herbert

Outstanding right-hand bat between 1919 and 1945, who scored more than 50,000 runs in his first-class career at an average of 52.02 with 151 centuries. The Yorkshireman played 54 Test matches for England scoring 4,555 runs at an average in excess of 60. He was part of 145 first-wicket century stands, notably with Jack Hobbs for England, and was a batsman of quite astonishing talent.

Swann, Graeme

Northants and Notts off-spinner, who has developed into one of the finest bowlers in the world. After making his Test debut in 2008, he quickly passed the 100-wicket mark and has proved to be England's match-winner on a number of occasions. A lively character, he is a useful and aggressive batsman with four first-class centuries to his name and has already taken more than 900 wickets in all forms of the game

Tattersall, Roy

A lanky Lancashire off-spin bowler between 1948 and 1964 who took 1,369 first-class wickets at a fraction above 18 runs apiece. He took five wickets in an innings on 99 occasions and 58 wickets in 16 Test match appearances for England. He achieved his best match figures of 12-101 in the Test against South Africa at Old Trafford in 1951.

Tendulkar, Sachin

Consistently impressive and well-equipped Indian batsman, known as The Little Master. Since his Test debut in 1989 he has broken virtually every batting record in the game. He has scored the most runs and hundreds in both Tests and One Day Internationals. He has a top Test score of 248 not out and in 2010 made the first ever One Day International double century, off only 147 deliveries with 25 fours and three sixes against South Africa.

Thomson, Jeff

Right-arm fast bowler for Australia, often in partnership with Dennis Lillee, who took exactly 200 wickets in 51 Test matches and a further 55 in 50 One Day Internationals. He bowled aggressively with a low, slinging action that could produce dangerous and sometimes unplayable deliveries. In his first-class career he took 675 wickets despite fitness problems later on.

Thorpe, Graham

Left-handed Surrey batsman who played exactly 100 Test matches for England between 1993 and 2005, making 16 centuries and averaging nearly 45. He also appeared in 82 One Day Internationals for his country and in his first-class career scored nearly 22,000 runs and made 49 centuries. In the one-day format, he scored over 10,800 runs.

Trueman, Fred

Fast bowler for England, Yorkshire and Derbyshire between 1949 and 1972. He was the first Test bowler to take more than 300 wickets and took over 2,300 in his first-class career. In Test cricket his best return was 8-31 in 1952 against India, his bowling average was a shade over 21.50 and he took five wickets in an innings on 17 occasions. A born storyteller, a summariser for BBC's *Test Match Special* after retirement and one of cricket's legendary characters.

Ufton, Derek

Played 149 matches for Kent between 1949 and 1962, claiming more than 300 victims as wicketkeeper during this time. Also played as a centre forward for Charlton Athletic and won one England cap in 1953.

Vaughan, Michael
Played county cricket for Yorkshire, despite being born in Manchester, and 82 Test matches for England between 1999 and 2008. He scored over 5,700 Test runs with 18 centuries and played in 86 One Day Internationals. He was one of England's most successful post-war captains and led his country when they regained the Ashes in 2005 after an 18-year gap. His career was hampered by injury and since retirement in 2009 he has joined the BBC's *Test Match Special* as a summariser.

Vettori, Daniel
New Zealand all-rounder who has played more than 100 Test matches and over 260 One Day Internationals since 1996, having debuted for his country at the age of 18. One of the few players to have achieved the double of 300 Test wickets and 3,000 runs, he was also an impressive captain of his country. Has scored six Test centuries and taken five wickets in an innings on 19 occasions with best figures of 7-87 against Australia in 2000.

Walcott, Sir Clyde
West Indian wicketkeeper-batsman between 1948 and 1960 who played 44 Test matches, scoring 3,798 runs at an average of over 56. One of the famous three Ws – Walcott, Weekes and Worrell – he scored 11,820 runs and took 187 dismissals behind the stumps in his first-class career. He was knighted in 1994, and was tour manager and selector among other senior appointments before his death in 2006.

GLOSSARY OF PLAYERS

Walsh, Courtney

Awesomely fast West Indian bowler between 1981 and 2000 who took 519 Test wickets in 132 matches as well as a further 227 in 205 One Day Internationals. His best Test figures of 7-37 were against New Zealand at Wellington in 1995. Took more than 1,800 wickets in 429 first-class matches but was no batsman, making 43 ducks in Test matches.

Wardle, Johnny

Yorkshire left-arm spinner who played 28 Test matches for England, taking 102 wickets at 20.39 apiece. Produced his best bowling figures for England against South Africa at Cape Town in 1957, when he took 7-36 to dismiss the hosts for 72 in their second innings as England won by 312 runs. His first-class career lasted from 1946 to 1968, during which time he took 1,846 wickets, but his Test appearances were limited due to the presence of Tony Lock.

Warne, Shane

One of the game's great characters and a fine leg break and googly bowler. Played in 145 Test matches for Australia, during which he missed out on a century by just one run. With the ball, he took 708 Test wickets, second only to Muralitharan, with best figures of 8-71 against England at Brisbane in 1994. He played 194 One Day Internationals, taking 293 wickets, and in 2000 was rated one of the five greatest cricketers of the 20th century. Now an entertaining and informative cricket pundit.

Washbrook, Cyril

Lancashire opening batsman who made 37 Test appearances between 1937 and 1956, often in partnership with Len Hutton with whom he enjoyed many successful stands. He made six Test hundreds and more than 34,000 runs in his first-class career. In

1956, five years after his last Test, he was a selector when asked to return to the side at the age of 41. In the match against Australia, which England won, Washbrook made 98.

Wasim Akram
Outstanding left-arm fast bowler who took 414 wickets for Pakistan and scored nearly 3,000 runs in 104 Test matches between 1985 and 2002. He also played in 356 One Day Internationals. In England he played for Hampshire and Lancashire and took a total of more than 1,000 first-class wickets with a supreme mix of swing and seam.

Watts, Hugh
Cambridge University and Somerset left-hand batsman who made 72 first-class appearances between 1939 and 1952, with a best score of 110. After retirement he finished his career as secretary and captain of the St Enodoc Golf Club in Cornwall.

Weekes, Sir Everton
Legendary West Indian batsman who played in 48 Test matches between 1948 and 1958, scoring 4,455 runs and making 15 centuries with a highest score of 207 against India in 1953. An attractive stroke-maker, he made over 12,000 runs in his first-class career averaging well over 50. After retiring from the game he became an ICC referee and was knighted in 1995.

Willis, Bob
Surrey and Warwickshire fast bowler who made 90 Test appearances for England, taking 325 wickets at a shade over 25 runs apiece. He also played in 64 One Day Internationals, taking 80 wickets. His best Test figures of 8-43 came in the famous 'Botham' match against Australia in 1981, and he was just one

short of 900 first-class wickets when he retired in 1984. Now a cricket pundit and commentator with Sky.

Worrell, Sir Frank
West Indian all-rounder who played in 51 Test matches between 1948 and 1963, averaging a shade under 50 with the bat while taking 69 wickets with his left-arm deliveries. He scored over 15,000 runs in first-class matches and took 349 wickets. The first non-white captain of a West Indies team, he was knighted in 1964 but died three years later at the age of just 42.

Wright, Doug
Fine leg spinner for Kent and England who took 108 wickets in 34 Test matches. He took 2,056 wickets in his first-class career at under 24 runs apiece, and five wickets in an innings 150 times and 10 in a match on 42 occasions. He took 100 wickets in a season 10 times, achieved seven hat-tricks and retired in 1957 at the age of 43.